OXFORD HISTORICAL MONOGRAPHS

D1346793

The Bridges of Medieval England

Transport and Society 400–1800

DAVID HARRISON

CLARENDON PRESS · OXFORD

OXFORD
UNIVERSITY PRESS

Great Clarendon Street, Oxford OX2 6DP

Oxford University Press is a department of the University of Oxford.
It furthers the University's objective of excellence in research, scholarship,
and education by publishing worldwide in

Oxford New York

Auckland Bangkok Buenos Aires Cape Town Chennai
Dar es Salaam Delhi Hong Kong Istanbul Karachi Kolkata
Kuala Lumpur Madrid Melbourne Mexico City Mumbai Nairobi
São Paulo Shanghai Taipei Tokyo Toronto

Oxford is a registered trade mark of Oxford University Press
in the UK and in certain other countries

Published in the United States
by Oxford University Press Inc., New York

First published 2004

First published in paperback 2007

British Library Cataloguing in Publication Data
Data available

Library of Congress Cataloging in Publication Data
Data available

Typeset by Laserwords Private Limited, Chennai, India
Printed in Great Britain
on acid-free paper by
Biddles Ltd,
King's Lynn, Norfolk

ISBN 978-0-19-927274-7 (Hbk.)   978-0-19-922685-6 (Pbk.)

1 3 5 7 9 10 8 6 4 2

For Eric Stone

PREFACE

One of the most impressive and least noticed achievements of Anglo-Saxon and medieval England was the construction and upkeep of a very large number of bridges and causeways. Perhaps the best indication of this is that there were almost as many bridges in 1250 as there were in 1750. At a significant number of these sites there had been an Anglo-Saxon bridge. Before 1100 bridges were timber decked but from that date they began to be rebuilt at great expense with stone vaults. By 1500 the majority of major bridges were entirely stone. Many of them survived until the late eighteenth century. As a result of the English love of topographical illustration, many were painted or sketched and subsequently engraved. Between 1770 and 1870 most were demolished, but over 200 have survived into the twenty-first century. Some are modest, simple structures of one or two small arches, but others are major pieces of civil engineering—like Piercebridge with its three large, lofty arches which bestride the River Tees, or the twenty-four-arched bridge at Bideford which is c.700 ft. long (plates 22 and 19). Despite the impressive quality of these structures, their numbers, their importance for road transport, the serious involvement of countless individuals who made bequests, and of the state and the church in constructing, repairing, and maintaining them, historians have shown little interest in bridges and there has been no scholarly history of the subject.

This book is intended to fill that gap. It has several purposes. Part I traces the stages by which an extensive network of bridges was established and looks at its relationship to the new, post-Roman road system which was created at the same time. Part II outlines major developments in the design and construction of bridges and examines the effectiveness of the work done to keep them in use. Part III is concerned with the economics of bridges and with social questions. How much did it cost to build them and keep them in use? How was the work organized? What was the role of the Old English state in compelling a workforce to work on bridges, and the role of charitable donations and of tolls? The findings have important implications for our understanding of the nature of the state and of the pre-industrial economy and society. What these implications are is considered in the final chapter.

Bridges can be readily identified and counted and we can detect improvements in quality. As a result, changes in the network of bridges can be studied over a very long period. Accordingly it seemed important to take the opportunity to broaden the period studied beyond the years when the network of bridges was first constructed and then reconstructed in stone: hence this book seeks to cover the 1,400 years from the end of Roman rule to the great changes which began to occur in the late eighteenth century.

Although no history of English bridges before the eighteenth century has been written, this book is clearly indebted to a number of earlier studies. Foremost are the pocket-sized volumes published between 1928 and 1938 by Charles Henderson and Henry Coates (*Old Cornish Bridges and Streams*) and by Edwin Jervoise (covering the rest of England). Jervoise's books contain the results of his survey of ancient bridges undertaken under the auspices of the Society for the Protection of Ancient Buildings. Their greatest virtue is that they identified the location of, and described the surviving ancient bridges. The National Monuments Record entries on bridges are still heavily dependent on Jervoise's work. They also contain much information about the history of individual bridges, both surviving and lost.

For about fifty years after Jervoise began his researches, apart from the important information included in the volumes of the Victoria County History very little was published about pre-eighteenth-century bridges. Since the 1970s, however, there has been a small but steady increase in interest in the subject. The published works fall into two broad categories. First, there have been studies of individual bridges or groups of bridges: Renn on the Wey bridges, Goodfellow on bridges in Northamptonshire, culminating with Simco and McKeague's comprehensive study of Bedfordshire bridges in 1997. This category includes contributions by engineers, both county bridge surveyors, such as Mr Wallis of Dorset, and academics, notably Professor Heyman and Dr Padfield. In the last ten years there have been two major studies of a single bridge: the multi-author volume to mark the six-hundredth anniversary of the new bridge at Rochester, and the Musem of London Archaeological Service's detailed archaeological and historical study of London Bridge. Secondly, there are works on particular periods or types of bridges, including Professor Brooks's important studies of bridges in Anglo-Saxon England and their European setting, Dr Chalkin on the construction and repair of bridges in the seventeenth and eighteenth centuries, Ted Ruddock on the transformation of bridge construction in the eighteenth century, and Dr Rigold on timber bridges.

Medieval bridges were first suggested to me as a research topic by Paul Hyams, who as my college tutor was well aware of my interest in medieval history, economics, and architecture. At the time I had little idea of just how interesting and important the subject would be or what uncharted territories I was entering. My supervisor, who guided me through them, was the late Eric Stone, who was a constant source of encouragement, support, and inspiration. Following his all too early death, I was extremely fortunate that James Campbell agreed to see my thesis through to completion. Thereafter he acted as Advising Editor to the present work. His kindness and helpfulness in reading through several earlier drafts of this book and suggesting many improvements have been invaluable.

A subject as ambitious as this study attempts has inevitably taken me into areas well beyond the bounds of any specialist knowledge I might claim to have. Dr Padfield read the relevant chapters of my thesis on structure, and pointed out some of its many shortcomings. He also directed me to further relevant reading, in particular the important work on masonry arches and bridges which he and Professor Heyman have undertaken. The book undoubtedly has failings which will immediately be apparent to an engineer, but fewer than it would otherwise have had. Dorian Gerhold read the sections relating to road transport after 1500, helped me avoid a number of errors, and made many useful suggestions.

I am grateful to many others who have helped me: John Gillingham and others at the medieval history seminars at the Institute for Historical Research in London; Christopher Dyer, who as Editor of the *Economic History Review* gave me a great deal of help in preparing an article on bridges and economic development, 1300–1800 which acted as a springboard for the present book; Susan Irvine for translating from Middle English; Peter Spring for his high-quality photographs of a number of engravings; Anne Gelling and her colleagues at OUP for prompt and helpful replies to my enquiries; and the many people who have sent me references to bridges from scattered sources, including Paul Brand, Paul Hyams, John Maddicott, and David Palliser.

In 1997 I became Clerk of the Environment, Transport and Regional Affairs Committee under the joint chairmanship of Gwyneth Dunwoody MP and Andrew Bennett MP. Through them, the transport specialists who worked for the Committee, and the Specialist Advisers who advised it, I gained many valuable insights into transport policy in general. Finally I should like thank my wife for reading several drafts of the book, to which she brought the unerring eye of a classics teacher, drawing attention to grammatical and stylistic infelicities.

CONTENTS

LIST OF ILLUSTRATIONS

The illustrations are to be found between pp. 140–141

LIST OF MAPS

LIST OF TABLES

LIST OF ABBREVIATIONS

Abingdon Chron.   *Chronicon Monasteri de Abingdon*, ed.
                   J. Stevenson, 2 vols. (RS, 1858)

         Alberti   L. B. Alberti, *The Ten Books of Architecture, The
                   1755 Leoni Edition*, facsimile edn. (New York,
                   1986)

       Ann. Mon.   *Annales Monastici*, ed. H. R. Luard, 5 vols. (RS,
                   1864–9)

            ASC   *The Anglo-Saxon Chronicles*, trans. and ed. by
                   M. Swanton (London, 2000)

           Bede   *Bede's Ecclesiastical History of the English People*,
                   ed. B. Colgrave and R. A. B. Mynors (Oxford,
                   1969)

Boyer, *French Bridges*   M. Boyer, *Medieval French Bridges: A History*
                   (Cambridge, Mass., 1976)

'Bridges of Bedfordshire'   A. Simco and P. McKeague, 'Bridges of
                   Bedfordshire', *Beds. Arch. Monographs*, 2 (1997)

Bridges in Oxfordshire   J. Steane, *Medieval Bridges in Oxfordshire*
                   (Oxford, 1981)

Britnell, 'Rochester Bridge'   R. H. Britnell, 'Rochester Bridge, AD 1381–1530',
                   in Yates and Gibson, *Traffic and Politics*

Brooks, 'Military Obligations'   N. P. Brooks, 'The Development of Military
                   Obligations in Eighth- and Ninth-Century
                   England', in P. Clemoes and K. Hughes (eds.),
                   *England Before the Conquest: Studies in Primary
                   Sources Presented to Dorothy Whitelock*
                   (Cambridge, 1971), 69–84

Brooks, 'Rochester Bridge'   N. P. Brooks, 'Rochester Bridge, AD 43–1381', in
                   Yates and Gibson, *Traffic and Politics*

Brooks, 'Medieval Bridges'   N. P. Brooks, 'Medieval Bridges: A Window
                   onto Changing Concepts of State Power',
                   Haskins Soc. Jnl., 7 (1995), 11–29

Brooks, 'Burghal Hidage'   N. P. Brooks, 'The Administrative Background
                   to the Burghal Hidage' in D. Hill and A. R.
                   Rumble, *The Defence of Wessex: The Burghal
                   Hidage and Anglo-Saxon Fortifications*
                   (Manchester, 1996), 128–50

Cal. Inq. Misc.	*Calendar of Inquisitions Miscellaneous, Preserved in the P.R.O.* (1916–)
Cal. Inq. p. m.	*Calendar of Inquisitions Post Mortem and other analagous documents in the P.R.O.* (1891–)
Cameron, *Place Names*	K. Cameron, *English Place Names* (London, 1996)
CCR	*Calendar of Close Rolls* (1892–)
CChR	*Calendar of Charter Rolls* (1903–)
CEH:	E. A. Labrum (ed.), *Civil Engineering Heritage:* (London, 1994–)
Chalkin, *Public Building*	C. Chalkin, *English Counties and Public Building, 1650–1830* (London, 1998)
CLibR	*Calendar of Liberate Rolls* (1916–)
Cooper et al., 'Hemington Bridges'	L. Cooper, S. Ripper, and P. Clay, 'The Hemington Bridges', *Current Arch.*, 140 (1994), 316–21
Cornish Bridges	C. Henderson and H. Coates, *Old Cornish Bridges and Streams* (Truro, 1928)
CPR	*Calendar of Patent Rolls* (1891–)
Crook, *Medieval Bridges*	M. Crook, *Medieval Bridges* (Princes Risborough, 1998)
CS	*Cartularium Saxonicum*, ed. W. de G. Birch, 3 vols. (1885–93) (quoted by number of document)
Darby, *Medieval Fenland*	H. C. Darby, *The Medieval Fenland*, 2nd. edn. (Newton Abbot, 1974)
DB	*Domesday Book*, 4 vols. (Rec. Com., 1783–1816)
Defoe, *Tour*	D. Defoe, *A Tour through the Whole Island of Great Britain*, 2 vols. (London, 1974)
Devon Bridges	C. Henderson and E. Jervoise, *Old Devon Bridges* (Exeter, 1938)
DNB	*Dictionary of National Biography*
EcHR	*Economic History Review*
EETS	Early English Text Society (original series)
EHR	*English History Review*
English Medieval Architects	J. Harvey, *English Medieval Architects: A Biographical Dictionary Down to 1550* (London, 1954)
EPNS	English Place-Name Society
Ekwall, *Dictionary*	E. Ekwall, *The Concise Oxford Dictionary of English Place-Names*, 4th edn. (Oxford, 1960)

EYC *Early Yorkshire Charters*, ed. W. Farrer and
C. Clay, 12 vols., Yorks. Arch. Soc. Rec. Ser.,
extra series (1914–65)

Fiennes *The Journeys of Celia Fiennes*, ed. C. Morris (1947)

Flower, *Works* *Public Works in Medieval Law*, ed. C. T. Flower,
2 vols., Seldon Soc., 32, 40 (1915–23)

Goodfellow, 'Northants Bridges' P. Goodfellow, 'Medieval Bridges in
Northamptonshire', *Northamptonshire Past and
Present*, 7 (1985–6), 143–58

Hamill, *Bridge Hydraulics* L. Hamill, *Bridge Hydraulics* (London, 1999)

Hill, 'Burghal Hidage Sites' D. Hill, 'Gazetteer of Burghal Hidage Sites', in
D. Hill and A. R. Rumble, *The Defence of
Wessex: The Burghal Hidage and Anglo-Saxon
fortifications* (Manchester, 1996), 189–231

Hindle, *Medieval Roads* B. P. Hindle, *Medieval Roads*, 2nd edn. (Princes
Risborough, 1989)

Hopkins, *A Span of Bridges* H. J. Hopkins, *A Span of Bridges* (Newton
Abbot, 1970)

H. Hunt. Henry of Huntingdon, *Historia Anglorum*, ed.
D. Greenway (Oxford, 1996)

Irish Stone Bridges P. O'Keefe and T. Simington, *Irish Stone Bridges:
History and Heritage* (Dublin, 1991)

Jackman, *Transportation* W. T. Jackman, *The Development of
Transportation in Modern England*, 2 vols.
(Cambridge, 1916)

John of Worcester *The Chronicle of John of Worcester*, vol. 2, ed.
P. McGurk (Oxford, 1998)

King's Works *The History of the King's Works*, ed. H. M.
Colvin, 6 vols. (1963–82)

Leland *The Itinerary of John Leland in or about the
Years 1535–43*, ed. L. Toulmin Smith, with a
foreword by T. D. Kendrick, 5 vols. (repr.
London, 1964)

Liebermann, *Gesetze* F. Liebermann, *Die Gesetze der Angelsachsen*, 3
vols. (Halle, 1903–16)

London Bridge B. Watson, T. Bingham, and T. Dyson, *London
Bridge: 2000 Years of a River Crossing* (London,
2001)

Margary, *Roman Roads* I. D. Margary, *Roman Roads in Britain*, 3rd. edn.
(London, 1973)

Mid and Eastern E. Jervoise, *The Ancient Bridges of Mid and
Eastern England* (London, 1932)

Rye, 'Burton-on-Trent Bridge'   H. A. Rye, 'The Great Bridge of Burton-on-Trent', *Burton-on-Trent Nat. Hist. and Arch. Soc.*, 5 (1903–6), 4–21

Salzman, *Building*   L. F. Salzman, *Building in England Down to 1540*, 2nd edn. (Oxford, 1967)

South   E. Jervoise, *The Ancient Bridges of the South of England* (London, 1930)

Statutes of the Realm   *Statutes of the Realm*, 11 vols. (Rec. Com., 1810–28)

Stenton, 'Road System'   F. M. Stenton, 'The Road System in Medieval England', in D. M. Stenton (ed.), *Preparatory to Anglo-Saxon England, Being the Collected Papers of F. M. Stenton* (Oxford, 1970), 234–52 (originally published in *EcHR* 7 (1936), 7–21)

Symeon   Symeon of Durham, *Tract on the Origins and Progress of This the Church of Durham*, ed. and trans. D Rollason (Oxford, 2000)

Taylor, *Roads*   C. Taylor, *Roads and Tracks of Britain* (London, 1979)

Test. Ebor.   *Testamenta Eboraciensia*, ed. J. Raine, Surtees Soc., 30 (1855)

Thomas, 'Devon Bridges'   D. L. B. Thomas, 'The Chronology of Devon's Bridges', *Reports and Trans. Devon Assoc.*, 124 (1992), 175–206

Traffic and Politics   N. Yates and J. Gibson, (eds.), *Traffic and Politics: The Construction and Management of Rochester Bridge A.D. 43–1993* (Woodbridge, 1994)

VCH   *Victoria County History* (London 1900–) (cited by volume title)

Wales and Western   *The Ancient Bridges of Wales and Western England* (London, 1936)

Wallis, *Dorset Bridges*   A. J. Wallis, *Dorset Bridges* (Sherborne, 1974)

Wayfaring Life   J. J. Jusserand, *English Wayfaring Life in the Middle Ages*, trans. L. Toulmin-Smith, 4th edn. (London, 1950)

YNR Bridge Book   *Book of Bridges belonging to the North Riding of the County of York, 1805* (North Yorkshire County Record Office)

YWR Bridge Book   *Book of Bridges belonging to the West Riding of the County of York, 1752* (West Yorkshire County Record Office)

NOTE ON THE TEXT

Places are identified here with reference to the counties before the reorganization of local government in the 1970s. Lengths are given in both imperial and metric measures (in particular of the spans of the arches bridges), depending on the sources being quoted.

I

Introduction

The autumn of 1069 was a frustrating time for William the Bastard, later known as the Conqueror. His way north to attack his enemies in York was blocked at Pontefract ('the broken bridge') by the River Aire, which was swollen by heavy rains. Orderic Vitalis records that: 'his way was barred . . . by the river, which was neither fordable nor safe for navigation. He rejected all advice to turn back . . . They were delayed there for three weeks. At length a knight of outstanding courage . . . made a determined effort to cross the river, riding up and down stream in search of a ford. At last he found a place that could be forded with great difficulty, and with sixty gallant knights made the crossing . . .'[1]

Crossing rivers in such conditions was very dangerous. Almost 700 years later Bonnie Prince Charlie, retreating from England into Scotland, faced a similar problem to William. He had to ford the River Esk near Longtown, a few miles north of Carlisle. Although the river here was only 60 yards broad, there was talk of it being unfordable because there had been several days of rain and the waters were 4 feet deep over the bed of brown rock. After guides tested the water using the tallest horses in the army, the Prince went in on his own horse. Then the 'foot marched in, six abreast, and in good order as if they were marching in a field, holding one another by the collars'. The heads of the Highlanders were 'generally all that was seen above the water . . . The deepness and rapidity of the river, joined to the obscurity of the night, made it most terrible'. It was considered very fortunate that only two camp-followers died in the passage.[2]

Only those who had a very good reason to make a journey, like William or Charles Edward Stuart, would use a ford or even a ferry when it had been raining heavily and the river was flowing quickly. Even in good weather fording

---

[1] Oderic Vitalis, *Historia Ecclesiastica*, ed. M. Chibnall, 6 vols. (Oxford, 1968–80), ii. 230–1.
[2] The account of the crossing is taken from C. Duffy, *The '45* (London, 2003), 339–40.

major rivers like the Aire cannot have been an appealing prospect. Moreover, rivers are unpredictable: a traveller might find little more than a trickle of water on the riverbed one day, but the next, after a heavy downpour, a raging torrent.

Reliable, safe, and regular road travel required bridges and causeways. Medieval accounts of the construction of new bridges stress both the lives which will be saved and the increased prosperity which increased traffic will bring. A mid-fifteenth-century poem, which commemorates the construction of bridges across several branches of the Thames in and near Abingdon (plate 15), contains the following lines which refer to both benefits:

> Another blessed business is bridges to make
> In places uncrossable after great showers.
> What a pity to pull a dead body out of a lake
> Who was baptized in a stone font, a fellow of ours.[3]

By the sixteenth century the bridge was judged to have made a major contribution to Abingdon's increased prosperity.[4]

By the eighteenth century there were many impressive bridges. Travellers, like Daniel Defoe, commented on the number and quality of the structures. In Yorkshire: 'The River Wharfe seemed very small, and the water low, at Harwood Bridge, so that I was surprised to see so fine a bridge over it . . . [however], coming another time this way after a heavy rain, I was convinced the bridge was not at all too big, or too long, the water filling up to the very crown of the arches . . .'[5] Describing the road to Nottingham, he observed: 'When I said the bridge over the Trent had nineteen arches, I might as well have said the bridge was a mile long; for the Trent being, at the last time I was there, swelled over its ordinary bound, the river reached quite up to the town; yet a high causeway, with arches at proper distances, carried us dry over the whole breadth over the meadows, which, I think, is at least a mile.'[6]

Several similar structures across the Trent valley were to be found within a relatively short distance upstream of Nottingham. Causeways were not confined to the Trent; some, like the long causewayed approach to Gloucester from the west, were, if anything, even longer (plate 1). Nor was Harewood Bridge a lone example of a lofty, large spanned bridge. The north was full of them (plates 3, 5, 14, 16, 22, 27). In the south too there were many fine stone bridges, including a number of very large structures. One was at Rochester, where the

---

[3] Leland, v. 116. The original text is as follows: 'Another blissid besines is brigges to make, There that the pepul may not passe after greet showres, Dole it is to drawe a deed body oute of a lake, That was fulled in a fount stoon, and a felow of oures.' The poem is discussed at greater length in Chap. 7.
[4] Leland, v. 1.   [5] Defoe, *Tour*, ii. 211.   [6] Ibid., ii. 145.

Medway was crossed by 'the largest, highest, and the strongest built of all bridges in England, except London-Bridge'.[7] The evidence from the first large-scale county maps of the second half of the eighteenth century confirms the impressions of travellers. There was a dense network of bridges and causeways in every part of the country.

This book tells the story of their construction and upkeep. It argues that the bulk of the network had come into being early. In an article in 1992 I sought to demonstrate that many bridges had been constructed by the end of the middle ages and that there were approximately the same number in the mid-eighteenth century. The substantial improvements in road transport of the second half of that century were therefore built on an existing and impressive infrastructure which dated back centuries. Indeed it was probable that most of the pre-industrial network of bridges was in place by the thirteenth century.[8] The present book takes the story further back. It argues that the first bridges at most sites were constructed in the 500 years between 750 and 1250. Thus a significant number of eighteenth-century bridges were on the site of a bridge which had been built in the Saxon period. The same is true, *mutatis mutandis*, elsewhere in Europe.[9]

In putting forward these arguments I am rejecting a long and widely held view that major improvements in transport were a post-medieval phenomenon. Even up to the 1970s many historians believed that while early eighteenth-century roads and communications were poor, those of earlier centuries were worse, and that a high proportion of bridges were built at a late date.[10] As late as 1973 H. C. Darby took for granted that 'before 1750, large rivers were usually crossed by fords and ferries'.[11] Subsequently the importance of road transport from the sixteenth to the nineteenth century was reassessed, but often the revisionists continued to consider the medieval road system primitive.[12] Albert, Chartres, and Pawson challenged older interpretations of the sixteenth, seventeenth, and eighteenth centuries, but not of the middle ages.[13] Of course,

---

[7] Ibid., i. 105.

[8] D. F. Harrison, 'Bridges and Economic Development, 1300–1800', *EcHR*, 2nd ser., 45 (1992), 240–61.

[9] Brooks, 'Medieval Bridges', 12.

[10] This observation was made by G. H. Martin, 'Road Travel in the Middle Ages', *Jnl. Trans. Hist.*, NS 3 (1975–6), 159–60. For a classic statement of the poor state of roads, see S. Webb and B. Webb, *English Local Government: The Story of the King's Highway* (London, 1920).

[11] H. C. Darby, 'The Age of the Improver: 1600–1800', in id. (ed.), *A New Historical Geography of England After 1600* (Cambridge, 1973), 74–5.

[12] The reinterpretation is described in T. Barker and D. Gerhold, *The Rise and Rise of Road Transport, 1700–1990* (Basingstoke, 1993).

[13] J. A. Chartres, *Internal Trade in England, 1500–1700* (London, 1977); W. A. Albert, *The Turnpike Road System in England, 1663–1840* (Cambridge, 1972); E. Pawson, *Transport and Economy: The Turnpike Roads of Eighteenth Century Britain* (London, 1977).

this tradition has never been universally accepted. A few medieval historians long ago presented a more positive picture of medieval transport. In the 1920s and 1930s J. Willard stressed that the medieval sources he studied portrayed a world in which carts and trade were common, and travel was reasonably cheap and easy, and quick when necessary.[14] In the last twenty years a growing body of research has confirmed this impression, including J. Langdon's study of road haulage and C. Dyer's of trading networks.[15]

There had been bridges and causeways in England long before the arrival of the Saxons. Man-made timber tracks constructed with vast amounts of timber, dating from the Neolithic period, have been found on the Somerset levels.[16] A Bronze Age bridge which crossed a former channel of the Thames has been excavated near Eton.[17] Later the Romans built a road system which was so thoroughly engineered that parts of it, including the remains of a number of important bridges, are still visible.

Impressive though the Roman road network was, not only did most bridges disappear relatively soon after the end of Roman rule, but many stretches of the roads themselves ceased to be used. In their place a new road system was established which owed surprisingly little to the Roman network. It can first be seen in some detail in the fourteenth century, but it is likely that much of the new road system, like many of the new bridges which were key parts of it, was in place by the late Saxon period. Once established, it proved remarkably stable. The main roads broadly retained their medieval alignment into the twentieth century; in some places they still keep to it. The principal river crossings of the middle ages continue to influence the modern road system. Between Northamptonshire and Yorkshire the A1 follows the same broad line as the Old North Road did in the middle ages, crossing major rivers in the immediate vicinity of former medieval bridges at Wansford, Stamford, Newark, Ferrybridge, and at Wetherby where, although now bypassed, the medieval bridge is still visible sandwiched between later widenings.

---

[14] J. Willard, 'Inland Transportation in the Fourteenth Century', *Speculum*, 1 (1926), 361–74; id., 'The Use of Carts in the Fourteenth Century', *History*, NS 17 (1932), 246–50; and see O. Coleman, 'Trade and Prosperity in the Fifteenth Century: Some Aspects of the Trade of Southampton', *EcHR*, 2nd ser., 16 (1963), which shows that carts laden with commodities made regular journeys to many parts of England.

[15] J. Langdon, 'Horse Hauling: A Revolution in Vehicle Transport in Twelfth and Thirteenth Century England', *Past and Present*, 103 (1984), 37–66; id., *Horses, Oxen and Technological Innovation: The Use of Draught Animals from 1066 to 1500* (Cambridge, 1986); C. Dyer, 'The Hidden Trade of the Middle Ages: Evidence from the West Midlands', in id., *Everyday Life in Medieval England* (London, 1994), 283–303.

[16] B. Coles and J. Coles, *Sweet Track to Glastonbury: The Somerset Levels in Prehistory* (London, 1986).

[17] T. Allen and K. Welsh, 'Eton Rowing Lake', *Current Arch.*, 148 (1996), 124–7.

Before the twelfth century most bridges were timber or had timber roadways and stone piers. While it was long known that some important vaulted stone bridges were built in the following centuries, it was assumed that the majority of major medieval bridges remained wooden. The small exhibit about bridges until recently displayed at the Science Museum, South Kensington, reflected these views. The present book argues, in contrast, that between 1100 and 1500 the bridge network was rebuilt so that by the sixteenth century most major bridges were constructed with stone vaults. These may have been the first such bridges ever constructed in lowland England where rivers have substantial flows all the year round, since there is no evidence that the Romans built arched bridges at these locations. By the sixteenth century major timber bridges were uncommon except around the middle Thames and possibly in East Anglia.

An impressive number of stone medieval bridges survive of all shapes and sizes, including some which are very substantial structures, such as the long estuarine bridges at Barnstaple and Bideford spanning the mouths of the Taw and Torridge with many narrow arches (plate 19), and the impressive series of bridges across the Tees at Yarm, Croft, Piercebridge, and Barnard Castle (plates 8 and 22). Many more bridges survived until the late eighteenth century, but were subsequently demolished in the hundred years between 1770 and 1870. This means that we know a good deal about them from descriptions and illustrations.[18] The bridges mirrored the remarkable engineering feats of medieval cathedral builders, and they shared the same technology, particularly in the use of stone vaults. The same clients paid for both bridges and cathedrals. Bishop Flambard ordered Framwellgate Bridge in Durham to be built at the same time as the vaulted nave of his cathedral was being constructed (plate 5). Masons too designed bridges and major churches. Henry of Yevele was involved in the construction of the new bridge at Rochester (over 500 feet long and completed *c.*1391–2) at the same time as he is thought to have been designing the nave of Canterbury Cathedral.[19] Although the bridges had to be constructed in far more difficult conditions than major churches, by the end of the middle ages there were bridges in the north with arches which are of greater span than are to be found in any church of the period. They are as impressive as many of the arched bridges built in the late eighteenth century.

Because bridges are built in water, not only is their construction particularly difficult, but maintenance and repair are very important, probably more so than for almost any other structure: small problems can very quickly turn into

---

[18] See Chap. 5.   [19] See Chap. 7.

big ones and bring disaster. To construct and maintain a massive transport infrastructure was an immense task. This was, in large measure, a social feat. It is a testimony to the powers of the Anglo-Saxon state that it was able to build a series of major bridges and to enforce, as contemporary laws and charters indicate, a widespread public duty to maintain and repair them. It was an achievement which ranks alongside other major public works, including the construction of a network of *burhs* or Offa's Dyke.[20] In some instances the liabilities imposed in the Anglo-Saxon period survived in one form or another, certainly into the eighteenth and probably into the twentieth century, but from the eleventh and twelfth centuries there is an increasing amount of evidence that bridge construction and maintenance were being financed in other ways, which reflected what seem to have been changes in the way the state operated.[21]

Strange as it may seem to us in the twenty-first century, the construction and repair of bridges was seen as an important act of charity. New bridges from the eleventh century, and probably earlier, were funded by private bequests, like hospitals, schools, and almshouses. The state assisted those building and repairing bridges in several ways, for instance by permitting them to take tolls on goods passing over the bridge, but most of the money was provided by wealthy people with strong local connections who, in some cases, made huge contributions. Their motives were a mixture of charity, civic pride, and self-interest mixed in many different proportions.[22] The extent of the effort that went into bridge repair and maintenance can be seen in a variety of ways, not least in the work of countless numbers of bridge wardens who supervised it; some of their accounts survive which record their expenditure in minute detail. Although it was an unceasing struggle, these efforts largely succeeded in keeping the network of bridges in use, notwithstanding some dramatic collapses.[23]

Total expenditure on building and maintaining bridges was huge. Repairs to one of them, Tyne Bridge, Newcastle, were estimated at £1,500 in the late fourteenth century. The cost of building a new bridge at the site would have been far in excess of this figure. A contract from 1421 survives for the construction of a bridge of three large arches at Catterick (plate 16), where the Great North Road crosses the River Swale; the masons were to be paid over £170, but that sum did not include the cost of most of the materials, including stone, iron, and timber, or of their transportation to the site. Catterick Church was rebuilt at roughly the same time for *c*.£100. There were hundreds of similar major bridges and thousands of smaller ones.[24]

Because they are readily identified and can be counted, bridges are most unusual, perhaps unique, in allowing us to construct accurate and useful data-series over very long periods. As a result the transport infrastructure of the eighteenth century can be placed in the context of the middle ages and earlier. The findings of this study have important implications for our understanding of transport and the economy in pre-industrial England. They show that a major part of the transport infrastructure had come into being at an early date and was adequate to serve the needs of the English economy on the eve of the industrial revolution.[25]

There are several reasons for this, but an important part of the explanation may be that the transport needs of the pre-industrial English economy and society did not change fundamentally between the middle ages and the seventeenth and early eighteenth centuries. Population levels may not have reached their medieval peak again until the eighteenth century, and there is some evidence that the economies were not of a different order of magnitude. It brings home to us that when we speak of pre-industrial England we are dealing with a society where the economic fundamentals remained similar for many centuries. In the late eighteenth century the situation began to change out of all recognition, but the improvements, including the construction of new bridges and the widening of existing ones, built on an already very impressive and sophisticated achievement.

---

[24] See Chap. 10.
[25] The implications of this study for our understanding of transport and the economy are discussed in Chap. 12.

PART I

Bridge Construction and the Creation of
the English Road System

2

Numbers

At Derby in December 1745 the Young Pretender made the fateful decision to return with the Jacobite army to Scotland and to defeat at Culloden. The retreating army took a route to the north-west through Ashbourne, Stockport, Manchester, and Wigan. There it joined the main west coast road, passing through the towns of Preston, Lancaster, and Carlisle, which stand on the banks of three of the major rivers, the Ribble, the Lune, and the Eden, which run west from the Pennines. En route, at Penrith, it had to cross the River Eamont which flows out of Ullswater.[1] At each of these rivers was an important ancient bridge, as there was at Mayfield near Ashbourne (over the River Dove), at Stockport (River Mersey), and Manchester (River Irwell). Some of these bridges he used, others, as happens in wartime, had earlier been broken to delay his advance. Two of the bridges survive: Hanging Bridge, Mayfield, where the pointed arches are visible behind later widening; and Eamont Bridge, Penrith, which is probably the bridge built *c.*1425 when indulgences were granted for the building of 'a new stone bridge across the waters of the Amot'.[2] Although the other bridges were demolished between 1750 and 1850, illustrations of them suggest that the structures were medieval. Three had been drawn and engraved a few years before 1745 by Samuel and Nathaniel Buck. Lune Bridge, Lancaster, is depicted with four large pointed arches and the bridge at Manchester is shown with similar arches.[3] The Buck brothers' Ribble Bridge, Preston, was the same bridge which John Leland had described 200 years earlier, with its 'V *great* arches'. It was probably the stone bridge which we know from the Patent Rolls was under construction in 1403 to replace a timber bridge.[4]

---

[1] The route of the retreat is described in Duffy, *The '45*, 315–38.

[2] *North*, 114.

[3] The engraving are reproduced in R. Hyde, *A Prospect of Britain: The Town Panoramas of Samuel and Nathaniel Buck* (London, 1994), plates 34, 47, 60.

[4] Leland, iv. 8; *CPR* (1401–5), 236.

At Carlisle, where the Eden divided into two, there was a bridge over each stream. Neither was illustrated by the Buck brothers, but the southern was drawn in 1815 by Joseph Farington. It had nine pointed arches.[5]

There had been bridges at these sites for centuries. All had been constructed by the sixteenth century. Eden Bridge existed by the early twelfth century; the bridge at Lancaster had been built by 1216.[6] They may have been old by then. The west coast route itself was ancient. It is shown on the earliest road map of the fourteenth century, and was used more than once by King John.[7]

FROM THE THIRTEENTH TO THE NINETEENTH CENTURY

Post-1500

The situation on the west coast main road was typical of national highways in most of the country. There were also bridges on secondary roads where they crossed large and small rivers. We know this because in almost every part of the country reasonably precise estimates of the numbers of bridges can be made with the aid of scattered, but nevertheless numerous sources. In some areas the estimates are very accurate. Many of the main conclusions in the present work are based on a study of bridges across twenty-four English rivers in three periods—the early sixteenth century, the third quarter of the eighteenth century, and the early nineteenth century—which is summarized in Tables 2.1–4.

The first column in each table shows the number of bridges standing *c.*1540; the second, those recorded on the first large-scale county maps, most of which were published in the third quarter of the eighteenth century; and the third those on the first edition of the Ordnance Survey maps of the first half of the nineteenth century. The information for the eighteenth and nineteenth centuries is based on relatively accurate surveys made for mapping.[8] The earlier numbers derive from a wide variety of sources, none of which are comprehensive. The twenty-four rivers in the sample include all the largest rivers (Great Ouse, Midlands Avon, Ouse and Ure, Severn, Thames, and Trent), and over

---

[5] *North*, 118.   [6] Ibid. 118, 132.

[7] Hindle, *Medieval Roads*, 34–5.

[8] The bridges can usually be easily identified; problems do occur, e.g. near mills where it can be difficult to tell whether there were a series of bridges across all the channels of the river. For example, Jefferys's map of Bedfordshire shows some sort of crossing over the four channels of the Great Ouse at Oakley Mill in Bedfordshire; in fact, there may have been small foot bridges over some of the channels, but just a ford for vehicles slightly downstream of the mill (*Bridges of Bedfordshire*, 46).

TABLE 2.1. *Number of known bridges over the great rivers,* c.*1540 to the nineteenth century*

Rivers	c.1540	c.1765–75	1st edn. OS
Avon (Midlands) (downstream from Finford Bridge)	14 (17*)	18	20
Great Ouse (from Claydon Brook to Ely)	17	24	36
Severn (from Montford Bridge)	10	10	16
Thames (from Lechlade)	17	23	36
Trent (from Stoke-on-Trent)	16	23	30
Ure and Ouse (from Bainbridge)	10	12	16

Note: *Figure includes bridges marked on the Sheldon Tapestry Map (*c.*1580).
Sources: Column 1: a great variety, including Leland; English Place-Name Society vols.; *VCH* vols.; local record society publications; printed government publications. Column 2: the following maps: Anderson, Dury, and Herbert, *Kent* (1769); Andrews and Dury, *Wiltshire* (1773); Burdett, *Derbyshire* (1767); Chapman, *Nottinghamshire* (1776); id., *Staffordshire* (1776); Davis, *Oxfordshire* (1797); Jefferys, *Bedfordshire* (1765); id., *Huntingdonshire* (1768); id., *Durham* (1768); id., *Bedfordshire* (1765); id., *Buckinghamshire* (1770); id., *Yorkshire* (1771); Rocque, *Shropshire* (1752); id., *Middlesex* (1754); id., *Berkshire* (1761); Taylor, *Hampshire* (1759); id., *Dorset* (1765); id., *Worcestershire* (1772); Yates, *Warwickshire* (1793). Column 3: first edition Ordnance Survey maps.

TABLE 2.2. *Number of known bridges over Yorkshire rivers,* c.*1540 to the nineteenth century*

Rivers	c.1540	c.1760–75	1st edn. OS
Aire (downstream from Coniston)*	16*	20	21
Calder (from Sowerby Bridge)	7	11	
Derwent (from Ayton Bridge)	9	9	12
Nidd (from Ramsgill)	13	17	18
Wharfe (from Kettlewell)*	11*	13	15
Swale (from Grinton)	7	8	11
Tees (from Eggleston)	5	7	9

Note: *Known bridges by c.1600.
Sources: See Table 2.1.

TABLE 2.3. *Number of known bridges over other major rivers, c.1540 to the nineteenth century*

Rivers	c.1540	c.1760–75	1ˢᵗ edn. OS
Avon (Bristol) (downstream from Malmesbury)	13	18	21
Avon (Hants.) (from Salisbury)	7	10	11
Medway (from Tonbridge)	8	10	12
Stour (Dorset) (from Blandford)	6	7	7
Tame (Staffs.) (from Water Orton)	6	9	9
Wear (from Stanhope)	9	12	15

Sources: See Table 2.1.

TABLE 2.4. *Number of known bridges over lesser rivers, c.1540 to c.1797*

Rivers	c.1540	c.1797
Cherwell (downstream from Banbury)	6/7	10
Thame (from Thame)	6	8

Sources: See Table 2.1. The 1797 figures are derived from Davis, *Oxfordshire* (1797).

half of the thirty major rivers of England as well as a number of smaller ones such as the Cherwell in Oxfordshire and the neighbouring Thame.[9]

The first and important conclusion is that by the early sixteenth century a very large number of bridges had been built (see Maps 1 and 2). Furthermore, the increase in number between that date and even the late eighteenth century was relatively slight. Thus, over the Midlands Avon there were seventeen bridges *c.*1580 and eighteen in the late eighteenth century. On some rivers, such as the Derwent and the Severn, there was no change in the number of bridges in the 300 years up to *c.*1770. On sixteen of the twenty-four rivers more than three-quarters of the bridges depicted on the eighteenth-century maps were on the site of a medieval bridge.

---

[9] In the long period this book covers river channels moved about the flood plain, here making some arches redundant, there requiring the erection of new arches or bridges, but most rivers continued to flow through the same river valleys. The exceptions were in marsh or fenland where there were numerous changes, e.g. in the fens waterways became extinct as a result of the silting up of the Wisbech estuary and artificial waterways were created, like that from Littleport to Lynn (Darby, *Medieval Fenland*, 94–100). For this reason, Table 2.1 does not examine the bridges over the Great Ouse downstream from Ely.

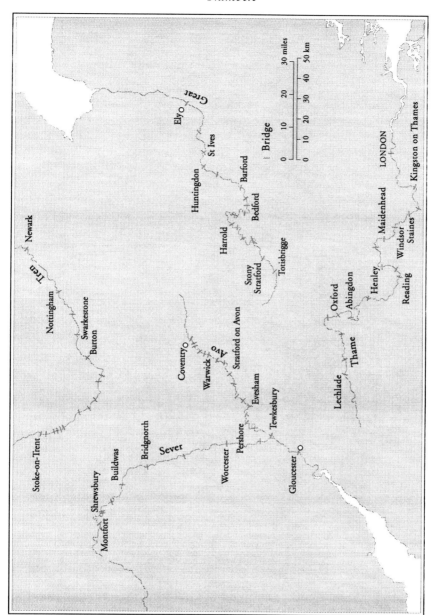

Map 1. Bridges in *c*.1540 across the great rivers of England south of the Humber

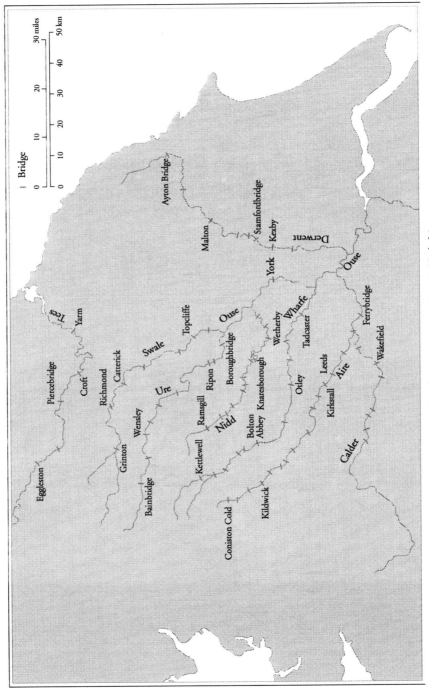

Map 2. Bridges in *c*.1540 across rivers in Yorkshire

The difference in the number of bridges *c.*1540 and the mid- as opposed to the late eighteenth century was even less than this. This is because new bridges at new locations began to be built in some numbers after 1760, a little before the publication of the maps on which the late eighteenth-century figures are based.[10] For example, Table 2.2 shows that five of the seven bridges over the Tees marked on Jefferys's Map, which was published in 1771, were medieval or on the site of a medieval bridge.[11] The other two were built in 1762–3 (at Winston) and 1770 (Stockton).[12]

Moreover, the figures for the early sixteenth century are minima, reflecting the patchy nature of the printed records searched. There were almost certainly more bridges. While the available printed sources invariably record the more substantial bridges on the lower sections of the rivers, only where there are exceptional collections of printed material are all the bridges on the upper reaches of rivers revealed; for instance, there seem to be significant omissions in respect of the upper reaches of the Trent, the Great Ouse, the Aire, and the Wharfe. There can be little doubt that more bridges could be identified by further research, but this would require a comprehensive examination of local, unprinted, primary sources. Where, as in Nidderdale in the Yorkshire dales, there has been such a detailed study, it can be shown that there were many minor upstream bridges by the later middle ages.[13]

Sources

The sources used to compile the statistics for medieval bridges shown in the tables are diverse. They include some documents containing material specific to bridges, such as the account rolls relating to the income and expenditure of bridge estates like those of Rochester and London Bridge, and surviving contracts, including those for Catterick Bridge, and Lady Bridge, Sheffield.[14] Much also depends on passing mentions, for example to a bridge as a way of identifying the location of a meadow. Such casual references, which occur in records of many kinds, not infrequently provide the earliest evidence for the existence of a bridge.

One source, however, stands out because it mentions so many bridges. In 1533 John Leland, a scholar in his late twenties, received a commission 'to search monastic and collegiate libraries for forgotten "monuments of ancient writers"

---

[10] Tables 2.1–4 also make clear the large increase in the number of bridges across some rivers between the county maps of *c.*1760–75 and the OS maps produced in the first half of the 19th cent.

[11] T. Jefferys, *Map of the County of York, surveyed by J. Ainslie, T. Donald and J. Hodskinson, 1767–70* (1771).

[12] Pevsner, *Durham*, 150, 505.

[13] B. Jennings (ed.), *History of Nidderdale* (Huddersfield, 1967).

[14] For the accounts and contracts, see Chaps. 9–10.

[so that] they may be brought "out of deadly darkness to lively light" '. After the Dissolution of the Monasteries this meant removing the 'monuments' to new homes. Over the next ten years he travelled widely through England and Wales, turning from 'a studious librarian into a tireless travelling antiquary'.[15] He showed a remarkably keen interest in archaeological sites and topography, and during his journeys made descriptive notes of the places and the nature of the country he passed through. These notes, which were first published by Thomas Hearne in 1710–12, include a record of many of the bridges he came across.[16] The following is a typical entry: 'Under Castelleford bridge of vii arches rennith Aire ryver, and a [3.] miles above this west up into the land is Swillington bridg on the same ryver, and 2. Miles beneth Castelforde is Fery bridge.'[17] Possibly no one until the twentieth century was as interested in collecting information about English bridges. His *Itinerary* has its limitations. It is not a comprehensive record, and he by no means lists all the bridges in the areas he visited; for instance, there were more than the three bridges he records across the River Aire. Nor did he travel to every region, scarcely venturing into most of Norfolk and Suffolk or Sussex. Nevertheless, he provides information about the number and fabric of bridges in many parts of the country, from the River Fowey in Cornwall to the River Kent in Cumbria, and from the River Rother which divides Kent and Sussex to the River Till near the Scottish border.

Others listed and described the bridges which they saw on their journeys, although none come near to matching the number recorded by Leland. They include William of Worcester, whose travels were undertaken in the previous century, as well as later travellers such as Celia Fiennes and Daniel Defoe. In 1675 Fiennes's contemporary, John Ogilby, published the first detailed maps of the principal routes in the country, marking many bridges.

A good deal of information is also contained in the royal and other administrative documents, produced in increasing numbers from *c*.1200. Amongst them, the Patent Rolls record the right to take tolls at bridges, the Close Rolls gifts of oaks for bridges, and bishops' registers the grants of indulgences for the benefit of bridges. However, bridges on smaller and middling rivers are not recorded in large numbers until the late middle ages. Most of the sources for this period are the same as they were earlier, but there are more of them, for example, of wills recording money left for the repair of bridges and legal disputes relating to bridge repair. Some have been printed, often by local record societies. Many court cases—although but a fraction of those which have

---

[15] Leland, i, Foreword.   [16] Ibid., p. xix.   [17] Ibid. 42.

survived—were collected by C. T. Flower of the Public Record Office together with cases relating to other public works such as roads and sewers. They were published in two volumes in 1915 and 1923 by the Selden Society as *Public Works in Medieval Law*. It is a treasure trove of information about bridges.

Much of the evidence which had been printed up to the early 1930s was brought together by Edwin Jervoise to form brief histories of many of the country's bridges. He undertook this research as part of a survey of ancient bridges, and descriptions of the bridges and 'information about their history and about the history of many of those bridges which have been replaced by more modern structures' were published between 1930 and 1936. Each book covered the bridges of a region: the south of England, mid- and eastern England, the north of England, and Wales and western England.[18] In his interest in bridges Jervoise might be described as the twentieth-century Leland. His survey was made river by river, following each from source to mouth. The pocket-book format followed that adopted by Charles Henderson and Henry Coates, who had published *Old Cornish Bridges and Streams* in 1928. Henderson died while preparing a volume on Devon bridges which was completed by Jervoise and published in 1938.

Jervoise's books were the fruits of a commission from the Society for the Protection of Ancient Buildings in 1926 to discover the state of the surviving ancient bridges of England, at a time when the pressure to demolish old bridges, which had to 'sustain a traffic whose volume, weight and speed are utterly beyond the conception of their designers', was beginning to make itself felt. Jervoise travelled the country inspecting over 5,000 bridges, and recording what he found. His work still underpins the information kept by the National Monuments Record. It must have been a delightful job. Despite the concern at the time about the increase in the use of motor vehicles, traffic levels were minute in comparison with today, nearer to the calm of Leland's time. In the introduction to the work, the Chief Inspector of Ancient Monuments announced that it had been undertaken with the intention of enlisting public interest in the bridges' preservation.[19] In this it was successful: the great majority of the ancient bridges Jervoise surveyed are still standing, although there have been serious losses.[20] Perhaps the saddest was not a medieval bridge but

[18] There are a number of other brief gazetteers of the surviving bridges, probably largely derived from Jervoise, e.g. H. Casson (ed.), *Bridges* (London, 1963); J. M. Richards, *The National Trust Book of Bridges* (London, 1984).

[19] *South*, p. vi.

[20] Bedfordshire has suffered particularly badly; losing a medieval bridge at Stafford and a 17th-cent. bridge at St Neots since the 1950s ('Bridges of Bedfordshire', 50, 20).

Rennie's masterpiece, Waterloo Bridge, which was opened in 1817 but demolished in 1934.[21]

Although few bridges have been destroyed, their settings have often been ruined, especially in towns. To choose one from many similar examples, the view of what Jervoise called 'the finest medieval bridge in this part of England', at Huntingdon, is marred by a modern footbridge jammed up against its upstream face, and the A1 bypass which is too near the bridge and town (plate 12). When Jervoise saw the bridge the High Street came right up to the northern bridge head in a picturesque grouping of shops and bridge; subsequently a new inner ring road was constructed, destroying houses and shops and leaving the area round the bridge cut off from the southern end of the town.

The work of Jervoise, Henderson, and Coates takes us some way to building up a list of the bridges which existed in medieval England, although it is far from comprehensive. While Jervoise produced a thorough survey of extant ancient bridges, his histories of the individual bridges are much less complete. This comment is not intended as a criticism: it was not his purpose to produce a comprehensive list of medieval bridges. Accordingly, there is very little about the history of many significant bridges in his books, and there is no reference at all to some, even though they are on the site of medieval bridges across substantial rivers. More detailed information has more recently been provided by the relatively small number of studies which are the result of an exhaustive inquiry, making use of unprinted records. The most notable are the more recent and comprehensive volumes of the Victoria County History (VCH) and the English Place-Name Society (which record early references to bridges). There are also a few very thorough local studies, including the *History of Nidderdale* mentioned above, and a recent survey of Bedfordshire bridges, a collaborative work undertaken by engineers, planners, archaeologists, and historians.[22] Such works, based on detailed research, reveal the medieval origins of many upstream bridges and even of obscure local crossings on smaller rivers and streams.

Unfortunately the coverage of these studies is limited: the volumes of the VCH and English Place-Name Society published in the last twenty years cover only a small part of the country. The upshot is that of the two main secondary sources, one, Jervoise, provides a history of the whole country but with less

[21] S. Croad, *London's Bridges* (London, 1983).

[22] Jennings, *History of Nidderdale*; *Bridges of Bedfordshire*. Other thoroughly researched local studies include Goodfellow, 'Northants Bridges'; Phillips, *Thames Crossings*, Thomas, 'Devon Bridges'. Examples of works by practising bridge engineers include Wallis, *Dorset Bridges*; G. H. Jack, 'Ancient Bridges in Herefordshire and their Preservation', *Antiq. J.*, 6 (1926), 284–93.

detail than we would wish, and the other, the VCH, has a very full account of bridges in some of the areas it covers, but omits many areas. Nevertheless, these two fundamental works provided the invaluable starting point for compiling the information set out in Tables 2.1–4.

The Thirteenth and Fourteenth Centuries

It is very likely that most of the bridges recorded in the early sixteenth century had been in existence for some time. Although counting them becomes more difficult as we peer back beyond the fifteenth century, it seems probable that the majority of medieval bridges had been constructed by the thirteenth century at the latest. Many bridges, large and small, are recorded in thirteenth- and fourteenth-century sources. There are, with a few exceptions, relatively comprehensive references by 1350 to the bridges over some of the biggest rivers. We know that there were at least eight bridges over the Severn by *c*.1350, ten by *c*.1540, and the same number by *c*.1770.[23] Across the Thames seventeen bridges were recorded in the early sixteenth century; 200 years earlier there had been thirteen and probably more;[24] the comparable figures for the Great Ouse were seventeen and fourteen.[25] There is evidence of about two-thirds of sixteenth-century Trent bridges by the mid-fourteenth century.[26] Other research has produced similar results: for example, P. Goodfellow has shown that all but two of the medieval bridges over the Nene in Northamptonshire were referred to in documents by 1350.[27]

These figures undoubtedly underestimate the number of bridges built by the mid-fourteenth century. While a few bridges were first constructed between 1350 and 1550—for instance, the first bridges across the Thames at Abingdon and Chertsey and across the Great Ouse at Great Barford were constructed in the fifteenth century—others recorded after 1350 may have been built before that date. These would include bridges at Sonning, Godstow, and Newbridge (Thames) and at Castle Mills and Stafford (Great

---

[23] *CPR (1334–8)*, 228; *Wales and Western*, 135; A. W. Ward, *The Bridges of Shrewsbury* (Shrewsbury, 1935), 127; *CPR (1327–30)*, 249; *Cal. Lib. Rolls (1245–51)*, 52; *CPR (1266–72)*, 639; *(1321–4)*, 400; *(1313–17)*, 377; *(1317–21)*, 119; *VCH Glos.*, iv. 242–3.

[24] See below for the 11 Thames bridges recorded before 1250; Maidenhead Bridge is first mentioned in 1297 (*CPR* (1292–1301), 324).

[25] For the bridges at Newport Pagnell, Olney, Sherington, and Stony Stratford, see *CPR (1272–81)*, 91; Flower, *Works*, i. 24–5; A. C. Chibnall, *Sherington: Fiefs and Fields of a Buckinghamshire Village* (Cambridge, 1965), 8–9; *CPR (1348–50)*, 263; for the other 9 bridges recorded by 1200, see below.

[26] *VCH Staffs.*, viii. 177; *Mid and Eastern*, 2–3; Leland, v. 21; *CCR (1234–7)*, 141, 310; *CPR (1281–92)*, 115; K. Cameron, *The Place-Names of Derbyshire* (Cambridge, 1959), iii. 660–1; *CPR (1345–8)*, 160; *(1358–61)*, 2.

[27] Goodfellow, 'Northants Bridges'.

Ouse).[28] It is possible that much of the apparent increase in the number of bridges between 1350 and 1500 derives from the differential survival of evidence.

There is good information about the lower reaches of the Yorkshire rivers, though not about the upper stretches. Four bridges are recorded downstream from Ripon on the Ure and Ouse before 1350, at Ripon itself, Bridge Hewick, Boroughbridge, and York, and there were no more bridges across this stretch of the river until the end of the eighteenth century.[29] Similarly, over the Wharfe downstream of Bolton Bridge all but one of the bridges which were standing at the end of the middle ages had been recorded by the mid-fourteenth century, that is, those at Otley, Harewood, Wetherby, and Tadcaster (the exception being Ilkley Bridge).[30]

Not only is it certain that a high proportion of bridges existed by 1350, but there is good reason to suppose that many of them were there by the early thirteenth century or even before. This can be demonstrated for the bridges of the Thames and Great Ouse, for which there is particularly good evidence. Across the Thames at least eleven major bridges had been built by 1250. On the upper reaches were: St John's Bridge, Lechlade, and Radcot Bridge, where the medieval bridge, repaired after it had been damaged by Thomas, duke of Gloucester, in the 1380s, survives. Downstream there was Grandpont, Oxford, and a bridge at Wallingford, both of which still contain medieval flood arches. Below the Goring Gap, bridges at Reading, Henley, Marlow, Windsor, Staines, and Kingston as well as London Bridge are all referred to before 1250 (plate 7).[31] Similarly, of the fourteen Great Ouse bridges recorded by 1350, nine existed by the early thirteenth century.

By the thirteenth century there were also large numbers of bridges for carts, horses, and pedestrians over streams, brooks, and the smallest water courses.[32] A good example of a substantial small stone bridge is the two-arched Sutton Bridge across Potton Brook, a tributary of the River Ivel in Bedfordshire, recently discovered to be of the mid-thirteenth century by radio-carbon dating of elm beams which formed a building platform for the abutments and pier.[33]

---

[28] Leland, v. 113–8; i. 106; *VCH Surrey*, iii. 404; *Register of Henry Chichele*, ed. E. F. Jacob, 4 vols., Canterbury and York Soc., 42–7 (1937–47), ii. 412; Leland, i. 111; v. 73, *VCH Oxon*, iv. 77; Leland, i. 101–2; *English Wills, 1498–1526*, ed. A. F. Cricket, *Bed. Hist. Rec. Soc.*, 38 (1957), 76.

[29] *CPR (1317–21)*, 476; Flower, *Works*, ii. 271–5; *EYC*, i. 75, 211.

[30] I. Kershaw, *Bolton Priory* (Oxford, 1973), 121–3; *Register of Archbishop Gray*, ed. J. Raine, Surtees Soc., 56 (1890), 20, 60–1; *EYC*, vii. 71; *CPR (1345–8)*, 197; see also *North*, 96–9.

[31] *CCR (1227–31)*, 82; *Rot. Lit. Pat.*, 87b; *Abingdon Chron.*, ii. 15, 25, 284; H. Hunt., 758–61; *CCR (1227–31)*, 499; *(1234–7)*, 146; *Rot. Lit. Claus.*, ii. 198; *CCR (1234–7)*, 392; *CPR (1225–32)*, 197; *Rot. Lit. Claus.*, i. 558.

[32] There are many examples in Flower, *Works*.   [33] 'Bridges of Bedfordshire', 74.

Some, like this bridge, were impressive structures, although others were little more than planks. A mid-thirteenth-century inquisition, which was published by the Record Commission together with the *Placita Quo Warranto Rolls*, recorded liabilities for the repair of more than eighty small bridges across small tributaries of the River Lea between Stratford and Ware.[34]

BEFORE 1200

The Twelfth Century

It is one thing to show that bridges were numerous by the mid-thirteenth century, another to determine how early this situation prevailed. Very obviously one might be led astray by the deficiency of sources in the earlier period. There are no extant Close Rolls before the second year of King John, or Patent Rolls until the following year. However, what evidence there is hints at a world in which bridges were common. Narrative sources tell us of a few major building projects in the eleventh and twelfth centuries.[35] The evidence, in particular of charters, suggests that a significant number of bridges may have been built by the end of the twelfth century. By 1200 there were bridges over the Severn at Shrewsbury, Atcham, Bridgnorth, Worcester, and Gloucester (plates 10 and 1).[36] Indeed, bridges had been erected at most important towns, for instance, at Carlisle, Leicester, and Exeter (plate 2).[37]

Fortunately in one area, encompassing the middle reaches of the Great Ouse (that is, those parts of the river in Bedfordshire, Cambridgeshire, and Huntingdonshire), there is excellent early source material. There are particularly good collections of pre-1200 printed sources, including a number of Bedfordshire charters, which show that nine of the bridges on this section of the river were in existence by the twelfth century. They also indicate that bridges were not confined to major towns. These nine bridges represent three-quarters of the bridges on this stretch of the river which were standing in 1500. In the short distance between Turvey Bridge, on the border of Bedfordshire and Buckinghamshire, and Bedford there were three bridges by 1200, and a fourth at Biddenham is recorded early in the thirteenth century. A charter issued between 1136 and 1146 refers to 'three acres of my lord's meadow next to Harrold Bridge';[38] in another charter of 1138/47 Robert de Blosseille, with the

---

[34] *PQW*, 284–6.   [35] See Chap. 3.
[36] *Wales and Western*, 132, 137; Ekwall, *Dictionary*, 64; John of Worcester, 25; *VCH Glos.*, iv. 242–3.
[37] *North*, 119; *Mid and Eastern*, 44–5; *Wales and Western*, 171; *Devon Bridges*, 62.
[38] C. R. Cheney, 'Harrold Priory, a Twelfth Century Dispute', *Bed. Hist. Rec. Soc.*, 32 (1952), 12.

consent of his lord, Samson le Fort, granted 'two acres of meadow next Turveie Bridge' to Harrold Priory.[39] Ancient bridges and causeways, though generally considered to be of a slightly later date, exist at both these sites.[40] A charter of Simon de Beauchamp of 1179/94 recorded a grant to the hospital of St John of Bedford of a chapel on Bedford Bridge.[41] A few miles to the west of Bedford the Great Ouse flows from north to south, and here, at Biddenham, was a bridge, first recorded in 1224 when it was repaired to ensure that siege engines could be taken to Bedford, where the castle, held for the great military captain Fawkes de Breaute, was withstanding royalist forces.[42] Downstream the bridge at St Neots was recorded by 1180 and Huntingdon Bridge by 1194, when it was the subject of a dispute about bridge repair, so that it must have been older.[43] At the beginning of the twelfth century the Ramsay Cartulary recorded the gift of a meadow at St Ives on which the bridge stood. Not far beyond Huntingdon and St Ives were the fens.[44] The causeway and bridges which carried the road from Cambridge to Ely crossed the river at the bridge of Aldreth in the middle ages. It seems to have been built, or possibly rebuilt, in the eleventh century; later in the century we learn that work on the causeway had been owed 'ex antiquo' from men of Ramsey Abbey in Chatteris. Further east, the causeway between Soham and Stuntney which links Ely with Bury St Edmunds was constructed in the twelfth century.[45]

Anglo-Saxon England

There is far less information about bridges before the Norman Conquest. The sort of detailed evidence we have about the Great Ouse in the twelfth century is not available earlier about any river, but this does not mean that bridges were rare before 1100. Two things seem to indicate the numbers and importance of bridges in late Anglo-Saxon England. First, there are references to specific bridges, often at major crossing points, and secondly, there are several indications that there were many more bridges than those which are recorded.

Many of the known structures must have been substantial. Amongst them are major causeways as well as bridges at some of the longest and most important river crossings. These include what were until the late eighteenth or

---

[39] G. H. Fowler, 'Early Records of Turvey and its Neighbourhood', *Bed. Hist. Rec. Soc.*, 11 (1927), 48–9.

[40] 'Bridges of Bedfordshire', 62–3, 56–7.

[41] F. M. Stenton, 'The Commune of Bedford', *Bed. Hist. Rec. Soc.*, 9 (1925), 177–80.

[42] G. H. Fowler, 'Munitions in 1224', *Bed. Hist. Rec. Soc.*, 5 (1920), 117–32.

[43] *VCH Hunts.*, ii. 337; *Rotuli Curia Regis, 1194–9*, ed. F. Palgrave (Rec. Com., 1835), 132; in fact, a bridge at Huntingdon was almost certainly first built in the Anglo-Saxon period (see this Chap. below).

[44] *Cartularium abbatiae Ramesiensis*, ed. W. H. Hart and P. A. Lyons, 3 vols. (RS, 1884–93), ii. 214.

[45] Darby, *Medieval Fenland*, 108–10.

nineteenth century the lowest bridges on the Thames, the Ouse, and the Dee at London, York, and Chester.[46] There were also major bridges on the road from London to the north, across the Great Ouse at Huntingdon, the Welland at Stamford, and the Trent at Nottingham. In the west, there were bridges at Worcester and at Bristol, not far from the mouth of the Avon;[47] in the east, the great bridge over the River Cam at Cambridge existed by the ninth century; in the south, Redbridge, the important crossing of the Test in the tideway, just before the river flows into Southampton Water, had been built by the tenth century.[48] These bridges were an impressive group, encompassing what were to remain some of the most important crossings in the country for almost a millennium.

We know of these bridges from a variety of sources, including the primary narrative accounts of the period. Charter bounds also provide evidence of bridges some of which were major structures. A charter of 958 shows that on or near the site of Radcot Bridge across the River Thames there was a stone bridge in the tenth century. A grant was made of 30 hides in the manor of (Longworth) near Faringdon. The boundaries of the estate are described, including the following clause: 'first to the stone bridge and from the stone bridge eastwards along the Thames . . .'[49] In Devon, charter bounds indicate that on the sites of Creedy Bridge, Bickham Bridge, and Kingsbridge there were formerly Anglo-Saxon bridges.[50]

The evidence of place-names is particularly valuable: for instance, Bristol is first recorded as *Brycgstow*, meaning 'the site of the bridge', in 1063.[51] Other place-names recorded by the eleventh century indicate the presence of major bridges, including Bridgwater, Somerset, on the lower Parrett; Doveridge, Derbyshire, where the route coming from the west towards Derby crosses the Dove; Stamfordbridge in Yorkshire (known as *Pons belli* in some twelfth-century sources in reference to the battle there in 1066) across the Derwent; and Attlebridge, Norfolk, which stands by the River Wensum on the main road to the north-west of Norwich.[52] In addition, the remains of a few Saxon structures have been uncovered, often during drainage work or quarrying.[53]

It is likely that these bridges and many others were bridges as we currently understand the word, but it needs to be stressed that this was not the case with all the structures termed *brycg*. Today the word bridge refers to a crossing with

---

[46] B. Watson, 'The Late Saxon Bridgehead', in *London Bridge*, DB, i. 298, 262.

[47] *DB*, i. 336b; *ASC*, 104; John of Worcester, 25; Ekwall, *Dictionary*, 66.

[48] Ekwall, *Dictionary*, 84, 383.   [49] *CS* 1028.

[50] Thomas, 'Devon Bridges', 189.   [51] Ekwall, *Dictionary*, 66.

[52] Ibid. 18, 64, 149, 436–7.   [53] See Chap. 6.

a hollow space below. In the Anglo-Saxon period a *brycg* seems to have been a man-made improvement to a crossing of a river or low-lying land. Accordingly it could mean, as well as a bridge, a causeway or raised track through marshland, as Cameron notes.[54] The latter meaning is likely where the first element denotes a muddy place, for instance Slimbridge in Gloucestershire, which is not situated by a river but is on low-lying land not far from the Severn estuary.[55] It is also how the word is used in the Old English poem *The Battle of Maldon*: when the tide went out Byrhtnoth found it necessary for the first time to send men to hold the 'brycge' (which was the causeway linking Northey Island to the mainland). The causeway appears later in the poem to be referred to as a 'ford'.[56] Similarly, Blair and Millard have demonstrated that a causeway with a stone ford on a small tributary of the Upper Thames which they excavated was referred to as a *stan ford* in one tenth-century charter and *stan bricge* in another contemporary charter.[57] In some districts a few place-names were influenced by the Scandinavian *bryggja*, which originally meant 'jetty, quay' as in Brigg, Lincolnshire.[58]

The Latin *pons*, which in late Saxon England was the usual translation for *brycg*, was used to describe both the whole bridge or causeway as well as the small bridges in the causeway; at Arundel timber was granted for the repair of a wooden bridge, which we would describe as being in the middle of the causeway or bridge ('ligni pontem est in medio pontis de Arundell').[59] Similarly, the long bridge and causeway at Oxford were known as 'Grandpont'. Possibly the introduction of the French term *causey* or causeway (Latin *calceta*) led to the common modern usage of bridge as the crossing of the main part of the river, with the artificial approach to it being described as a causeway. This is the way Leland used the words. Approaching Newbridge in the Upper Thames valley, he commented that 'the ground ther al about lyethe in low medowes often ovarflowne by rage of reyne. There is a longe cawsye of stone at eche end of the bridge. The bridge it selfe hathe vi. greate arches of stone.'[60]

While the references to specific bridges indicate the existence of a significant network, including structures of the greatest importance, the number of Anglo-Saxon bridges which we know of is small compared with later centuries.

---

[54] Cameron, *Place Names*, 170.   [55] Ibid. 170–1.

[56] D. Scragg, *Battle of Maldon AD 991* (Oxford, 1991), p. 24, ll. 74–81.

[57] J. Blair and A. Millard, 'An Anglo-Saxon Landmark Rediscovered: The Stan ford/Stan bricge of the Ducklington and Whitney Charters', *Oxoniensia*, 57 (1992), 342–8.

[58] Cameron, *Place Names*, 177.

[59] T. P. Hudson, 'The Origins of Steyning and Bramber', *Southern History*, 2 (1980), 11–29.

[60] Leland, v. 73.

There are, however, several reasons for thinking that there were many more by the eleventh century than can be identified. In the first place, most of the bridges recorded are referred to in only one source, suggesting that if more sources survived there would be references to more bridges. Secondly, where a detailed study can be made of a locality, it is clear that bridges over smaller rivers and streams are a common feature of the countryside. J. Blair has mapped the landscape revealed in a number of contiguous charter bounds in the lower Windrush valley, dating from the second half of the tenth century and the early eleventh century. It contained several bridges within a relatively small area: across the brook at Bampton was king's bridge; on two other streams to the east were two stone bridges, one of which was in fact a causeway with a stone ford on the bed; further east was Wenburh's bridge, and in Shifford we know from other sources that there was a knights' bridge; and finally, to the north of Bampton was the settlement of Curbridge, first recorded in the tenth century.[61] There is no obvious reason why this area should be different from the many others in lowland England with a similar topography.

Finally, there is the ubiquitous obligation to repair bridges. The frequency with which this liability is recorded in late Anglo-Saxon England suggests that it was taken very seriously and was widespread. It may also imply that bridges were common. The obligation is assessed in more detail below, but the key points need to be considered briefly here.[62] The main source of references are the many Saxon charters, granting land and rights, which frequently reserve to the Crown the three services of bridge work, borough work, and fyrd service (that is, the building or repair of bridges, the building or repair of (or garrisoning of) boroughs, and military service). These public works are also referred to in some of the Old English law codes.

We know what bridge work involved, because there is detailed evidence which shows how two major bridges, those at Chester and Rochester, were repaired in the eleventh century. At that time Rochester Bridge consisted of stone piers with a wooden deck formed from huge beams and planking for the road way. Certain estates, vills, or hundreds in a subdivision of Kent, known as the lathe of Aylesford, were responsible for the upkeep of each pier and associated road way. In Cheshire the whole county was responsible for the bridge.

Bridge repair continued to be organized in the same way in later centuries. The same estates which had repaired Rochester Bridge in the eleventh century

---

[61] J. Blair, *Anglo Saxon Oxfordshire* (Stroud, 1994), 130–2.   [62] See Chap II.

remained liable for its upkeep in the fourteenth century, and the pattern of liability for Chester Bridge was unchanged over the same period. In the thirteenth and fourteenth centuries the upkeep of other major bridges, including those at Cambridge and Huntingdon, was similarly organized. For instance, we are told that the four hundreds of Huntingdonshire were responsible for the bridge of the county town.[63] Below it is argued that the inevitable conclusion is that these arrangements, like those for Rochester and Chester bridges, date back to Anglo-Saxon England, which means, of course, that there were bridges at Huntingdon and Cambridge at that time.[64] In fact, we know that there was a bridge at Cambridge by the ninth century.[65]

In addition to the late medieval evidence about the repair of these major bridges, a large number of disputes about the repair of other, smaller bridges were also the subject of court cases. The arrangements for their repair seem to have a great deal in common with those for Chester and Rochester bridges. While the men of the county of Cheshire were responsible for the bridge of the county, elsewhere it was the men of other long-standing administrative units, in particular hundreds and vills: in *c*.1293 the tenants of Eyhorn Hundred in Kent had to repair half the bridge at Hawkenbury.[66] This looks very much like the way the repair of the Anglo-Saxon Rochester Bridge was organized in the eleventh century. It is possible that the men of Eyhorn were fulfilling a very ancient obligation, and that the bridge they were repairing was also very old.

Indeed, it may be that many of the obligations to repair bridges, whether of the county, the hundred, the vill, or the lord of the manor, which are recorded in the thirteenth century and later had their origins in the Old English system of bridge work.[67] Analysis of the responsibilities recorded in the late middle ages and later may then provide an indication of the scale of Saxon bridge building. Once again the evidence of the middle reaches of the Great Ouse is particularly suggestive. At least one-third of the medieval bridges over the river in the later middle ages—were repaired by liable local communities. Aldreth causeway and Huntingdon have been discussed already. Similar liabilities were recorded in 1389 for the repair of *Totisbrigge*, near Thornborough, upstream in Buckinghamshire.[68] As late as 1630 four bridges across the river in Willey Hundred in Bedfordshire—Bromham, Harrold, Stafford, and Turvey—were

---

[63] *Rot. Hun.*, ii. 407; *CCR (1369–74)*, 140.   [64] Chap. 11.
[65] See Chap. 3.   [66] Flower, *Works*, i. 197.
[67] Although not every bridge which was repaired by liable estates or individuals in the later middle ages was of Saxon origin, because there were ways in which liabilities could arise subsequently (see Chap. 11).
[68] Flower, *Works*, i. 28.

found to be the responsibility, at least in part, of local lords of the manor or inhabitants; for example, Harrold Bridge was repaired by the lords of the adjacent manors of Odell, Harrold, Charlton, and Chellington (plate 4).[69] It is not impossible that these obligations were ancient and that the bridges of Willey Hundred, like those of many other bridges repaired in a similar way, were first constructed some considerable time before the Norman Conquest.

[69] 'Bridges of Bedfordshire', 40, 48, 56, 62.

3

Change: 400–1250

If the situation on the Great Ouse and the Thames is representative of most of the rest of the country—and it is likely that it is—it follows that the bulk of the pre-industrial bridge network had been built by the first half of the thirteenth century. This means that most of the bridges standing in 1750 were on the site of a bridge constructed before 1250. When they were built is far less clear, since we know the construction date of only a handful of bridges. Nevertheless, there is sufficient information, albeit fragmentary, to show in broad outline the stages by which a network of bridges replaced fords and ferries as the main river crossings.

Many of these new bridges were on different sites from those of the Roman river crossings. Together with major new centres, they were the focal points of a new road system which was significantly different from the Roman network. By the first half of the fourteenth century the new road system can be seen in considerable detail, but it is likely that it had been established centuries earlier. Here and there, parts of it can be seen by the late Saxon period.

AN AGE OF FORDS: FROM THE FIFTH TO THE EIGHTH CENTURY

Roman Roads and Bridges

The Roman road system in Britain is well known from both Roman sources and subsequent archaeological investigations. The Antonine Itineraries, a road book of AD 210, lists the towns and staging posts along the chief roads of the Roman Empire. The main routes and many secondary routes in Britain have been traced on the ground for centuries by scholars. The first full description of them was published by Thomas Codrington in 1903. It was updated in the

1950s to take account of the many discoveries made in the intervening period by Mr Margary, a Sussex landowner who became interested in Roman roads in 1929, when he found an aerial photograph which showed traces of an unrecorded Roman road passing through Ashdown Forest near his home. Like Jervoise, who had set off on his travels in search of ancient bridges in the mid-1920s, Margary travelled over the whole Roman road system in Britain, covering 20,000 miles. He devised a system of road numbering, using single figures for important roads, double for secondary roads, and three figures for minor roads.[1]

The main roads and most of the secondary roads are now well established, but the extent of other roads is disputed. An experienced group, who called themselves the Viatores, undertook a very detailed study, which was published as *Roman Roads in the South-East Midlands*.[2] They rightly argued that there were many more minor roads than had hitherto been realized, but, as R. W. Bagshawe has pointed out, the contributors (and he was one of them) were a little over-zealous, including roads laid out as a result of late eighteenth-century enclosure awards. He gives an approximate estimate of 10,000 miles as the total mileage of the paved Roman road system in Britain, comprising 7,400 of known roads and 2,000 miles which are still to be found. In addition there would have been an array of minor unmetalled roads, many of them prehistoric tracks.[3]

While the Roman roads of Britain are well known, there is far less information about Roman river crossings. There are hundreds of books and articles on the road system, but few contain detailed references to bridges, fords, and ferries. The basic work on Roman bridges in Britain is still D. P. Dymond's important but brief twenty-nine page article, which was published in 1961.[4] He listed fewer than 100 sites where it was either probable or possible that there had been a Roman bridge. While only a handful more have been uncovered since then, the known bridges must represent a fraction of those built in the province. There were surely many more.[5]

[1] T. Codrington, *Roman Roads in Britain* (London, 1903); Margary, *Roman Roads*, 29–33; and see R. W. Bagshawe, *Roman Roads* (Princes Risborough, 2000), 8–11.

[2] The Viatores, *Roman Roads in the South-East Midlands* (London, 1964).

[3] Bagshawe, *Roman Roads*, 7, 10; Taylor, *Roads*, 78–83; O. Rackham, *The History of the Countryside* (paperback edn., London, 1987), 252–7.

[4] D. P. Dymond, 'Roman Bridges on Dere Street, County Durham, with a General Appendix on the Evidence For Bridges in Roman Britain', *Arch. Jnl.*, 118 (1961), 136–64; there is also a brief but informative discussion of Roman river crossings in Taylor, *Roads*, 71–7; see also O'Connor, *Roman Bridges*, 147–8; the design of the bridges is discussed in more detail in Chap. 6.

[5] e.g. D. A. Jackson and T. M. Ambrose, 'A Roman Timber Bridge at Aldwincle, Northants.', *Britannia*, 7 (1976), 39–72.

This does not, however, mean that there was a bridge at every crossing. At some sites bridges probably collapsed before the end of Roman rule, at others there was never a bridge. Dymond claimed that fords were relatively common even on main roads: some were carefully constructed with steps down to the river, and a few of these have been found.[6] Place-names, in particular the 'Stratfords', may provide additional evidence. Ekwall pointed out that all were on Roman roads. For example, a Roman road crossed the river at Stratford-upon-Avon, which is first mentioned at the early date of 691–2 (*aet stretfordae*). Some were very important crossings. In Buckinghamshire are Fenny Stratford and Stony Stratford on Watling Street, and Water Stratford on the Alchester/Towcester Road. Stratford in Middlesex is close to where the main road from London to Colchester crossed the River Lea. Among the others are Stratford St Mary in Suffolk (where the major road from Colchester to Caistor St Edmund (*Venta Icenorum*) crossed the valley of the Stour), and Stratford sub castle and Stratford Toney in Wiltshire. Other forms are found: there is Strefford in Shropshire, which is on Watling Street.[7] It has been argued that the names indicate Roman bridges which had rotted away,[8] but they may be evidence of Roman fords.

The Early Anglo-Saxon Period

With the departure of the Roman armies the impressive road network began to change. Sections of roads ceased to be used; these would rapidly have become overgrown.[9] Most timber bridges would have become unuseable before the end of the fifth century if they were not maintained. Margary envisaged the breakdown of the Roman road system in the following manner: 'The effect of this increasing disorganization upon the road system can well be imagined. The wooden bridges would be the first to go, and if some local owner did not carry out the repair the road would be broken at that point unless a ford was available nearby; wash-outs would occur in hilly districts, severing the road at culverts and creating very awkward obstacles.'[10]

Some roads remained in use. It is possible to distinguish a number of places where a road survived by diverting to a neighbouring ford. For instance, at Acton Burnell, Shropshire, a hollow-way descends from the Roman road to a ford upstream of the Roman bridge.[11] The same process can be observed where Ermine Street met the Nene. The road ran from Alconbury Hill northwards,

---

[6] Dymond, *Roman Bridges*, 149.
[7] The 'Stratfords' are listed in Ekwall, *Dictionary*, 449–50, 439.
[8] Rackham, *Countryside*, 261.   [9] Ibid. 257.
[10] Margary, *Roman Roads*, 23.   [11] Dymond, *Roman Bridges*, 162.

just to the west of the fens, to cross the river near Water Newton (Roman *Duro-brivae*, meaning 'fort by the bridge'), where stone piers have been observed.[12] After the Roman period travellers left the Roman road not far from Water Newton and took what must have been a local track to the nearest ford over the river at Wansford. This had presumably happened by the tenth century when the settlement is first recorded, but the diversion may have been in use centuries earlier.[13] Subsequently a bridge was built, not near the site of the former Roman bridge, but at the ford where the road now went. By far the most plausible explanation for this diversion is that the Roman bridge had collapsed. Wansford remains today the main crossing of the A1. The ancient bridge, which partly dates from 1577, is now bypassed, but is visible from the main road. The story of the crossings at Stamford is similar: Ermine Street crossed the River Welland to the west of the present town, but the Saxon road shifted to the stony ford further downstream where the river flowed through a series of shallow channels.[14]

Roman bridges were scarce after 400, but they probably did not completely disappear. A few may have survived for several centuries. Bede observed that: 'The Romans had occupied the country south of the earthwork which . . . Severus built across the island, as cities, forts, bridges and paved roads bear witness to this day.'[15] He was surely referring to bridges with stone piers and timber decks such as those at Corbridge, Piercebridge, Newcastle, and Rochester, which may have been in intermittent use through to the mid- and late Anglo-Saxon periods, incorporating at least the foundations and parts of the stone piers of Roman bridges.[16]

In addition to these important survivals, it is likely that some new timber structures, were constructed in the Dark Ages between the fifth and seventh centuries, either on the site of an earlier bridge or at new sites. There is no evidence of such bridges before 700, but it is clear that craftsmen of the period had the ability to construct large wooden buildings: the earliest great timber hall to be excavated at Yeavering, Northumberland, which was probably built *c.*600, had a length of nearly 25 metres and a width of 11 metres.[17]

However, the number of bridges, be they surviving Roman or new structures, was small. The weight of the evidence is that bridges were scarce before the eighth century, certainly in comparison to the dense pattern of bridges of the later middle ages. There is no archaeological evidence of an Anglo-Saxon

---

[12] Margary, *Roman Roads*, 224; for the history of the road, see Taylor, *Roads*, 122.
[13] Ekwall, *Dictionary*, 496.   [14] Taylor, *Roads*, 97–9.
[15] Bede, 40–1.   [16] See Chap. 6.
[17] Welch, M., *Anglo-Saxon England*, (London, 1992), 18, 29, 44–53.

bridge before 700, and no document mentions bridges until a few years later.[18]

In contrast, there is positive evidence that fords were the normal form of river crossing in early Anglo-Saxon England. It is striking that there are many place-names with a -ford element where there was a bridge in the later middle ages. There were bridges in the fifteenth century across the Thames at Lechlade (from the Old English *gelad*, meaning 'passage'), Oxford, and Wallingford, across the Severn at Montford, and across the Great Ouse at Water Stratford, Stony Stratford, Stafford, Great Barford, and Bedford.

It is likely that these place-names reflect conditions prevailing in the early Saxon period. It is not known exactly when they came into being, but probably many were formed at an early date. Professor Gelling is of the view that place-names containing a topographical element, including -ford, are in some areas among the oldest English settlement names.[19] The following names were recorded before 731: Bestlesford, Brentford, Daylesford, Fordstreate (now lost), Hertford, Hreutford (now Redbridge), Somerford (now Somerford Keynes), and Twyford (now lost).[20] More place-names containing a -ford element were recorded by the tenth century, including places where there were later important bridges: Aylesford (by the River Medway); Burford (Windrush), Castleford (Aire), Guildford (Wey); Hereford (Wye); Leatherhead (Mole)—the name means 'grey ford'; and Watford (Colne).[21] Most were probably established long before they first appear in documents.

Many other -ford place-names appear in Domesday Book, and there are also some, but far fewer, -bridge names. Ekwall's *Concise Oxford Dictionary of English Place-Names* lists over 400 of the former recorded before 1100 and just over sixty of the latter. No -bridge name is recorded until the late ninth century. It seems that in earlier centuries, when so many place-names were formed, fords were far more common than bridges.

Early narrative sources, notably Bede, give a similar impression. None of the events recounted in the *Ecclesiastical History of the English People* (written in 732) takes place near a bridge (or at least none are described as taking place near a bridge). In contrast, several meetings were held near fords or at settlements by a ford. A synod was held under the presidency of Archbishop Theodore in the presence of King Egfrid where Cuthbert was elected bishop of the church of

---

[18] Bede, Book 1, Chapter 11.

[19] M. Gelling, *Signposts to the Past: Place-Names and the History of England* (Chichester, 1997), 118–19, 126.

[20] B. Cox, 'The Place-Names of the Earliest English Records', *English Place-Name Society Journal*, 8 (1975–6), 12–66.

[21] Ekwall, *Dictionary*, 20, 34, 74, 89, 130, 355, 493, 207, 236, 292, 501; Cameron, *Place Names*, 49.

Lindisfarne. He was reluctant to accept the office, and only agreed to do so after the king himself and others had taken a boat to his island retreat and begged him. From our point of view, the interest lies in the fact that the meeting was held 'near the river Alne (in Northumberland) at a place called Twyford or the Two Fords'. Another important synod was held at Hertford in 670. One of the stories which Bede relates about St Aidan, the missionary from Iona sent to King Oswald of Northumbria in the 630s, provides an interesting insight into travel in the north of England at the time: the saint 'had been given an excellent horse, and although he usually walked, he would ride it when he had to cross a river'.[22] It is likely that in the seventh century it was a good idea to have a horse to ford rivers and streams because there were few bridges.

BUILDING BRIDGES: FROM THE EIGHTH TO THE THIRTEENTH CENTURY

The Eighth and Early Ninth Centuries

By the eighth century there is evidence that the situation had begun to change. The earliest known major Anglo-Saxon crossing is a large piled causeway linking Mersea Island to the Essex mainland, which has been dated to *c*.700.[23] It would be surprising if there had not been other similar structures. In the middle of the century we first hear of the obligation to work on bridges, which was to be a constant aspect of later Anglo-Saxon charters and was a sufficiently important duty to be mentioned in several law codes. Aethelbald, king of Mercia (716–57), the dominant ruler of the southern English kingdoms, held a council in 749 at Gumley where he issued important privileges to the church. *Inter alia*, church lands were freed from all works and various specified burdens, including feeding the king, but they were to contribute to certain public works. These were work on bridges and fortresses, as laid down in a royal edict: 'sola quae communiter fruenda sint, omnique populo edicto regis facienda iubentur, id est instructionibus pontium vel necesariis defensionibus arcium contra hostes non sint renuenda.'[24] The Gumley charter may have been confined to Mercia, since it was only witnessed by Mercian bishops. Two charters

---

[22] Bede, 436–7, 348–9, 258–9. [23] See Chap. 6.

[24] The most important article on the introduction of bridge work and the other two public services is Brooks, *Military Obligations*. The issues have been considered by many others: e.g. R. P. Abels, *Lordship and Military Obligations in Anglo-Saxon England* (London, 1988); E. John, *Re-assessing Anglo-Saxon England* (Manchester, 1996), 50–2; P. Wormald, 'The Age of Offa and Alcuin', in J. Campbell., *The Anglo-Saxons* (Oxford, 1982).

of King Uhtred of the Hwicce, a sub-kingdom under Mercian lordship, of 767 and 770, which freed lands from other services, use the same formula to refer to the liability to build bridges.[25] By the end of the century charters were referring to military service in addition to the two other public burdens.[26]

It is not exactly clear what was happening in the 740s, but it appears that a few years before 749 Aethelbald had made changes to the services which land held by the church contributed to the state. During the years 745 to 747 Boniface, who was in Germany, sent a series of letters to England in which he objected to the king's proposals. To Cuthbert, the archbishop of Canterbury, he referred to the 'forced labour of monks upon royal buildings and other works'.[27] Possibly the decision at Gumley in 749 was a compromise reached as a result of these representations. Historians have long debated whether the burden of constructing bridges and forts was newly imposed in this decade. Did the exemption clauses appear at this time because for the first time an attempt was made to impose the obligation on church and/or other lands? We cannot be certain and, as we might expect, historians have taken different views.[28]

It is likely that some form of liability for maintenance survived from Roman Britain if bridges continued to be repaired.[29] Then, in the eighth century, it seems that the liability was extended in two ways. Not only were existing bridges to be maintained, but new bridges were to be built at sites where there had not been bridges before. Church lands were to share the burden of constructing and maintaining them. A notable feature of the relevant charters is the reference to *instructio* (rather than *restauratio* or *reparatio*). It is possible that Aethelbald had decided on a programme of building bridges and fortifications, and was transforming an existing burden to achieve it.

Why did he do this, and what were the results? The reasons for building bridges are not stated anywhere, but since the charters link bridges and forts together, it is likely that the aims were military and political. A well-located bridge next to a fortified centre could help control a whole region. Haslam has argued that Offa, Aethelbald's successor, constructed a series of such fortified bridge-heads.[30]

This seems plausible. Unfortunately, identifying the bridges which Aethelbald, Offa, and their successors built is more difficult. A small number

[25] *CS* 202, 203.   [26] Brooks, *Military Obligations.* 78.   [27] Ibid. 77.

[28] See Abels, *Lordship*, 52–7; Wormald, *Age of Offa and Alcuin*, 122; E. John, *Land Tenure in Early England* (Leicester, 1960), 64–79; Brooks, 'Military Obligations', 74–8.

[29] Brooks, 'Rochester Bridge', 14–15.

[30] J. Haslam, 'Market and Fortress in England in the Reign of Offa', *World Arch.*, 19: 1 (1987), 76–93; and see Brooks, 'Military Obligations', 72.

of defended settlements of about this period are known in Mercia, albeit the archaeology is often difficult to interpret. At Tamworth, what was considered to be a Mercian royal site, a 'palace complex', was excavated together with a defensive circuit lying beneath the late tenth-century rampart. The abutment of a tenth-century bridge has been found, but not an earlier crossing.[31] Other possible locations include major estate centres such as Northampton, where a massive late eighth- or early ninth-century timber hall has been found, although there is no evidence of defences.[32] At Hereford a most impressive eighth-century settlement has been uncovered, founded on a virgin site, not far from where a Roman road crossed the River Wye. Excavations have shown that 'sometime in the eighth century a grid of streets was laid out . . . and by the middle of the ninth century they were surrounded by a defensive rampart'.[33] Here, on the border with Wales, where Offa's Dyke is assumed to have run near the River Wye, would have been the perfect location for a fortified bridge-head. All that is missing is evidence of an eighth-century bridge.

There are two settlements on the borders of Mercia where it is claimed that substantial work on the river crossing took place. It has been argued that a major project was undertaken on the Thames crossing at Oxford, which was on a major route from Mercia to Winchester and Southampton. The work is said to have involved, not the construction of a bridge, but other improvements to the route across the several channels of the river. A clay bank, forming a cause-way which led to the Thames and which may be artificial, has been excavated. Between the mid-eighth and mid-ninth centuries it is thought that the bank was heightened and a gully lined with wattle fences was dug into it, running down to the river in the same direction as the modern road. J. Blair, in his recent study of Anglo-Saxon Oxfordshire, concluded: 'What emerges as reasonably certain is that earth-moving and construction works of some mag-nitude took place at the Oxford river-crossing in the reign of King Offa [757–96] or King Coenwulf [796–821].'[34] Subsequently excavations have uncovered timbers from what is thought to be a trestle bridge; one of these was dated by radiocarbon to AD 660 to 900,.[35]

We are on more certain ground with the bridge across the Cam at Cambridge. It was probably built some time between the 730s and 870s. Bede described a visit by the community at Ely to a nearby ruined city,

[31] H. Clarke, and B. Ambrosiani, *Towns in the Viking Age* (London, 1991), 39; Crook, *Medieval Bridges*, 11.

[32] Clarke and Ambrosiani, *Towns*, 37.

[33] Ibid. 45.

[34] Blair, *Anglo-Saxon Oxfordshire*, 87–92; and see B. Durham et al., 'The Thames Crossing at Oxford: Archaeological Studies 1979–82', *Oxoniensia*, 49 (1984), 57–100.

[35] A Dodd (ed) *Oxford before the University* (Oxford, 2003), 15, 123–4.

called *Grantacaestir*, to look for stones to make a new coffin for St Ethelreda.[36] By 875 it was known as *Grontabricc* (the bridge over the Granta). Many years ago A. G. Gray argued that the bridge was designed to secure Mercian control of this important river crossing which controlled access to East Anglia. If this were so, it might well have been constructed in the second half of the eighth or the early ninth century, when the Mercian kings held an overlordship of East Anglia which was periodically overthrown. It is notable that all but one (and that disputable) of the hidage-based payments, which continued to be made into the eighteenth century, came from west of the River Cam, which suggests that they may antedate the creation of Cambridgeshire as a county.[37]

While there are only one or may be two examples, it is possible that there was a strategy beginning in the 740s to improve a number of important Mercian river crossings, particularly those on its borders. This would have been the first attempt since the Romans to establish a network of crossing places. However, its scale can only be guessed at. If just a handful of bridges were constructed, it would not have been the first ambitious programme in history to peter out with scant results, but there are two reasons for thinking that something substantial was achieved. First, the construction of bridges and fortresses continued to be exempted in the charters. Why do this if neither had been built, and if any programme had failed? Secondly, the contemporary construction of Offa's Dyke, a huge project, shows that eighth-century English society was quite capable of major works of civil engineering, including the construction of a network of bridges and fortresses. The function of some of these bridgeheads, like the Dyke itself, may have been to control the routes between Mercia and its neighbours.

From the Ninth Century to the Norman Conquest

Between the ninth and eleventh centuries the evidence is much better. Many bridges were built, both smaller and larger structures, at towns and forts and in the countryside. Most of the information is about the former, but it is clear that a great number of rural bridges were built in this period. A study of references to fords and bridges in authentic Anglo-Saxon charters suggests a very significant increase. Cooper has found that in 91 authentic sets of charter bounds from the seventh, eighth and ninth centuries, only one bridge is mentioned and it is not 'above suspicion'; by contrast there are 50 fords. Tenth century charters present a different picture with many more references to bridges.[38]

---

[36] Bede, 394–5; *VCH City of Cambridge*, iii. 2.

[37] A. G. Gray, 'The Ford and Bridge at Cambridge', *Camb. Antiq. Soc. Com.*, 14 (1910), 126–39; I. W. Walker, *Mercia and the Making of England* (Stroud, 2000), 1–21.

[38] A. Cooper, *Bridges, Law and Power in medieval England, 700–1400* (Woodbridge, 2006), 8–9.

Occasionally, there is direct evidence of the construction of bridges in the country; for instance, bridges were built as part of improvements to the road to London by Leofstan, abbot of St Albans (d. 1066).[39]

The liability to build and repair bridges became more important. During the late eighth and ninth centuries charters in other parts of England followed those from Mercia in reserving bridge work. Most of the exemption clauses in charters from the late eighth century refer to military service as well as work on bridges and *burhs*. This triple obligation is first recorded in authentic charters in Kent in the 790s and Wessex from the 840s or 850s.[40] It has been argued that some of the *burhs* in Wessex were having their defences built or repaired by customary annual labour-services from the 850s.[41] Thereafter there is good evidence about the construction of fortified centres. Through the reigns of Alfred and Edward the Elder they were built at an astonishing rate, playing an important role in the wars against the Danish armies in the late ninth and tenth centuries.

Their history is now well-trodden ground.[42] *Burhs* were part of a European movement at this period: similar fortifications were constructed in several countries.[43] Those that existed in Wessex (together with a few others) are listed in a document known as the Burghal Hidage, a text which was originally drawn up in the late ninth or early tenth century.[44] It shows that in a short space of time a system of fortifications had been constructed such that nowhere in Wessex was more than about 20 miles from one. In the early tenth century, as Mercia was taken from Danish control, many more were established.[45] Between 912 and 914 Aethelflaed, Lady of the Mercians, constructed *burhs* at *Scergeat*, Bridgnorth, Tamworth, and Stafford, at Eddisbury Hill between Manchester and Chester, and at Warwick. Edward the Elder, her brother, had *burhs* built at Witham near Maldon in Essex, and on either bank of the River Lea at Hertford and of the Great Ouse at Buckingham; he also received the surrender of the Danish army based in Bedford.[46]

Burhs varied considerably in size, from small promontory forts like Eashing, Lydford, and Lyng to large centres like Oxford, Winchester, and Wallingford.[47] They had a variety of functions. They provided a place of refuge and a centre for defence. Some were temporary forts in out-of-the-way places; others may

---

[39] *Gesta Abbatum monasterii sancti Albani*, ed. H. T. Riley, 3 vols. (RS, 1867–9), i. 39.
[40] Brooks, 'Burghal Hidage', 129.   [41] Ibid.
[42] The principal work is D. Hill and A. R. Rumble, (eds.), *The Defence of Wessex: The Burghal Hidage and Anglo-Saxon Fortifications* (Manchester, 1996).
[43] Sturdy, *Alfred*, 58–9.   [44] Hill and Rumble, *Defence of Wessex*, 2.
[45] Walker, *Mercia*, 91–126.   [46] Ibid. 100–2.   [47] Hill, 'Burghal Hidage Sites'.

have been planned from the first as towns. Many were designed to control road and river communications.

The exemption clauses in charters suggest that bridges were constructed in conjunction with *burhs*. Unfortunately we do not know nearly as much about bridges as we do about the burghal defences. In addition to the considerable documentary evidence about the latter, earth works survive at several sites, sometimes, as at Wallingford, on an impressive scale; in contrast, evidence about even major bridges is very limited.[48] No document comparable to the Burghal Hidage lists their names, and remains are almost non-existent. Nevertheless, there are several reasons for thinking it likely that a significant number of major bridges were built at *burhs* in the late ninth or tenth century. Not only did the liability to work on bridges continued to be referred to in the charters, but also, for the first time, it is possible to document the construction of a small number of bridges, which must be representative of many others.

Whereas once bridges were largely ignored by the historians of Anglo-Saxon England, recently they have attracted more notice. Some studies have argued that they were common, and, in particular, have stressed that they played an important role in controlling the movement of Danish boats along rivers. The clearest picture of this function comes from Francia. Some years before Alfred, Charles the Bald had initiated a policy of building forts and bridges at key places along major rivers in north-west France to block the passage of viking boats.[49] At Trilbardou in 862 he rebuilt a bridge across the Marne and stationed troops on both its banks. In the same year he built a fort at Pont-de-l'Arche, which was seen as a turning-point in the wars: 'Charles caused all the leading men of his realm to assemble about 1 June, with many workmen and carts, at the place called Pitres, where the Andelle from one side and the Eure from the other flow into the Seine. By constructing fortifications on the Seine he closed it off to ships sailing up or down the river. This was done because of the Northmen.'[50]

Alfred was influenced by Charles the Bald's successes. He may have constructed *burhs* at Wareham and Exeter before 875–6; both were a short distance from the sea on rivers which would have provided ready access to Danish boats.[51] The Anglo-Saxon Chronicle for 895 shows how similar Alfred's

---

[48] Hill, 'Burghal Hidage Sites', 219–21.
[49] J. M. Hassall and D. Hill, 'Pont de l'Arche: Frankish Influence on the West Saxon Burh?', *Arch. Jnl.*, 127 (1970), 188–95.
[50] *The Annals of St-Bertin*, ed. and trans. J. L. Nelson (Manchester, 1991), 100.
[51] A. P. Smith, *King Alfred the Great* (Oxford, 1996), 68.

strategy was to Charles's. A Danish army had built a fortress on the Lea, 20 miles above London:

one day the king rode up along the river and looked to see where the river might be obstructed, so that they [the Danes] could not bring out the ships. And then they did so: made two fortifications on the two sides of the river. Then when they had just begun that work and had camped by there, the raiding army realized that they could not bring out the ships. Then they abandoned them and went overland so that they arrived at Bridgnorth on the Severn.[52]

We get some idea of how a bridge might be used for defensive purposes from Snorri Sturluson's accounts of an attack on London Bridge which took place in the early eleventh century. The Danes, who held the bridge, had fortified its southern end at Southwark, digging ditches and building a wall with wood, stone, and turf. On the bridge were fortifications and parapets as high as a man's waist. Under the bridge were staves (that is, vertical timber poles), which were probably placed there to prevent boats from passing under.[53] Remarkably, in the last century the remains of a bridge were found in Norwich which seems to have been defended in just the way Snorri Sturluson described. In the river bed were a mass of timber poles, restricting the passage in the centre of the stream to a single boat. At the time it was thought that the bridge was Roman, but on very slight grounds; a Viking Age date is just as likely.[54]

Several historians have argued that the strategy of building bridges to control movement along rivers was important and widely applied.[55] The maximalist view has been put by Haslam, who has argued that a system of small *burhs* (Barnstaple, Totnes, Plymouth, Kingsbridge, and possibly Kingsteignton), which were associated with bridges at the heads of estuaries, was established in Devon between *c*.904 and 910. Some of these locations would have required huge bridges: at Barnstaple the river is about 700 feet wide. Haslam claims that their construction makes most sense if it is seen as part of 'a policy for the systematic defence of the whole of southern England against Viking seaborne attack . . . They must be seen as the prototypes of the usually larger *burhs* set up by Edward in the Midlands, after 911, for which the same function can be postulated.'[56] This argument raises two questions. How likely is it that bridges

[52] *ASC*, 89.

[53] J. R. Hagland, 'Saxo-Norman London Bridge and Southwark—The Saga Evidence Reconsidered', in *London bridge*, 232–3. Suorri's account was written in the 13th cent., but the attack was mounted by King Olaf of Norway, at the time the ally of King Aethelred.

[54] See Chap. 6.   [55] e.g. Hassall and Hill, *Pont de l'Arche*, 189, 191.

[56] J. Haslam, 'The Towns of Devon', in J. Haslam, ed., *Anglo-Saxon Towns in Southern England* (Chichester, 1984), 249–83.

were constructed at all these sites? Was their chief function the control of movement along rivers?

We know of at least one bridge built by King Alfred, at Lyng in the
Somerset levels. Asser's Life of Alfred records that: 'He ordered the foundation
of two monasteries: one for monks in the place which is called *Aethelingaeg*
which is surrounded on all sides by very great swampy and impassable
marshes so that no one can approach it except by punts or by a bridge which has
been made by laborious skill between two fortresses.'[57] The bridge at Athelney
was no doubt substantial and indicative of what could be built, but it was not
central to the nation's communications. Two other bridges built around this
time were: one was the bridge over the Trent at Nottingham, built shortly after
the Danish borough there was taken by Edward the Elder. This was a national
event of some importance since it was recorded in the Anglo-Saxon Chronicle—the only time the erection of a bridge merited inclusion in this central
text. We are told that before midsummer in 920 Edward 'went to Nottingham
with an army, and ordered a stronghold to be made opposite the other on the
south side of the river, and the bridge over the Trent between the two strong-
holds'.[58] That such an entry should be made is not altogether surprising; the
bridge was a formidable undertaking of great strategic importance. Not for 200
years would there be a bridge further downstream. An even bigger project was
the bridge over the Thames in London, which seems to have been constructed
late in the century. By *c*.1000 there are documentary references to it. The earliest archaeological evidence for the bridge also comes from this period. Two
large timbers, from a tree felled *c*.987–1032, were found *ex situ*, reused in the
foundations of a later bridge. They have been interpreted as part of the southern abutment of a timber construction.[59]

It is likely that a number of the major bridges extant in the eleventh century
had been built in the previous century, including those at Chester, Stamford,
and Worcester.[60] Ouse Bridge, York, seems to belong to this period too.[61] In
907 Chester was captured by Aethelred of Mercia, the Roman walls restored,
and the town garrisoned. Long ago R. Stewart-Brown pointed out that the

[57] S. Keynes and M. Lapidge, *Alfred the Great: Asser's Life of King Alfred and Other Contemporary Sources*
(Harmondsworth, 1983), Chap. 92.
[58] *ASC*, 104.   [59] Watson, *Late Saxon Bridgehead*, 57.
[60] *DB*, i. 262; i. 336b; John of Worcester, 25.
[61] Under the Scandinavians the Coppergate area, to the east of the Minster, became the centre of York,
and the route of the main street changed, leading to a new river crossing, downstream of the Roman bridge
(Clarke and Ambrosiani, *Towns*, 94). At this site Ouse Bridge had probably been constructed by 1086;
Domesday Book states that there was land in the geld of the city, performing the three works of the king (*DB*,
i. 298).

works may have subsequently included the erection or reconstruction of a bridge over the River Dee, noting that the eighteenth-century historian Grose recorded that a friend had communicated to him the following passage from a now-lost manuscript: 'After the death of Elfleda . . . her brother Edward . . . finished the bridge over the Dee at Chester which was begun by his sister Elfleda, before which time there was a ferry for passengers under St. Mary's Hill at the Shipgate.'[62] There was certainly a bridge here by 1066.

This is, alas, about the limit of the documentary evidence. It is likely that there were many bridges, but we cannot know whether there was a bridge at almost every *burh*, as Haslam has suggested. Archaeological evidence may, as it has at London, fill some of the gaps, but it will not be in the near future. It is possible that bridges were intended but not constructed until long after the burghal defences. Asser mentions the extraordinary burden of military service and *burh* construction.[63] Bridges were probably less important militarily than the fortifications, and may therefore have been left until last.

There must also be doubts about Haslam's second proposition, that bridges were built as part of a strategy to control the movement of boats up and down rivers. They were used for this purpose, but were probably not essential to it. Forts on either bank may have been sufficient, perhaps with stakes driven into the river bed and/or a heavy chain across the river to block boats. It is perhaps of interest that, in discussing Alfred's plans to block the River Lea to Danish ships, the Anglo-Saxon Chronicle makes no reference to a bridge.

It is also important not to overlook the traditional role of bridges: providing strategic road crossings.[64] Forts at either end of the bridge helped to secure control of the land crossing as well as river traffic. Most of the few bridges which we know for certain were constructed at this period were, or became, major foci of the road system. The Saxon bridge at Stamford carried the Great North Road across the River Welland. Nottingham was the most important crossing of the Trent, and the nub of the road system in the east Midlands.

From the Norman Conquest to the Thirteenth Century

Although major structures had been built by 1066, the number of bridges which can be identified is but a fraction of those recorded by the thirteenth century. This is in large part a reflection of the rapid increase in the number

---

[62] R. Stewart Brown, 'The Old Dee Bridge at Chester', *J. Chester Arch. Soc.*, NS 30 (1933), 64–5.

[63] Keynes and Lapidge, *Asser's Life*, Chap. 91.

[64] See R. P. Abels, *Alfred the Great: War, Kingship and Culture in Anglo-Saxon England* (London, 1998), on the role of the *burhs* of Wessex in controlling the road system. In my opinion, he wrongly supposes that the road system still in use was Roman. See below.

of documents generated in, and surviving from, the intervening period, but not entirely. Some important bridges were first built in place of fords and ferries after the late eleventh century.

We know of some of these, particularly where the construction of a new bridge was controversial or because it was worth mentioning as one of the good works of a great man or woman. In the second quarter of the twelfth century Alexander the Magnificent, bishop of Lincoln, decided to build a bridge across what was then the course of the Trent at his borough of Newark. He obtained permission for the project from the Crown. A writ (1129–33) states: 'Sciatis quod consessi Alexandro episcopo Linc' ut faciat fieri unum pontem super acquam Trente ad castellum suum de Niwerca ita quod non noceat civitati mee Linc' neque burgo meo Not'; quod firma mea propter hoc non decidat. Et si nocuerit ita talem eum faciat qui non noceat. Testibus etc.'[65] The bridge was built, and it was being repaired three decades later in 1169.[66] Bishop Alexander probably obtained the writ for two main reasons. First, as the nephew of Henry I's chief minister, Roger, bishop of Salisbury, he was in an exceptional position to secure the government's favour. Secondly, he needed this support because the project provoked considerable opposition. It had consequences for trade and communications over a wide area, affecting the fortunes of surrounding towns, in particular Nottingham, which was upstream, and Lincoln to the east. It looks as if the men of both these places were worried about their livelihood and some royal officials were concerned about royal revenues.

Over the following centuries other bridge-builders sought the government's permission for their plans. For instance, in 1416 the Crown licensed the construction of a number of bridges in or near Abingdon.[67] The scheme is likely to have faced stiff opposition from the men of the neighbouring town. According to Leland: it was 'a gret decay to Wallynford, for that the Glostershire men had usyd Walyngford that now go by Abyndun.'[68] Subsequently an act of parliament was granted in favour of the bridge. In later centuries acts were regularly sought to authorize bridge construction.[69]

It was probably unusual to seek the permission of central government at an earlier period, but proposals to build bridges of any significance were surely considered by major figures in the area. There is one piece of evidence that this is what happened. A dispute about tolls taken at the important bridge at Atcham across the Severn led to a case in the royal courts in 1221 which reveals

---

[65] *The Registrum Antiquissimum of the Cathedral Church of Lincoln*, ed. C. W. Foster, Lincoln Rec. Soc., 27 (1931), 38–9.

[66] *Eastern*, 55.   [67] *CPR (1416–22)*, 33.   [68] Leland, i. 306.

[69] For a 16th-cent. example see *Wales and Western*, 120.

the background to its construction. The abbot of Lilleshall had formerly had a ferry at the site and decided to replace it with a bridge. The eyre rolls record that: 'By common counsel of Lord William fitz Alan and other magnates it was provided that the abbot should make a bridge there and take from every loaded cart belonging to Shrewsbury 1d and from others 1/2d and that bridge is now finished except for an arch and in this way he takes that custom.' William fitz Alan was sheriff of Shropshire in the late twelfth century; it is possible that the proposal to build the bridge was discussed in the county court.[70]

We know of a number of other major projects between 1066 and 1200. They include two bridges at Durham, a massive causeway across the fens from Soham and Stuntney to the Isle of Ely, a causeway and bridges over channels of the River Lea at Stratford, near London, and Grandpont, Oxford, which, according to the Abingdon Chronicle, was built as a good work by a penitent, Robert d'Oilly, the castellan of Oxford.[71] These and a few other prominent examples of new construction, together with the continuing growth in population, the economy, and new towns, have led to the widely held assumption that the twelfth and thirteenth centuries were a period of great improvements in transport when many new bridges were built.

R. H. Britnell has observed that: 'The years between 1000 and 1300 saw much bridge construction, which included the rebuilding in stone of some earlier works', S. Reynolds that: 'With the increasing pace and volume of exchange, transport facilities were also becoming more important.' She points, for example, to the importance of the construction of a new bridge at Salisbury (Harnham Bridge, 1244) in the growth of the town. M. W. Beresford referred to the role of new bridges in the establishment of several new towns.[72]

Were these years, then, from the Norman Conquest to the thirteenth century, the key period of bridge construction in pre-industrial England—a period like the late eighteenth and nineteenth centuries when new bridges at sites where there had not previously been a bridge were to be found everywhere? The answer is, bluntly, that we do not know. Considering the thousands of bridges built in the middle ages, and the hundreds of bridges over major and middling rivers, there is not a large number of sites where the earliest bridge can be securely dated between the late eleventh and thirteenth centuries. It was not

---

[70] *Select Pleas of the Crown, A.D. 1200–25*, ed. F. W. Maitland, Seldon Soc., 1 (1887).

[71] For Stuntney causeway, see Darby, *Medieval Fenland*, 108, for details of the other bridges, see Chaps. 7 and 11.

[72] R. H. Britnell, 'Commercialisation and Economic Development, 1000–1300', in R. H. Britnell and B. M. S. Campbell (eds.), *A Commercialising Economy: England 1086 to c. 1300* (Manchester, 1995), 17; S. Reynolds, *An Introduction to the History of Medieval Towns* (Oxford, 1977), 64; M. W. Beresford, *New Towns of the Middle Ages* (London, 1967), 112–20, 137, 176.

the intention of Beresford, Britnell, and Reynolds to provide a comprehensive list of new bridges, but had they wanted to, it would not have been a long one.

Unfortunately, records, like those relating to Newark Bridge, which reveal the background to the construction of new bridges are extremely rare. The main problem is that we usually first hear of a bridge not because of proposals to build it or because it had just been built, but because there was a dispute over its repair, or because it provided a convenient topographical reference, perhaps in a land transaction. Historians have been inclined to take the earliest reference to a bridge as a record of the construction of the first bridge on the site. Britnell reports Hoskins's opinion that most of the bridges across the Exe, Dart, and Tamar were first built in the thirteenth century, but in fact all we know is that the earliest references to the bridges were at this time. The sources do not record their erection, and the most recent study of Devon bridges is extremely cautious about the date of their first construction.[73] Even when there is a reference to construction, it is often difficult to know whether it is referring to the construction of a bridge in place of a ford or ferry on the site or whether there had been an earlier bridge which was being rebuilt. The verb used in the sources is often *facere*.

What then can be made of the limited evidence? We know that in the two centuries after the Norman Conquest there was, as Britnell argued, massive investment in transport. Much of it was spent on reconstruction, but some of it consisted of major bridges at new sites. However, we do not know the scale of new building. The relatively few examples of the construction of new major twelfth-century bridges may be the only records that have survived of a great twelfth-century building boom which essentially established the medieval (and later) bridge network. On the other hand, they may be late and important additions to a bridge network which was already largely complete in 1100. To put it another way, it is highly likely that some of the many bridges standing in the twelfth and thirteenth centuries had been constructed by the late eleventh century, but we do not know how many bridges this was. Was it a quarter? A half? Three-quarters?

The history of other important structures, in particular mills, may help to suggest an answer to this question, or at least provide a basis for an educated guess. Like bridges, we know of relatively few mills in late Anglo-Saxon England. However, whereas references to bridges remain comparatively rare until the thirteenth century, several thousand mills are listed in Domesday Book. They are recorded in the survey because they generated income; bridges

[73] W. G. Hoskins, *Devon* (London, 1954), 147–8; Thomas, 'Devon Bridges', 175–206.

did not. There were possibly about 6,000 mills in 1086; by 1300 the number of mills may have doubled: that is, there may have been as many as 12,000 wind-mills and watermills.[74] Perhaps a similar doubling in the number of bridges over the same period would not be out of place. If this were the case, it would imply that a high proportion of bridges standing in the mid-eighteenth century were on the site of an Anglo-Saxon bridge. It would also point to the scale of construction in the twelfth century.

THE CREATION OF A NEW ROAD SYSTEM

The Post-Roman Road System

The network of bridges, mainly constructed between the eighth and thirteenth centuries, were among the principal foci of a new, post-Roman road system. New roads, created from a patchwork of different types of earlier routes, joined new centres to one another, to former Roman towns, and to the new bridges. The history of this new English road system remains obscure, because for centuries it is only possible to glimpse small fragments of it. Then, in the fourteenth century, we can see it in detail because of the survival of a single source, the Gough Map. This unique map of England depicts major towns and some other settlements, rivers and, most importantly, roads. It shows all the main national roads spreading out from London as well as a number of cross-country routes. Some are shown as lines between towns. Others, equally important, are represented by the settlements along the road. For instance, the Ipswich Road is marked by indicating in the correct order: Brentwood, Chelmsford, Witham, Colchester, Cattawade Bridge, and Ipswich. As Richard Gough, the eighteenth-century antiquarian who bequeathed the map together with the rest of his collection to the Bodlean Library, said: 'the greatest merit of this map is, that it may justly boast itself the first among us wherein the roads and distances are laid down.'[75]

The map seems to have been produced by officials in central government for their use, and is comparatively large, approximately 4 feet by 2 feet. E. J. S. Parsons observed that it 'could be considered as an official map of Great Britain preserved in some central office for all to consult'.[76] It had probably been taken from the central government records in the early eighteenth century, and was

---

[74] R. Holt, *The Mills of Medieval England* (Oxford, 1988), 107, 116.
[75] Parsons, *Gough Map*, 10.
[76] Ibid. 2.

subsequently purchased by Gough for half-a-crown.[77] It is all the more remarkable because nothing comparable was to be produced for several centuries.[78] It was not until 1675, when Ogilby's *Britannia* was published, that very detailed descriptions of the main and secondary roads of England, depicted on a series of strip maps, were available.[79] The Gough Map differs markedly from earlier maps. It does follow certain traditions: as with other medieval Christian maps, east is at the top, with Britain shown lying on its back. However, it is a world away from the Hereford *Mappa mundi* of the early fourteenth century. It has some similarities with the much less detailed Matthew Paris maps of the previous century, one of which shows the road from Dover to Newcastle, but represents it by a straight line through the middle of the country, with the east coast drawn roughly parallel to it and very poorly represented.[80] In contrast the Gough Map is outstandingly consistent and accurate. This can perhaps best be seen by comparing the routes it depicts with those of Ogilby's Road Book. While the latter describes more cross-country and secondary routes, its main roads largely follow the routes set out in the Gough Map, passing through the same towns and crossing the same bridges.[81]

One of the most notable features of the road system shown on the Gough Map is the extent to which it differs from the Roman. Admittedly, some Roman roads did remain in use and others formed sections of the medieval road system. The Dover Road largely coincided with the Roman route; the road to Colchester took the line of the Roman route for most of the way.[82] However, it would be a gross exaggeration to claim, as B. P. Hindle has, that: 'There is considerable evidence to show us which were the most important routes. Our starting point must be the Roman road system, large parts of which were clearly still in use, as shown by the Gough Map and the royal itineraries.'[83]

Of the seven main medieval roads centred on London, only the two just described, to Dover and Colchester, followed the line of a Roman road for most of their course. Sections of two others, to York and Chester, incorporated

---

[77] It was probably obtained by Peter Le Neve, when he was deputy chamberlain of the exchequer. His widow married Thomas Martin, an antiquarian. Gough bought it at the sale of part of Martin's collection (ibid. 1–2).

[78] Ibid. 10. A road book was published in 1571 by Richard Grafton, but roads were not shown on a map of England until Thomas Jenner published his map in 1671.

[79] The frontispiece to *Britannia* describes the volume as *An illustration of the Kingdom of England and Dominion of Wales by a Geographical and Historical Description of the Principal Roads thereof* (Ogilby).

[80] Parsons, *Gough Map*, 4–5.   [81] Ibid. 18.

[82] Ibid. 16; Margary, *Roman Roads*, 14.   [83] Hindle, *Medieval Roads*, 26.

stretches of the Roman roads, Ermine Street and Watling Street, but ignored them for long distances. The Roman Watling Street ran from London to Wroxeter (in Shropshire) via St Albans and Towcester. At Stretton the Chester Road branched off to the north, heading to its destination through Whitchurch. The medieval road took a quite different course for all but a relatively short stretch. It went to St Albans not on Watling Street, but via Barnet. Soon after St Albans the medieval and Roman routes coincided, but after 40 miles they diverged completely, the medieval road passing through the towns of Daventry, Coventry, Lichfield, and Newcastle under Lyme. The southern part of the Gough Map road to York broadly followed the course of Ermine Street, although the track it indicates goes a few miles to the west through the obscure settlement of Ogerston.[84] North of Grantham the roads diverged completely, the medieval route passing through Newark, en route for Doncaster.[85]

The three other major medieval roads emanating from London, namely the roads to Exeter, Gloucester, and the Great West Road, owed even less to their Roman predecessors. This was despite the fact that Exeter, Gloucester, and Bath (just off the Great West Road) were Roman towns which had been linked to London by a Roman roads. The medieval Exeter Road avoided the Roman roads, except for the last few miles of the journey from Honiton to Exeter.[86] The same is true of the medieval Gloucester Road. The route shown on the Gough Map followed the Roman road from Gloucester to Cirencester only for the short distance to the Cotswold escarpment at Birdlip, before striking off to follow for most of the way the modern A40 via Oxford into London.[87]

How and When the English Road System Was Created

Anglo-Saxon England

The new road system described on the Gough Map was formed, as F. M. Stenton observed in his article on 'The Road System of Medieval England', from ancient pre-Roman tracks, some sections of Roman road, and from a myriad of village lanes, formerly used for local traffic only.[88] W. G. Hoskins described this process in some detail, showing the creation *c*.1200 of a network of roads to link the new town of Market Harborough with the neighbouring towns. He demonstrated how the present through-route from Leicester was

---

[84] The only trace of this route is a modern lane which passes a farm on the site called Ongutein Manor (Taylor, *Roads*, 120–1).

[85] The Roman roads are described in Margary, *Roman Roads*, the York and Chester roads and several other major medieval roads in Taylor, *Roads*, 193–7.

[86] Parsons, *Gough Map*, 36.   [87] Ibid.   [88] Stenton, 'Road System', 238.

built up out of a series of inter-village paths, with entirely new pieces here and there to fill in the gaps.[89] Tracks established between major centres would subsequently be upgraded, mended with gravel and stones, and ditches would be dug to improve drainage. Since fords proved the most difficult and dangerous part of many journeys, the construction of bridges was of special importance. Once constructed, they played a key part in fossilizing a route, as traffic was diverted from neighbouring ferries and fords.

There have been few serious attempts to examine the development of the post-Roman road system. The principal work to do so, apart from Stenton's article which was written over fifty years ago, was C. Taylor's *Roads and Tracks of Britain*, published in 1979. Both came to the same conclusion, that a new road system had been created long before the fourteenth century: 'the primary layout was there by the time William the Conqueror arrived in England. It was perhaps centuries old by that time. All we have done since is to modify it slightly to meet with changing circumstances.'[90] However, Stenton and Taylor have had surprisingly little effect. Historians have been reluctant to accept that such a new road system was appearing in the Saxon period, and have tended to assume that Roman roads remained the most important channels of communication until the eleventh century and even later.

This attitude is reflected in the convention that even scholarly books about Anglo-Saxon England have maps of the Roman road network and books about the thirteenth century and later describe a road system based on the Gough Map; those writing about the eleventh and twelfth centuries find themselves in a quandary. The practice of plotting the sites of late Anglo-Saxon England on a map which assumes that the Roman road system remained in place leads to the ridiculous situation that major new towns, including those listed in the Burghal Hidage, appear to be unconnected to that road network; in fact, like Market Harborough at a later date, they would have been joined to it very quickly. A road map of the eighteenth century or even the early twentieth century may provide a more accurate picture of the routes of late Anglo-Saxon England than the Roman roads which are usually depicted.

It is not difficult to understand why Stenton's and Taylor's views have been largely ignored, and why most historians have continued to believe that the Roman roads remained the country's national highways until after the Norman Conquest. There are no contemporary descriptions of a post-Roman route

[89] 'The Origin and Rise of Market Harborough', in W. G. Hoskins, *Provincial England* (London, 1965), 54–63.
[90] Taylor, *Roads*, 110.

network before the Gough Map. Of course, a few Saxon roads which subsequently became major routes have been traced, for instance, the roads described in estate boundaries, such as *herepaths* (usually translated as a track used by an army, but probably meaning a secondary road).[91] However, indicating that sections of some modern roads have their origin in Saxon tracks is a long way from delineating a systematic Saxon route system comparable to the Roman.

There is also very strong evidence that some Roman roads, not shown on the Gough Map, remained in use until the late Saxon period. An example is provided by the construction of a fort at Sashes, an island in the Thames near Cookham, which is referred to in the Burghal Hidage. Here or very near here the Roman road from Silchester to St Albans had crossed the river. The construction of the fort at the site implies that the Roman road remained in use.[92] Even more impressive evidence is provided by the references in twelfth-century legal compilations to four national roads which were protected by the King's Peace. The *Leges Edwardi Confessoris* contain the following statement: 'Pax regis multiplex est . . . alia quam habent quatuor chemini, id est Watlingstrete, Fosse, Hikenilde-stret, Ermingstre, quorum duo in longitudinem regni, alii vero in latitudinem distenduntur.' The *Leis Willelme* contain a similar statement.[93] The same four roads, although not mentioned in the other compilation of this period, the *Leges Henrici Primi*, are described by Henry of Huntingdon and later in other chronicles.[94] Three of them, Watling Street, Ermine Street, and Foss Way, appear to be Roman roads; the fourth, the Icknield Way, was a prehistoric track. The inference is clear: in around 1100 major Roman roads continued to be used and formed, together with an even older track, the backbone of a national road system.

Moreover, there are strong a priori reasons for thinking that Roman roads must have survived as the main routes. They were such impressive and visible structures, which stretched out to every part of Roman Britain, that it seems obvious that they would have continued to be used by future generations of travellers wherever possible. The paved roads were, as we might expect, still apparent to Bede in the eighth century.[95] Even in recent times Margary found

[91] Rackham, *Countryside*, 259.

[92] The place-name probably commemorated some prominent artificial landmark pole erected hereabouts at an ancient ford of the Thames (J. McN. Dodgson, 'A Linguistic Analysis of the Place-Names of the Burghal Hidage', in Hill and Rumble, *The Defence of Wessex*, 119).

[93] Liebermann, *Gesetze*, i. 637, 511; the four roads are not referred to in the *Leges Henrici Primi*, which simply refers to *herestrete* 'which are completely the concern of the king'; it also states that the '*via regia* is always open . . . which no one can close . . . which leads into a city or fortress (*burgum*) or castle or royal town (*portum*)' (*Leges Henrici Primi*, ed. and trans. L. J. Downer (Oxford 1972), 109, 249.

[94] H. Hunt., 22–3.   [95] Bede, 40–1.

places on Ermine Street where the *agger* was to be seen 4 or 5 feet high and 45 or 50 feet wide, especially where it had remained in use, thereby preserving it from the effects of ploughing.[96] Finally, many of the Roman roads still went where people wanted to travel: London remained a major centre in Anglo-Saxon England, and, needed to be well connected with many important former Roman towns, including Chester, Colchester, Dover, Exeter, Gloucester, Winchester, and York.

However, despite these reasons why it should have survived, the Roman road network did not. While it is true that sections of the Roman roads remained in use for long periods, and that the new roads which evolved in Anglo-Saxon England are difficult to identify, there are good reasons for thinking that a new road system had been created by the eleventh century which differed significantly from the Roman. First, some parts of the road system, as we have seen, became unusable. Secondly, even where they survived, other routes became more popular. Defoe made the interesting observation that even where travellers followed the line of a Roman road, they did not necessarily walk or ride on top of the road, but chose to go on either side.[97] Most importantly, new roads came into being to link together major new Anglo-Saxon settlements, not connected to the former Roman road system. These included some of the trading entrepots such as Ipswich and the earliest fortified *burhs*. Later there were ever more non-Roman settlements, including many of the *burhs* established by Alfred and his successors. There were shire towns of the Midlands as well as important sites in Wessex, including Bedford, Buckingham, Malmesbury, Nottingham, Shaftesbury, Wallingford, Wareham, and Warwick. It is quite frankly incredible that travellers between these places would have made for the nearest Roman road, however far it took them out of their way. The new settlements also led to major changes in long-distance roads. Travellers preferred to take a route which ran through a town which provided them with accommodation, food and drink, company, and other services for their journey rather than follow a Roman road which offered none.

Some of the major post-Roman roads which provided links to new towns, and new routes to former Roman towns, can begin to be traced in the tenth and eleventh centuries.[98] A case in point is the road from London to Oxford. Oxford grew up on the gravel terrace at the confluence of the Thames and the Cherwell. It was obviously very well placed to take advantage of river commu-

---

[96] Margary, *Roman Roads*, 20.   [97] Defoe, *Tour*, ii. 120.
[98] The development of new roads around both Winchester and Tamworth is described in Taylor, *Roads*, 99–102.

nications and it had good road links in some directions, but not to the east. Once established as a major settlement, it was inevitable that the land route to London and the south east would be improved. There were Roman roads to the east of the town, including a north–south Roman road from Alchester to Dorchester-on-Thames which passed some miles to the east of Oxford, but this was not the shortest route to London.[99] That is marked by the A40 (which survived as the main road until the building of the M40 in the 1970s) through Uxbridge, High Wycombe, Tetsworth, and Wheatley. Through the evidence of place-names and charter boundaries it is possible to show that the river crossings on this road were in place by the tenth century, and hence, presumably, so was the road itself. The road left London following the Roman road to Bath, but soon turned off to the north-west. It crossed three main rivers on its way to Oxford: the Colne, the Thame, and the Cherwell. The bridge across the Colne at Uxbridge is likely to have been built at an early date; the name, which means 'settlement by the bridge of the Wixan', is first recorded in the twelfth century, but since Wixan is a name referred to in the Tribal Hidage, it is almost certainly much older. At Wheatley, where the road crossed the Thame, there was an important ford, described as the 'herpath ford' in the tenth century. A bridge was subsequently constructed at the site, and a medieval arch is hidden under one of the arches of the modern bridge. By 1004 there was a bridge across the Cherwell on the site of Magdalen Bridge on the eastern side of Oxford, and on the east bank of the river was a settlement known as the *brycg-gesett* ('bridge settlement').[100]

By the late Saxon period we can also trace what was probably then the main road from London to the north through Nottingham and Doncaster. Domesday Book refers to a section of it as the road towards York in Nottinghamshire. It passed through Blyth and Doncaster on its way to York. This section of the road may already have been in use in 868 when the Danes, based in York, seized Nottingham. Here there was a ford of the Trent. Just over fifty years later the importance of the route was firmly established by the construction of the bridge which channelled north–south traffic to this key crossing.[101] It was by far the most important crossing of the Trent in the eleventh century. William the Conqueror used this road when passing to and from the north on his major campaigns in 1068 and in the spring and autumn of 1069.[102]

[99] Margary, *Roman Roads*, 163–4.
[100] Ekwall, *Dictionary*, 488; CS 945; M. Gelling, *The Place-Names of Oxfordshire*, 2 vols. (Cambridge, 1953–4), i. 142; *Cartulary of the Monastery of St. Frideswide*, ed. S. R. Wigram, Oxford Hist. Soc., 29: 31 (1896), i. 8; Blair, *Anglo-Saxon Oxfordshire*, 161.
[101] *VCH Notts.*, i. 239.   [102] M. Bennett, *Campaigns of the Norman Conquest* (Oxford, 2001), 51, 54.

There is an obvious difficulty in reconciling this information about new routes with the post-Conquest references in the *Leges Edwardi Confessoris* and other legal compilations to the four national highways. If travellers from the south preferred to take the post-Roman road to York via Nottingham rather than Roman Ermine Street through Lincoln and across the Humber ferry at Brough, why do the legal compilations refer to Ermine Street? What may be the explanation for this discrepancy is that Ermine Street and Watling Street were names used in the legal compilations to describe the two great national north–south routes—the one to York, the other to Chester and the north-west—but the roads described were not Roman roads. Rather they were their more recent successors: thus Ermine Street meant the main road used in the eleventh century to the north, not the Roman main road. It is worth noting that Henry of Huntingdon described the Foss Way as the road from Caithness to Totnes (the Roman Foss Way went from Exeter to Lincoln); Daniel Defoe described Watling Street as the road through Stony Stratford, Daventry, and Coventry to Chester, that is, he was describing the road which was in use, and which is marked on the Gough Map, but he referred to it by its 'Roman' name.[103]

The Twelfth and Thirteenth Centuries

A road map drawn up at the time of Domesday Book would have shown that much of the medieval and later road network had been established and that, with some exceptions, Roman roads were no longer used as the major routes of the country. Nevertheless, it would also have differed in certain important respects from the road system of the later middles ages. As before, the two main driving forces behind the changes after 1100 were the need to connect new to existing settlements and the improvement of existing tracks. It is possible to show that the construction of a handful of important bridges in the twelfth and the thirteenth centuries transformed some secondary or minor routes into national highways.

Two of the most striking examples were the bridges at Newark and Maidenhead, constructed in the twelfth and thirteenth centuries respectively. Those who had opposed the construction of a bridge over the Trent downstream from Nottingham had been right to think that it would have major consequences. There must have been a road from Stamford to Newark earlier, and probably a ferry or ford for travellers to cross the Trent there, but the preferred route from London to York went through Nottingham, as we have seen. Once the bridge had been built at Newark, more traffic to the north was attracted to

---

[103] H. Hunt., 22–3; Defoe, *Tour*, ii. 126.

the Newark road. The Gough Map shows this route as the main highway to the north. Its basic alignment north of Stamford is still followed by the A1.

Much of the modern course of the Great West Road had been established by the Norman Conquest, but there were major changes in its alignment up to the thirteenth century.[104] The medieval and Roman roads left London and entered Bath together, but in between they diverged. The Roman road went west from London to the Thames at Staines, from there across the Berkshire heathland to Silchester, and thence north-west heading in the direction of Cirencester, crossing the Enborne and the Kennet before entering Thatcham (*Spinae*); soon afterwards it left the Cirencester Road and headed west in a very direct route to Bath. Throughout the middle ages the road to Staines, the Roman crossing of the Thames, remained in use, and the next section of the Roman road from Staines to Thatcham may have been used for some considerable time. A *weala brucge*, on or near the site of the Roman bridge over the Enborne near Thatcham, is recorded in the tenth century.[105]

However, during the ninth and tenth centuries Reading became the main settlement in the area.[106] The site was an ideal location both for navigation and defence at the junction of the Thames and Kennet. It was prominent in the wars with the Danes, who seized it and constructed a rampart between the two rivers. While it was founded because of its position on the Thames, once it was established road links were created to it and at some point it became the focus of the Great West Road. There is a hint that parts of the route were in being by the ninth century. In 871 Alfred attacked the fortification there and was defeated. According to a twelfth-century chronicler, he escaped, along what we must assume was at least a track, to the ford of the River Loddon at Twyford.[107] This was on the route of the later Great West Road; before 1250 a bridge had replaced the ford.[108] While initially traffic from London would have reached Reading via the crossing at Staines, the construction of a bridge at Windsor led to the development of a new road to Twyford and thence to Reading. This was the route which, as their itineraries show, was frequently taken by John, Edward I, and Edward II.[109] Windsor Bridge is recorded by the thirteenth century, but might have been in use by the late eleventh century when William the Conqueror built his chief castle on the middle Thames here (plate 7).

[104] The Roman and medieval routes are described in detail in O. G. S. Crawford, *Archaeology in the Field* (London, 1953), 68–73. See also Parsons, *Gough Map*, 17; Taylor, *Roads*, 195:
[105] Crawford, *Archaeology*, 68.
[106] G. G. Astill, *Historic Towns in Berkshire* (Reading, 1978), 75–86.
[107] Geffrei Gaimar, *L'Estoire des Engleis*, ed. A. Bell (Oxford, 1960), 94–5.
[108] *South*, 21.   [109] Hindle, *Medieval Roads*, 40.

Finally, in the thirteenth century one last and important change in the alignment of the road seems to have been made as a result of the construction of
Maidenhead Bridge to the north of Windsor. It is likely to have been built relatively late, possibly not before 1250, since it is not mentioned until 1297, that
is, over fifty years after the first reference to most of the other Thames crossings
in the vicinity.[110] By the next century it had become part of the Great West
Road and is marked on the Gough Map. Subsequently, the route through
Maidenhead and Reading, and from there to Marlborough, remained the main
road to Bristol and Bath for centuries.

Although it took its final form later than most other major roads, the Great
West Road was in many respects typical. It demonstrates well the types
of changes which were happening throughout England between the end of
Roman Britain and 1300. The key parts of the process were the linking up of
existing tracks of various kinds to form roads to new centres like Reading. Travellers preferred a long-distance route which passed through these centres to a
lonely Roman road through a deserted settlement like Silchester. Subsequently,
the new roads and tracks were improved in various ways, in particular through
the construction of bridges, which in turn attracted more travellers. Here and
there, as at Maidenhead, the construction of a new bridge led to the realign-
ment of a major road.

[110] *CPR (1292–1301)*, 324.

4

Stability: Bridges and the Road System After 1250

After over 500 years of change, when the major river crossings were bridged and a new road system established, there followed almost 500 years of stability. The stock of bridges changed little. The dense pattern of bridges which existed in the eighteenth century would have been recognizable to Englishmen five centuries earlier. Similarly, the routes established by the time of the Gough Map survived almost unchanged.

One of the principal characteristics of the English road system in this period is clear: travellers on major roads could be sure of dry and safe river crossings provided that the bridges had been kept in repair. It is no exaggeration to say that where a national highway met a river there was invariably a bridge. On secondary roads too, bridges were the norm, except on the downstream sections of rivers, where ferries were common. On minor roads, while bridges across major rivers were unusual, there were numerous bridges over streams and small water courses as well as countless fords and ferries.

This is not to say that there were no changes. Bridges were reconstructed. Some major bridges were built in place of ferries on secondary roads, but they represented a relatively small increase to the large existing stock of bridges. New bridges continued to be constructed after 1350, despite the effects of the Black Death. Then, in about 1550, the construction of important new bridges in place of fords and ferries largely ceased, although repair and some rebuilding continued.

In the eighteenth century, and especially after 1760, the situation changed again. New bridges were erected at many sites. The remaining ferries on secondary roads were replaced by bridges. This was the second great age of bridge construction, which has lasted to the present day. Nevertheless, the main river crossings were still, with a few exceptions, the same as they had been in the middle ages. Roads were improved, but despite changes in detail they continued to follow the same general alignment which they had five centuries earlier.

Bridges

1200–1350

The increasing number of administrative records in the period 1200 to 1350 means that there are more and more references to bridges. This has been taken as evidence of the quickening pace of bridge construction. In fact, it is probable that most of the references are the first record of bridges which had been built in previous centuries. There is a paucity of material relating to the construction of new bridges at new sites in this increasingly well-documented period, which tends to confirm this view.

Of course, some evidence points to the building of a few new major bridges at virgin sites: at Maidenhead for example.[1] The construction of a number of others is well documented. There is reliable information that a bridge (today known as Harnham Bridge) was built in 1244, linking the new town of Salisbury to the areas south of the Avon.[2] Another major project was the new causeway and bridge built later in the thirteenth century at Lichfield across the long marshy valley there.[3] Another was the bridge over the Nene at Peterborough. In 1346 an inquiry found that there was no bridge across the river until Godfrey, abbot at the beginning of the century, built one.[4] These bridges were important. Leland recorded a tradition in Salisbury about the consequences of building Harnham Bridge: 'and so was the high-way westward made that way, and Wilton way lefte, to the ruine of that towne.' Wilton had once been the county town. Taylor argues that the Lichfield causeway had similar effects, claiming it to have been the making of Lichfield's medieval prosperity.[5]

This seems to be impressive stuff, but it must be stressed that these bridges were modest additions to an already large stock. For instance, by *c.*1300, when the abbot is said to have built the bridge at Peterborough, other bridges across the River Nene had been recorded in Northamptonshire: at Great Billing, Wellingborough, Ditchford, Thrapston, and Wansford, and there were almost certainly others at Northampton and Oundle.[6] For all the importance

---

[1] See Chap. 3.
[2] *VCH Wilts.*, iii. 344; vi. 69, 87–9; *The Fifteenth Century Cartulary of St Nicholas Hospital, Salisbury*, ed. C. Wordsworth (Salisbury, 1902), 23.
[3] Taylor, *Roads*, 135–6; *VCH Staffs.*, xiv. 11, 41, 45.
[4] *CPR* (1345–8), 87; Goodfellow, 'Northants Bridges', 144.   [5] Leland, ii. 28; Taylor, *Roads*, 135–6.
[6] Goodfellow, 'Northants Bridges', 152–7.

of the new bridge built at Maidenhead (probably *c.*1275), it was but one of a number across the Thames in its vicinity at that date.

Moreover, on closer inspection much of the evidence for new construction is as ambiguous as it is scanty. It is often not clear whether the bridges were the first on the site or reconstructions. The authors of the relevant VCH volumes note the possibility that there were pre-thirteenth-century structures both across the Avon in Salisbury and at Lichfield. The problem in interpreting the evidence relating to the construction of a bridge over the Nene at Peterborough is different. Here the evidence seems unambiguous, but the problem is that it comes from a court case in which the abbey was attempting to deny liability for the repair of the structure. If there had not been a bridge on the site until recently and if its construction had been a matter of private piety, there could be no obligation to repair. It is, as is well known, difficult to prove a negative. The lack of evidence for new bridges does not prove that they were not built, but it does look as if, from the thirteenth century, expenditure was directed towards repair and reconstruction rather than bridging hitherto unbridged sites.

1350–1550

In 1349 the Black Death arrived in England. Perhaps one-third of the population died. It probably did not regain its pre-plague peak for over two centuries, possibly longer. Remarkably, these cataclysmic events seem to have had little long-term effect on the network of bridges. A few major bridges were lost after the late thirteenth century, and there are strong a priori reasons why their disappearance might have been related to dislocation in the second half of the fourteenth century. The regular process of maintenance and repair could have been disrupted, sometimes with ensuing collapse. Here and there fallen structures were not replaced. Bridges which had been out of repair before 1350 were not repaired or rebuilt. However, whatever dislocation occurred, by the fifteenth century new bridges were being constructed to replace ferries and fords. It is almost certain that there were more bridges in 1550 than there had been 200 years earlier.

The evidence of lost bridges is as follows. At Hemington, on the road from Leicester to Derby, a series of bridges were found in the 1980s across a disused channel of the Trent. They had been built from the eleventh to the thirteenth centuries; after the thirteenth-century bridge collapsed there was no bridge on the road across the river until Cavendish Bridge was erected nearby in 1758.[7] Further north, a bridge at Myton-on-Swale, which took what was then the

---

[7] Cooper et al., 'Hemington Bridges', 316–321; *Mid and Eastern*, 8.

main road from York to the Great North Road and to Ripon, had probably disappeared by 1354.[8] It has never been replaced. On the Thames a bridge is recorded at Shillingford as late as 1370, but by the next century there was a ferry on the site which remained until the eighteenth century.[9] Across the Tees there had been an important medieval bridge at Pounteys Bridge, which may have been unuseable by the late fourteenth century when money was given for its repair. Leland used a ferry at the site. This crossing must have been important, since the ferry there was on one of the main north–south roads described by Ogilby. Its foundations were still visible in the early nineteenth century.[10] Further north, on the Borders, bridges had always been sparse, but during the later middle ages some of this small number disappeared. In the twelfth century a person 'called in the English tongue Sproich' was employed by the almoner of Durham Cathedral to build a bridge over the North Tyne at Bellingham. A certain Walter of Flanders stole a hatchet sent to him to cut down timber for the bridge. After this there is no reference to a bridge at the site until the nineteenth century. Downstream there was a bridge at Hexham by 1263; it is referred to again in 1324, but not thereafter. Jervoise noted that in the fifteenth and sixteenth centuries the only method of crossing the river here was by ferry.[11] The precise circumstances of the loss of these bridges is not known, but it may be that without the conditions created by the fall in population and shortages of labour they would have been rebuilt.

On the other hand, there is usually a plausible alternative explanation. For instance, it is possible that Pounteys Bridge was not rebuilt because there was a convenient crossing at Croft Bridge a few miles upstream. The Gough Map shows this bridge as the site where the road from York to Newcastle via Northallerton crossed the Tees. The fine medieval structure with seven pointed arches still survives (plate 8).[12] The movement of bridges was not peculiar to the fourteenth century; the bridge at Bridgnorth replaced *Cwatbrycg* at nearby Quatford at a date after 900.[13] On the Borders the main problem was as likely to have been the constant warfare with the Scots as the effects of the plague.

More striking than the loss of bridges after 1349 was the construction of new structures; they were being built even in the 1350s. Whitaker, writing in the early nineteenth century, quoted a charter which granted permission to build a bridge at Ribchester across the Ribble in 1354: '. . . volo quod liberi homines eius patriae ibi edificent pontem de ligni vel lapide.'[14] In the fifteenth century

---

    [8] Flower, *Works*, ii. 270–3.   [9] *South*, 9.   [10] Leland, v. 68; Ogilby, plate 9; *North*, 57.
    [11] *North*, 15, 21.   [12] Ibid. 54.   [13] Ekwall, *Dictionary*, 64, 376–7.
    [14] T. D. Whitaker, *An History of the Original Parish of Whalley and Honor of Chitheroe*, 3rd edn. (London, 1818), 460.

there were more new bridges, for example, at Abingdon (Thames) and Great Barford (Great Ouse). We know these were not rebuildings: the deaths from drowning at the ford at Abingdon and the complaints of the inhabitants of the neighbouring town about the loss of trade resulting from the construction of Barford Bridge are well documented. Several bridges were first built in Cornwall at this period. Amongst them was probably Looe Bridge and certainly Wadebridge. In the fourteenth century the settlement was known as Wade (meaning 'ford'), which confirms Leland's story that there had not been an earlier structure at the site.[15] New bridges continued to be constructed in the first half of the sixteenth century. In listing the bridges over the Tamar, Leland noted 'Caulstock bridge next the see begon by Sir Perse Eggecumbe', who died in 1539.[16] Two years later, in 1541, the first bridge over the River Hull at Hull was erected.[17] These bridges were, as in the century before the Black Death, small additions to a huge pre-existing stock of bridges. Nevertheless, they are impressive evidence of the continuing investment in the bridge network at a time when it might be thought that its disintegration was more likely.

1550–1760

After 1550 there continued to be significant investment in bridges. Spending on maintenance remained high, and some bridges were reconstructed. However, few new major bridges were built at unbridged sites over the next 150 years. A rare exception was Downholme Bridge across the Swale, which John Hutton of nearby Maske sought permission to build in 1684.[18] At the small number of other sites where a bridge was built in place of a ferry, there had often been an earlier bridge. In 1597 an act of parliament authorized the construction of a new bridge at Ross-on-Wye in place of a ferry which had been there for some years. It was, however, not the first on the site: Leland had seen a wooden bridge there.[19] A bridge was erected at West Tanfield c.1609, on the road from Ripon to Middleham. Leland had crossed by ferry, but the entry in his *Itinerary* suggests that there may have been an earlier bridge which had collapsed.[20]

More bridges are recorded on most rivers in c.1770 than in c.1540, but mostly because minor bridges were built towards the end of the period. The situation on the Great Ouse is typical. All the bridges across that river shown on Jefferys's maps of Buckinghamshire, Bedfordshire, and Huntingdonshire

---

[15] *Cornish Bridges*, 68–9; Leland, i. 178; Ekwall, *Dictionary*, 490.
[16] Leland, i. 174; *DNB*, vi. 376.   [17] *VCH East Yorks.*, i. 389.
[18] *North*, 86.   [19] *Wales and Western*, 120–1.
[20] *North*, 79; Leland, i. 83. He states that he used the ferry 'for lak of a bridge', which may imply that there had formerly been a bridge on the site.

(1767–70)[21] and not recorded c.1540 were minor ones on the upper sections of the river; for example, a bridge at Wolverton Mill (near Stony Stratford) and another at Tyringham. These bridges today carry unclassified roads. The detailed work carried out on Bedfordshire bridges provides precise dates for the construction of post-medieval bridges in that county: after Sir Gerard Bray-brooke paid for the construction of Great Barford Bridge c.1430, no new bridge was erected over the Great Ouse in Bedfordshire for 300 years. The bridge, built in 1736, was a ramshackle timber structure constructed at Tempsford. It was made necessary by improvements to navigation that had made the ford more difficult to use.[22]

The situation on other rivers was similar. Across the Midlands Avon four bridges are marked on Yates's map of 1787–9 which had not been recorded c.1540 (although two bridges extant in the sixteenth century had disappeared by the late eighteenth).[23] Of the four new bridges, two were associated with country houses: one was a bridge near the entrance to Stoneleigh Abbey; the other an ornamental bridge designed by Robert Mylne, c.1765, in the grounds of Warwick Castle.[24] The other two were minor bridges on minor roads.

Roads

Just as the stock of bridges increased little in late medieval and early modern England, so the road system too proved remarkably stable. The best way to comprehend this is to compare the main roads of the Gough Map of the four-teenth century with those of Ogilby in the late seventeenth century. Take the routes radiating from London to the chief provincial cities of the country, which were classified as the A1, A2, A3, A4, and so on in the twentieth century. Ogilby described them as 'Direct Independants', Stenton as the principal highways in his account of the Gough Map roads.[25] To a very large extent these roads followed the same alignment, even though the maps are separated by more than 300 years. For instance, the main towns on the York Road are marked on both: Waltham, Ware, Royston, Huntingdon, Stamford, Grantham, Newark, Tuxford, and Doncaster. The Gough Map delineates a few cross-country routes; Ogilby describes more, calling them 'Cross Indepen-dants'. Some of these routes too were similar on both maps: on the Gough Map

[21] T. Jefferys, *The County of Buckingham, surveyed 1766–8* (1770); id., *The County of Bedford, surveyed 1765* (1767); id., *The County of Huntingdon, surveyed 1766* (1768).

[22] 'Bridges of Bedfordshire', 21.

[23] W. Yates and Sons, *A Map of Warwick drawn from an Actual Survey taken in the Years 1787–9* (Warwick, 1793); I. Taylor, *Map of County of Worcester* (1772).

[24] Pevsner, *Warwickshire*, 456.

[25] Stenton, 'Road System', 240.

there is a road from Bristol to Leicester via Gloucester, Worcester, Droitwich, Solihull, and Coventry.[26] This is shown by Ogilby as two cross-county roads: one from Bristol to Worcester, the other from Hereford via Worcester to Leicester.

Where there are differences between the two maps, they are slight. They occur for a variety of reasons, but usually because there were, as there still are, alternative long-distance routes; different cartographers might choose different routes. At a particular date one of these routes might be a little more popular, at a later date another, perhaps because of improvement to one of them. The medieval map marks the northerly route from Exeter to Cornwall via Okehampton; Ogilby shows the southern road via Plymouth, Looe, and Penzance, a route which involved ferry crossings of both Plymouth Sound and the Fowey estuary.[27] The availability of a number of options was important: one road might be better in dry weather, the other in wet; one might be particularly infested by robbers.[28] Some roads were more appropriate for certain types of traffic: waggons and carts might prefer one road, horsemen another, and drovers yet another.

There were also a variety of roads between towns. For instance, travellers had a choice of two routes on the Great West Road between Newbury and Marlborough. One went through Hungerford and Savernake Forest, which is roughly the present line of the A4, the other went to the north of the River Kennet via Ramsbury. Ogilby describes both roads.[29] The Ramsbury route seems to have been popular in the early days of coaching, possibly to avoid the steep gradients and medieval ruts in the descent from Savernake Forest; however, it subsequently fell into disuse when the medieval route was turnpiked. The *Cornhill Magazine* of 1864 told the story of an old coachman in the previous century who refused to heed the remonstrations of his passengers to use the new turnpike road; his father and grandfather had driven along the road through the Kennet valley and he was not going to change.[30]

The few new bridges built after the thirteenth century usually had little effect on the road system, although exceptionally, a new bridge might transform a minor road into a major highway. The network of bridges, causeways, and roads constructed in the vicinity of Abingdon succeeded in attracting those travelling from London to Gloucester who had formerly gone by

---

[26] Parsons, *Gough Map*, 36.
[27] Ibid.; Ogilby, plates 27–8.
[28] On the subject of highwaymen, see G. Spraggs, *Outlaws and Highwaymen* (London, 2001).
[29] Taylor, *Roads*, 195; Ogilby, plate 10.
[30] The story is told in Crawford, *Archaeology in the Field*, 69.

Wallingford.[31] The new route via Abingdon is not marked on the Gough Map, which was drawn before the bridges were built, but Ogilby's *Britannia* shows it as forming one of the main roads of the kingdom. It was marked as the road from London to St David's through Henley, Abingdon, Faringdon, and Gloucester. Most new bridges, however, did not create new main roads, but replaced ferries on well-established secondary roads. The bridge, built at Kexby *c.*1430 at the site of a ferry over the River Derwent on the road from Hull to York, did nothing to change the alignment of the route, which is marked on the Gough Map, but it did presumably make the journey between the two towns easier, more reliable, and safer.[32]

THE CHARACTERISTICS OF THE ENGLISH ROAD SYSTEM

National Highways

By the 1530s, the decade when Leland set off on his travels, there is sufficient information to see the road system in detail. The Gough Map lists the places through which roads passed, usually between about 5 and 20 miles apart; a more precise route between these places can in most cases be established from Ogilby, and other sources, like Leland, which describe certain sections of road. Thus we can plot the river crossings on the national highways. Two principal points stand out. The first is that on these roads there were bridges wherever they crossed a major river, and where there is the detailed evidence, it suggests that there were also bridges where they crossed minor rivers. Ferries were not employed on national highways, unless a bridge was out of repair. Fords too, which had been used as major river crossings in early Saxon centuries, were not in use except at a few streams and smaller water courses.

Secondly, the primary routes were relatively direct. The major national highways did not take long diversions to find a suitable bridge. Keeping to relatively straight routes, they went through a variety of landscapes, including long stretches along river valleys and over desolate heath. The main exceptions were where roads needed to avoid marshland: thus the Old North Road takes a detour to avoid Hatfield Chase and the fens at the confluence of the Trent, Ouse, and Aire.

It is possible to piece together vivid and very detailed descriptions of the main medieval roads which clearly demonstrate some of their chief characteristics. The Gough Map marks the route of the Exeter Road through

---

[31] Leland, v. 113–18.   [32] *CCR* (*1422–9*), 473.

Winchester and Salisbury.[33] Leland described the same road from London to Winchester.[34] It left London Bridge, and went by way of Kingston. Not far from the line of the M25, it crossed the Mole by the bridge at Cobham,[35] and subsequently went over another tributary of the Thames, the Wey, where the river has worn a gap in the chalk ridge at Guildford. The medieval bridge at the town lasted until 1900, when flood water swept timber under the arches, and the central one collapsed.[36] From Guildford the road went over the Hog's Back to Farnham, as it still does. This wild route was described by Defoe: 'the road to Farnham is very remarkable, for it runs along . . . the ridge of a high chalky hill, so narrow that the breadth of the road takes up the breadth of the hill, and the declivity begins on either hand, at the very hedge that bounds the highway, and is very steep . . . from this hill is a prospect either way, so far that 'tis surprising; and one sees to the north, or N.W. over the great black desart, call'd Bagshot-Heath.'[37] After Farnham the road went to Alton, and then to Alresford. Leland recounted how the water from the pond 'cummith into a narow botom and rennith thorough a stone bridge at the ende of Alresford toun', and over this bridge the road went.[38] Defoe again takes up the route: 'From hence, at the end of seven miles over the Downs, we come to the very ancient city of Winchester; not only the great church, which is so famous all over Europe . . . but even the whole city has, at a distance, the face of venerable, and looks ancient a far off.'[39] The city stretches from East Bridge over the Itchen, which had two stone arches in the sixteenth century, up the hill to the castle.[40]

From Winchester to Salisbury the route, completely ignoring the Roman road, passed over chalk downland intersected by the valley of the Test, which was crossed at Stockbridge. Leland described the road from Salisbury, that is, travelling in the other direction:

From Saresbyri to Thomas Beketes bridge of 2. stone arches a mile al by champayn. Under this bridg rennith a praty broke (the River Bourne). . . . Passing a 3. miles farther I left a mile of on the right hond Bukholt Woodde, a great thing, wher in tymes past by likelihood hath bene a chace for dere. Thens 8. miles al by champayn grounde baren of woodde to Stoke Bridge of . . . stone archis. . . . From Stoke to Winchestre 8. miles al by champayn ground baren of wodde. The soyle betwixt Saresbyri and Winchestre of white clay and chalk.[41]

The modern A30 goes from Salisbury to Wilton and then along the foot of the downs to Shaftesbury, but the medieval road, like Ogilby's, left the town by

---

[33] Parsons, *Gough Map*, 36. Ogilby shows the shorter road to Salisbury via Basingstoke, which remained the main road into the twentieth century.

[34] Leland, i. 275.   [35] *South*, 28.   [36] Renn, 'Wey Bridges', 80–1.

[37] Defoe, *Tour*, i. 145–6.   [38] Leland, i. 274.   [39] Defoe, *Tour*, i. 181–2.

[40] Leland, i. 274.   [41] Ibid. 269.

Harnham Bridge over the Avon, and went along the ridge top above the valley of the River Ebble, rejoining the modern road at Whitesheet Hill and then into Shaftesbury.[42] Defoe tells us that the road went over

> fine down or carpet ground . . . It has neither house or town in view all the way, and the road which often lyes very broad, and branches off insensibly, might easily cause a traveller to loose his way, but there is a certain never failing assistance upon all these downs for telling a stranger his way, and that is the number of shepherds feeding, or keeping their vast flocks of sheep, which are every where in the way, and who, with a very little pains, a traveller may always speak with. Nothing can be like it, the Arcadians plains of which we read so much pastoral trumpery in the poets, could be nothing to them.[43]

Between Shaftesbury and Sherborne the landscape changed: 'The country rich, fertile and populous, the towns and houses standing thick.'[44] The road crossed the Stour at High Bridge and the River Cale and Bow Brook at Five Bridges. Leland records: 'Thens to Fyvebridge upon Cale ryvar a bout a 2 myles. There be 5 principall arches, where of it takethe name, but ther joynethe hardon to a longe stone causey, in the whiche be dyverse archelets. Al the countre aboute Fivebridge is a flate vale of a greate cumpace environid withe high hills.'[45] From Sherbourne the route made for Yeovil, running parallel to the Yeo before crossing it where 'there is a bridge a litle from the toun of 3. great arches of stone apon Ivel, and is the highe way from Shirebourne westward'. Yeovil 'stondithe plesauntly on a rokky hille, and is meatly welle buildyd'.[46] The river ran north to the flat, Somerset levels, the Gough Map road on firmer land to the south-west through Crewkerne, Chard, and Honiton. The River Parrett flows between Haselbury Plucknett and Crewkerne, and a little north of the modern road on the line of the medieval route is a fine medieval bridge with two pointed arches and chamfered ribs.[47] At Crewkerne Leland saw 'nothing very notable', but Honiton was 'a fair long thorough fare and market toun, longging to Courteney of Powdreham: beyng just xij. miles from Excester by est in the high way to London'.[48] En route the road crossed the River Otter at Fenny Bridges, where the river was: 'devided into 4. armes by pollicy to serve grist and tukking milles. Apon 3. of these streames I roode by fair stone bridges. The first arme of the 4. was the leste, and had no bridg that I markid. On the north side of the first bridge was a chapelle now prophanid'.[49] In 1326 Bishop Stapledon had bequeathed 11*s.* 6*d.* to the repair of the bridge and causeway.[50]

---

[42] Taylor, *Roads*, 194   [43] Defoe, *Tour*, i. 218.   [44] Ibid.

[45] Leland, v. 110.   [46] Ibid. 109.   [47] *South*, 98.   [48] Leland, i. 160.

[49] Ibid. 240.   [50] Hoskins, *Devon*, 72.

This road Fiennes described as 'all fine gravell way the best road I have met withall in the West'.[51] It descended to the River Clyst at Clyst Honiton, where William of Worcester saw a bridge in 1478, and passing through the eastern suburb of Exeter entered the city, which was 'right strongly waullid and mainteinid' with 'diverse fair streates'.[52]

Secondary Roads

As well as the primary national routes there was a network of secondary roads which essentially linked market towns together and to the shire town and other regional centres. These roads are more difficult to trace than the national routes. A few are shown on the Gough Map, but they are not recorded comprehensively on any map before the eighteenth century. Nevertheless, there is a good deal of contemporary information about them. They were probably referred to as *herepath* or *herestrete* in Anglo-Saxon England, and it may be possible to trace some of them from charter bounds.[53] In the *Leges Henrici Primi* roads to towns and castles are described as the *via regia* (the King's Highway).[54] This term continued to be used for secondary as well as primary roads. A court case in the late fourteenth century refers to the *via regia* between Warwick and Southam, a dispute in 1375 to a causeway on the *via regia* between Bingham and Whatton.[55] These routes, like many others, can still be identified even after so many centuries with modern 'A' roads. The road near Warwick was on, or close to, the line of the present A425, the other road near the present A52 between Grantham and Nottingham. Through detailed work it is possible to reconstruct networks of secondary routes, as D. C. Cox has done in the Evesham area.[56]

Rough outlines of the networks of secondary roads are shown on county maps from the seventeenth century.[57] A good example is Warburton's map of Yorkshire of *c.*1720.[58] It does not mark any bridges, but since it shows the towns, principal roads, and rivers of the county, it is easy to see where the river crossings were. For instance, the roads indicated on the map crossed the River Swale at several places: Grinton, Richmond, Catterick, Morton-on-Swale, Skipton, and Topcliffe. Roads also met the River Nidd at Pateley Bridge,

---

[51] Fiennes, 271.

[52] *William Worcestre Itineraries*, ed. and trans. J. H. Harvey (Oxford, 1969), 19; Leland, i. 227–8.

[53] Rackham, *Countryside*, 259.   [54] *Leges Henrici Primi*, 248–9.

[55] Flower, *Works*, ii. 225, 108.

[56] D. C. Cox, *The Battle of Evesham: A New Account* (Evesham, 1988).

[57] The early county maps, including Saxton's *Atlas of England and Wales* (1579), did not show roads. A few road maps were produced by John Norden (1548–1626) under the title of *Speculum Britanniae*, but such maps remained uncommon until after Ogilby.

[58] *County Atlases of the British Isles published after 1703: A Bibliography Compiled by Hodson, D.*, vol. 1, *1704–42* (Welwyn, 1984), 178.

Hampsthwaite, Killinghall, Knaresborough, and Green Hamerton. All these places were the sites of medieval bridges. There are just a few places on the map where a road met a river where there had not been a bridge in the middle ages. Here ferries were used. There was one exception. The crossing of the River Ure between Middleham and Leybourn was by ford.[59] At most of these locations there were still no bridges in 1770.[60]

In other areas too, bridges were the norm. In the valley of the Great Ouse bridges linked riverside towns with areas on the opposite bank. At all the towns by the river—Buckingham, Stony Stratford, Newport Pagnell, Olney, Bedford, St Neots, Huntingdon, St Ives, and Ely—there had been a medieval bridge. Where other secondary roads crossed the river there had also been medieval bridges: for example, the road from Northampton to Bedford crossed the Great Ouse at Turvey Bridge, the route from Cambridge to Bedford at St Neots Bridge. There was just one ford on an important secondary route, at Tempsford.[61]

Many fords, of course, survived next to the bridges which had been built alongside them. They were essential next to foot or pack-horse bridges. Those next to cart bridges served a variety of purposes. Sometimes drivers of carts or riders preferred fords to bridges, especially when the water was low, because the horses could drink at the river. This may possibly be why at Hoveringham on the Trent Leland used the ferry, his horse the ford.[62]

There was one type of location where major bridges were rare, even on important secondary roads. This was in the large areas of low-lying wetland: there were no bridges over the Yorkshire Ouse below York or across the East Yorkshire Derwent where it approached its junction with the Ouse, or the Trent downstream of the Newark–South Muskham crossing, a distance of more than 50 miles.[63] On the downstream sections of these rivers ferries rather than bridges provided the river crossings, as at Gainsborough and Marnham on the lower Trent and at Littleborough, where the Roman road from Lincoln to York via Castleford had crossed the river.[64]

Ferries were also used to carry passengers across estuaries such as the Humber.[65] Journeys at such sites could be very difficult, as Celia Fiennes found when she crossed the Sound from Plymouth to Cremyll. This was

---

[59] Leland, i. 71, 84, 79.   [60] According to Jefferys, *Map of York*.
[61] Defoe, *Tour*, ii. 123. For the Great Ouse bridges, see Chap. 2.
[62] Leland, iv. 18; of course, there may simply have been no room on the ferry boat for his horse.
[63] H. R. De Salis, *Bradshaw's Canals and Navigable Rivers of England and Wales, A Reprint of A Handbook of Inland Navigation For Manufacturers, Merchants, Traders and Others* (Newton Abbot, 1969), 178–9, 412–3.
[64] *Cal. Inq. p. m.*, vii. 713; Leland, i. 32; *CPR* (1313–17), 397.
[65] *VCH East Yorks.*, i. 387–9; Flower, *Works*, ii. 306–9.

a very hazardous passage, by reason of 3 tydes meeting; had I known the danger before I should not have been very willing to have gone it, not but this is the constant way all people go . . . I was at least an hour going over, it was about a mile but indeed in some places, notwithstanding there was 5 men row'd and I sett my own men to row also I do believe we made not a step of way for almost a quarter of an hour, but blessed be God I came safely over.[66]

However, with these exceptions, the large number of bridges which carried the primary and secondary roads formed a dense network. Many rivers were bridged at intervals of less than 10 miles, and often under 5. There were similar spaces between bridges on many stretches of great rivers such as the Trent, the Ure and Ouse, the Great Ouse, and the Thames. Bridges at towns were often very close to one another to provide the traveller with the most direct access to the centre. This was particularly important before the automobile age, when traffic moved comparatively slowly and making a journey a few miles shorter could bring about a big time saving. At York, for instance, there were three bridges across the River Foss within a short distance of each other, Foss, Layerthorpe, and Monk, which carried each of the main roads out of the city to the north-east, east, and south across the River Foss.[67]

It is possible that the medieval secondary road system, although far less well constructed than the Roman, contained many more bridges. Our knowledge of Roman crossings is far from comprehensive, but comparisons are striking. For example, we know of just three Roman roads which crossed the Thames between Staines and Reading. These were at Staines (Roman *Pontes*), which carried the main road from London to the west; at Hedsor, near Cliveden, where the road from Verulanium to Silchester met the river, but where no bridge has been found; and near Henley, the site of a secondary route from Dorchester to Silchester. Here oak piles, possibly from a Roman bridge, have been uncovered.[68] In the middle ages, by contrast, there were more than twice as many major crossings, all bridges: at Reading, Sonning, Henley, Marlow, Maidenhead, and Windsor as well as at Staines.[69] They may imply, in turn, a more extensive and effective system of secondary roads.

Minor Roads

There were innumerable minor roads which linked villages to main roads, villages to towns, villages to villages, and joined villages to their fields and outlying settlements. Where a minor road met a major river, there was rarely a bridge. In fact, bridges at such locations were largely unknown before the

---

[66] Fiennes, 255.   [67] *North*, 84.   [68] Margary, *Roman Roads*, 85–6, 181, 167.
[69] For the full references, see Chap. 2.

eighteenth century. Ferries were used instead. There were several across the Thames in the vicinity of Oxford: at Bablock Hithe, Nuneham Courtenay, Sanford, and Clifton Hampden.[70] Here a splendid Victorian Gothic bridge was built in the mid-nineteenth century, but the road remained a local road, and is unclassified today.[71] Ferries were also common in towns. York was typical: the main road went over Ouse Bridge, but there also two ferries, one upstream and the other downstream.[72] There were also many fords on minor roads. In the Vale of Blackmoor Leland 'passid over Cale water at a greate forde'. In the north, where many of the riverbeds are stony and summer water levels can be low, he even crossed major rivers by ford when he wanted to make a detour from the main road. He used the ford over the Wear when he visited the Neville castle at Brancepeth; in Yorkshire, he passed 'over Ure at a forde byneth Huewik bridge [Bridge Hewick]'.[73]

Fords came into their own when neighbouring bridges were unuseable. At the extreme they were a necessity in time of war, when an enemy held a bridge or bridges or had destroyed them. For instance, the Battle of Boroughbridge centred both on the attack on the bridge and on a nearby ford. In many campaigns attempts were made to obstruct fords to prevent the enemy using them.[74] In a more mundane way they were used to avoid tolls. In 1350–1, when Dee Bridge, Chester, was broken down, it was reported that the ferry yielded £14. 19s. 3½d., 'and not more because the ford of the water of Dee was sufficient for horse men and foot passengers'.[75]

Whereas fords and ferries were the norm where a minor road met a large river, there were bridges of all kinds on minor roads across smaller rivers and streams as well as fords: there were bridges for carts, footbridges and horse-bridges, bridges consisting of planks, and some fine stone bridges. Where footbridges were built over such water courses, fords would be used by horses and carts. The sources provide an impression of the ubiquitous presence of small bridges. An inquisition held in 1252 found that the abbot of Abingdon and others were liable to make two bridges at 'Munekeye below Curmeror', a bridge at 'Horseylake', two bridges at 'Maideford', three bridges by the mill at 'Langeford' and a fourth at 'Briggebroc', and others at 'Goldhorde', 'Cornhullenor', 'Schirplake', and 'Enneylake'.[76]

---

[70] *South*, 4–8; Phillips, *Thames Crossings*, 65.   [71] *South*, 8–9.
[72] *VCH City of York*, 520.   [73] Leland, i. 71, 84.
[74] T. F. Tout, 'The Tactics of the Battles of Boroughbridge and Morlaix', *EHR* 19 (1904), 711–15; *CCR* (1261–4), 374.
[75] *Cheshire Chamberlain's Accounts 1301–60*, ed. R. Stewart-Brown, Lancs. and Cheshire Rec. Soc., 59 (1910), 179.
[76] *Cal. Inq. Misc. (1219–1307)*, 146.

POSTSCRIPT: THE SECOND AGE OF BRIDGE CONSTRUCTION,
1760 TO THE PRESENT DAY

In the eighteenth century, after 500 years of stability, there were rapid changes. Substantial bridges were built on the Thames soon after 1700: Datchet Bridge was constructed in 1706, Putney Bridge in 1729, Westminster Bridge, 1738–50, and Walton Bridge in 1750.[77] From the 1760s and 1770s new bridges became common in the rest of the country. It was then that the first post-medieval bridges were constructed over the Tees.[78] Between 1750 and 1850 over ten new Thames bridges were built.[79] Across the Severn there was the same number of bridges in 1770 as 1500, but in the following decade new structures were built at Stourport in 1775 and Coalport in 1777. Work also began in 1777 on neighbouring Ironbridge, which opened in 1781. The great central cast-iron arch remains today, much as it was over 200 years ago.[80]

In London the increase in bridges after 1750 was spectacular, reflecting the city's expanding area and population. Upstream of London Bridge, Southwark Bridge was built in 1815–19, Blackfriars Bridge 1769, Waterloo Bridge 1811–17, Vauxhall Bridge 1811–16, Battersea Bridge 1771–2, Hammersmith Bridge 1837, Kew Bridge 1758–9, and Richmond Bridge 1774–7.[81] There were similar increases in other rapidly growing cities in the nineteenth century. In Leeds there was only one bridge over the River Aire between the north and south parts of the town until 1818–19, when Waterloo (Wellington) Bridge was constructed; by 1842 a further four had been built.[82]

By the late eighteenth century bridges began to replace ferries on the lower reaches of rivers in eastern England. Over the lower Derwent, Bubwith Bridge, built in 1793, and Loftsome Bridge (1804) took the place of ferries on two main roads which joined the East and West Ridings. Both roads converged on Selby, where the Ouse was bridged in 1790. It was the first ever bridge over the river downstream of York. At Gainsborough a bridge was opened over the Trent downstream of Newark in the following year. By the first edition of the Ordnance Survey other bridges had appeared at Dunham and Aldwark on the lower reaches of the Trent and Ouse respectively.[83]

---

[77] Phillips, *Thames Crossings*, 127, 184; Ruddock, *Arch Bridges*, 240, 242, 238.
[78] Pevsner, *Durham*, 150, 505.
[79] Phillips, *Thames Crossings*, 14–15, 29, 37, 62, 67, 79, 83, 106, 149, 157.
[80] *Wales and Western*, 143, 139; R. K. Morriss, 'Bridges Over the Shropshire Severn', in R. K. Morriss (ed.), *The Shropshire Severn* (Shrewsbury, 1994), 103–7.
[81] Croad, *London's Bridges*.
[82] D. Fraser, *A History of Modern Leeds* (Manchester, 1980), 137.
[83] *VCH East Yorks.*, iii. 91, 53; *North*, 85; *Mid and Eastern*, 15.

In general, the new bridges, as in previous centuries, replaced ferries on existing routes; they were not built as part of a new road system. Turnpikes, which
were established in increasing numbers after 1700, similarly had surprisingly
little effect on route patterns. Roads were straightened, gradients reduced, and
sections of new road built. Eventually the productivity of road transport
increased significantly, in part because of these improvements.[84] There were
some consequences for the alignment of routes: where there had been a number of paths, improving one led many travellers to ignore the others. A few
roads did become much more important and popular. Following work by the
Alconbury Turnpike on a secondary road from Biggleswade to Alconbury Hill
(which included the construction of the timber bridge—reconstructed in
stone in 1820—at Tempsford), the Great North Road began to follow this,
its modern, course, crossing the Great Ouse here rather than at Huntingdon.[85]
However, essentially turnpikes brought about the improvement of existing
roads. The great majority of turnpiked roads continued broadly to follow
traditional alignments going through the same major settlements and using
the same river crossings.[86]

There was one outstanding exception. This was Telford's London-to-
Holyhead Road built in the 1820s to improve communications with Ireland. It
remains today as the A5. Telford ignored the medieval and early modern route,
but instead 'almost totally rebuilt' the road. The south-eastern part was essentially, albeit with new embankments and culverts and reduced gradients, the
Roman Watling Street, which had not been popular with travellers for
centuries.[87]

Nothing else on this scale was built, probably because in the next decade the
development of the railway system made it unnecessary. While on many roads
traffic increased to feed the expanding railway network, movement on some
through routes massively declined. In the 1890s an account of the Great North
Road recorded lengths 'of the broad old highway running straight and smooth
between wide grassy borders, the very spaciousness and emptiness of the road
possess a certain dignity and grandeur which are suggestive of long vanished
pomps and spectacles such as we shall never see again'.[88]

The brief period of largely empty highways was soon to change with the
advent of the car. No areas remain unaffected by new roads, bypasses, and

[84] D. Gerhold, 'Productivity Change in Road Transport before and after Turnpiking, 1690–1840', *EcHR*
49 (1996), 491–515.
[85] Taylor, *Roads*, 194; 'Bridges of Bedfordshire', 21–6.
[86] Taylor, *Roads*, 155–6.   [87] Ibid. 162–3, 192.
[88] A. H. Norway, *Highways and Byways in Yorkshire* (London, 1899), 3.

bridges. Nevertheless, despite these changes, the road system described on the Gough Map has proved remarkably enduring. Even after the plethora of bypasses, motorways, and inner ring roads transformed England in the twentieth century, the line of some of the main medieval routes is still followed by a trunk road.

PART II

Structure

5

Challenges, Options, Sources

CHALLENGES

The Elements

During the night of 16/17 November 1771 rain fell continually in northern England. Water levels rose, and tributaries of the Tyne swelled into raging torrents. Downstream, the water swirled round the piers of the 500 year-old bridge across the river at Newcastle. Nevertheless, the residents of the properties, mainly shops with dwellings above, which stood on the bridge, slept. The events of the night and an account of one of the most spectacular bridge collapses in English history are told by P. M. Horsley: 'The river, soon to reach a level unparalleled in living memory, began a headlong descent down the valley, sweeping all before it—crops, cattle and people. Far away in Newcastle the current swirled and sucked at the foundations of the old bridge, which stirred uneasily in the rain-swept night.' By 2 a.m. the flood water was close to the keystones of the arches, which were normally high above the water level. At 3.30 a.m. Weatherley, a shoemaker who lived on the bridge, awoke. He saw his neighbour Fiddas guiding his family to safety along the roadway, now awash. Dr Horsley continues: 'Hastily collecting his own family, Weatherley turned north. The next-door house crashed into the river. He turned south, only to face a huge gap. Two arches had fallen. Terror-stricken, numb with exposure, the family huddled for six interminable hours on a small slab until they were rescued.' Fiddas was less fortunate. He went back with the maid to retrieve her belongings. 'A distraught Mrs Fiddas, standing at the bridge-end, saw an arch collapse and carry with it her husband and the girl.' In the morning the extent of the catastrophe was clear. The river was running 8 feet above the high-water mark level. Low-lying property was flooded to a depth of 6 feet; ships had been lifted onto the quay. At Jarrow Slake the house of Patten, the draper of Tyne

Bridge, was found, afloat. In it unharmed, were the family pets, a cat and a dog. By four o'clock in the afternoon the flood waters had subsided.[1]

Old Tyne Bridge was not the only casualty in 1771. All but one of the other bridges over the Tyne were swept away. These included important bridges at Chollerford, Alston, and Haydon Bridge, which carried the main road from Carlisle to Newcastle. Hexham Bridge, which had only been completed in the previous year, collapsed too. The one structure which survived, at Corbridge, was almost overwhelmed as the river rose so high that people 'could by leaning over the parapets, wash their hands in the river'.[2]

The northern floods of 1771 were exceptional. Possibly they were the worst to occur in Newcastle in the 500-year life of the bridge. However, flooding, if not on the scale of 1771, was common. The more serious floods have always been memorable events. The brief Anglo-Saxon Chronicle entry for 1096 records as one of the major events of the year that London Bridge was 'well-nigh washed away'.[3] Under the year 1125 we are told that on 'the feast of St Lawrence (10 August) there occurred so great a flood that many villages and men were drowned and bridges broken down'.[4] After 1200, because there are more records, we know more about the areas and bridges affected. For instance, in July 1233 a flood destroyed stone bridges, walls, and roads near Waverley Abbey in Surrey.[5] In 1284 a great part of the long bridge at Burton-on-Trent was swept away.[6] In 1293–4 Huntingdon Bridge was demolished by a severe flood laden with ice.[7] The Parliament Rolls of Edward III's reign recount a particularly gory tale of the consequences of a flood on the River Severn. The king demanded 100 marks owed him by his chamberlain of North Wales; he was informed that a clerk, William of Markeley, had set off with the money, but had been drowned at Montford Bridge by the rising flood waters; he could not be found, and had presumably been devoured by beasts.[8]

In later centuries there is more detailed evidence. At Shrewsbury the two ancient bridges over the Severn, English Bridge and Welsh Bridge (plate 10), were frequently damaged. There were regular and severe inundations roughly every twenty to fifty years. The town's charter of 1446 explicitly referred to the 'no small damage [which] had happened to the arches and stonework of . . . the . . . bridges . . . by the too vehement and rapid course of the aforesaid

[1] P. M. Horsley, *Eighteenth Century Newcastle* (Newcastle, 1991), 1–14; and see J. Clephan, 'Old Tyne Bridge and its Story', *Arch. Aeliana*, NS 12 (1887), 135–49.

[2] *North*, 16–23. [3] *ASC*, 234. [4] *ASC*, 255–6.

[5] *Annals of Waverley*, *Ann. Mon.*, ii. 312. [6] *CPR (1281–92)*, 115.

[7] *Rolls and Register of Bishop Oliver Sutton*, ed. R. M. T. Hill, 8 vols., Lincoln Rec. Soc., 39–76 (1948–86), v. 123.

[8] *Rot. Parl.*, ii. 91.

water there so swiftly running along'. In 1545 'the major part of the stone gate [on English Bridge] fell by reason of a great flood'. The river is very fickle and thirty years later, in 1578, it was so dry that the Horse Fair was held in the middle of the river channel. In January 1599 there was another severe flood; three brothers bringing their barge downstream, 'thinckinge to shute the bridge', collided into Welsh Bridge, and two were drowned. In 1634 part of English Bridge was broken in an inundation caused by a thaw: a trowman (a trow was a type of barge used on the Severn) saved a woman from drowning, but was almost killed himself when his boat was sucked by the current under one of the arches. In 1672 the gate on Welsh Bridge and one of the arches fell, and 'considerable damage was done by a great rising of the river' to a pier of [English] bridge and 'watchmen were employed for three nights at eighteen pence per night' to keep a close eye on the structure. The water rose on this occasion to a tremendous height, the maximum being 19 feet $7\frac{1}{2}$ inches. To put this in context, the greatest depth of the river in dry weather was about 3 feet, and the highest arch was 17 feet 4 inches. above low-water level. There were severe floods in 1740, in 1770 while a new English Bridge was being built in place of the medieval structure, and in 1795. This was the worst flood yet. Neighbouring properties were flooded, including a local pub, the 'Severn Stars', where the event was recorded by a brass plate, with the following inscription:

> To our very great surprise,
> Severn to this place did rise.[9]

Devastation has continued into the twentieth century. In 1912 eighty bridges were destroyed in a massive inundation in Norfolk. In July 1930 the River Esk was afflicted by a major flood, which swept away several substantial bridges upstream of Whitby. Between 1964 and 1984 forty-six bridges were seriously damaged in Cornwall and Devon and a further thirteen were destroyed.[10]

Flooding is brought about in a variety of ways. Melting snow and ice have frequently been a cause, as in the Severn floods of 1634. During the hard winter of 1564–5 a sudden thaw caused 'such a water that it overthrew two bowes [arches] . . . [of Ouse Bridge, York] and twelve houses standing upon the same bridge, and by the fall thereof was drowned 12 persons'.[11] The most common cause of destruction have been heavy storms leading to sudden flash floods. They still are: in August 1952, in a gigantic cloudburst over Exmoor, a massive 8 inches of rain fell during one day over a considerable area. The rain quickly

[9] This account is taken from A. W. Ward, *The Bridges of Shrewsbury* (Shrewsbury, 1935), 19–22, 131–2.

[10] *North*, 64; L. Hamill, *Bridge Hydraulics* (London, 1999), 9–11.

[11] D. M. Palliser, *Tudor York* (Oxford, 1979), 3, 266.

fed the many tributaries of the East and West Lyn rivers. Under the headline 'Unparalleled Scene of Destruction', the *Western Evening News* of 18 August reported 'deaths on a wartime scale'. It recounted how: 'Rapidly mounting floods cascaded down the hillsides gathering in an immense wave of water which rushed seawards. Trees, boulders, buildings, and a mass of debris pounded up in vast quantities behind bridges in the upper reaches of the rivers. Then one bridge gave way and masses of water and debris hurtled down the narrow valley . . . then . . . the incalculable weight of water descended on Lynmouth and Barbrook.'[12]

The impact of flooding depends not just on the amount of rainfall but also on the nature of the terrain. River basins respond very differently to rainfall. In some, water levels rise very slowly following even heavy rain, usually because the rain is absorbed by vegetation and by porous, underlying rock like chalk; in others, rainfall rapidly runs off the ground and rushes into the river, creating flash floods. Although some lowland areas experience a rapid response, such floods are most common in the highland zone with its steep valleys and, in places, impermeable rock, as events in the Lyn valleys show.[13] There is also a difference in the response of the upper and lower reaches of the same basin. In his *Natural History of Lancashire, Cheshire and the Peak* of 1700, Charles Leigh compared the Dove and the Trent:

This river [the Dove] swells sometimes so much in twelve Hours time, to the great terror of the Inhabitants, that it carries down their sheep and other Cattle; yet in the same Compass of Time falls again, and returns to its old Bounds; whereas the Trent, when it overflows its Banks, keeps the Fields in float four or five Days: their Reasons are manifest, because in one the country is mountainous, the other is a large extended Flat.[14]

It can be several days before heavy rainfall on the watershed affects the lower reaches of longer rivers. It takes about five days for the crest of a flood to travel from the Pennines and North Yorkshire to the Humber.

The main reason why bridges collapse during floods is the scouring of the river bed. 'Scour' is the process whereby the action of the river removes material from the bed.[15] When this occurs near a bridge holes are created which

---

[12] P. Keene and D. Elsom, *Lyn in Flood, Watersmeet to Lynmouth* (Oxford, 1990).

[13] I. Galbraith, *Understanding the Physical World* (Oxford, 1995), 37–56. The Mole is a good example of a lowland river with rapid responses. Its upper reaches and tributaries flow over the impermeable clay of the Weald, and floods quickly follow heavy rain.

[14] C. Leigh, *Natural History of Lancashire, Cheshire and the Peak in Derbyshire.* (Oxford, 1700).

[15] Hamill describes scour as 'the excavation and removal of material from the bed and banks of streams as a result of the erosive action of flowing water' (Hamill, *Bridge Hydraulics*, 251).

can expose the foundations and undermine the piers and abutments. Unfortunately, scour is often at its worst in the vicinity of bridges because they make the
waterway narrow, creating eddies. As a result the river can be noticeably
deeper near bridge piers. The problem is exacerbated by the difficulty in detect-
ing scour holes, which can be created very quickly but can equally soon be filled
in by stones and other loose material. As a result, the loss of a firm river bed may
not be spotted.[16] A discussion of bridge collapse in Ireland concluded: 'Scouring of the subsoil under the foundations of piers and abutments was the cause
of collapse, partial and total, of the vast majority of the twenty bridges
described at the seminar. Scour occurred upstream and downstream, under
both masonry and concrete piers and abutments. The predominant type was
scour under the upstream ends and cutwaters of masonry piers.'[17]

An analysis of bridge failures in the United States identified another factor
in addition to scour: debris piled against the structure. The debris causes
damage in a number of ways: by crashing into the stonework, by exacerbating
scour through creating localized fast currents near the obstructions, and by
acting as a dam and blocking the river channels; the build-up of water in such
a situation can have devastating consequences. Surprisingly large objects,
including large trees and boulders, can be brought downstream by torrential
waters.[18] The medieval bridge over the main channel of the Trent at Swarkestone is reputed to have been demolished in 1795 by wood which came floating
down the Trent from a timber yard in a heavy flood.[19] In a similar event in 1900
flood water swept timber under the ancient bridge at Guildford, and the
central arch collapsed.[20]

Ice flows carried downstream on the spate present another danger. They can
be large and move very quickly, as a story told in the Annals of Dunstable
shows. After the cold winter of 1281–2, when the thaw came the ice broke near
Biddenham Bridge, Bedfordshire, beneath a woman and left her on a fragment
of it. The rapidly flowing river carried her several miles, firmly seated as far as
Bedford Bridge, but no one could reach her, the ice crumbled, and she was seen
no more.[21] The build-up of ice around the piers of bridges could also cause
damage; in that same severe winter the accumulation of ice at an already
weakened London Bridge brought about the collapse of five arches.[22]

A longer-term threat comes from the tendency of rivers to move over the
flood plain. The current is always faster on the outer bend of the river;

---

[16] Ibid. 16.   [17] *Irish Stone Bridges*, 90.   [18] Hamill, *Bridge Hydraulics*, 12.
[19] J. B. Firth, *Highways and Byways in Derbyshire* (London, 1928), 32.
[20] Renn, 'Wey Bridges', 81.   [21] *Annals of Dunstable, Ann. Mon.*, iii. 287.
[22] T. Dyson and B. Watson, 'London Bridge is Broken Down', in *London Bridge*, 129.

accordingly, that bank is eroded while material is deposited on the inner bend. The consequences of this natural phenomenon can be very serious. In the 1430s erosion on either side of the west 'breast' of Rochester Bridge exposed the stonework of the bridge to increased water and threatened to undermine the bridge abutment on the Strood bank.[23]

Constructing structures which could withstand these potentially devastating effects of flooding, ice, and shifting river channels was a huge challenge. While bridges might not be expected to cope with the extreme events which occur once in 500 years, they had to be designed for more frequent but still threatening conditions. Moreover, bridges were not easy to build. Stable structures had to be erected in very difficult conditions, where foundations were hard to lay.

In addition, other, if less demanding, challenges had to be met. Bridges not only had to support their own load, but also that of vehicles passing over them, including shaking carts, which were a regular concern, and very heavy loads such as cannon. While this was not normally a problem, it could be if arches or timbers were already weak. Carts, waggons, and other vehicles also frequently caused damage by crashing into parapets.[24] Finally, on navigable rivers bridges had to be designed to permit the passage of boats. Few, if any, other building types are subject to the same difficulties.

Locations

Different types of structures were required for a wide variety of locations, including small lowland water courses, steep upland river valleys, deep estuarine rivers with swift tides, and wide flood plains. Some were substantial, others simple structures, such as a few planks over a stream. In those parts of the uplands where bridges were frequently subject to violent flash floods, they required a wide, high waterway both to allow the passage of the water and to prevent debris becoming trapped in the arches. Devil's Bridge, Kirby Lonsdale, rises 45 feet above the water; the arches of Barnard Castle Bridge similarly soar above the normal water level (plate 27). It was essential that they did: in 1771 the River Tees rose so high here that 'the arch on the Yorkshire side could not contain so great a quantity of water, and the battlement was forced down'.[25] However, the bridge survived.

In estuaries it always difficult to establish foundations in loose sediments in tidal waters where the river is deep, fast-flowing, and wide. Among the widest is the Tweed at Berwick, where the river measures 270 yards.[26] A seventeenth-century bridge, built at great expense, still stands; it was preceded by various

[23] Britnell, 'Rochester Bridge', 71.   [24] Ward, *Bridges of Shrewsbury*, 128.
[25] *North*, 50.   [26] Ibid. 2.

bridges built intermittently since the twelfth century if not before. Structures had to be constructed in similar locations throughout the country. In the south-west alone bridges were built at or near the mouth of the Taw, Torridge, Camel, and Looe. In other parts of the country conditions made building large bridges even more difficult. Rochester Bridge was constructed in the tidal waters of the Medway which today have a daily difference of 14$\frac{1}{2}$ feet in winter and about 17$\frac{1}{2}$ feet in summer.[27]

Flood plains present different, but still demanding, challenges. For parts of most years they are under water and can only be crossed by causeways which are often raised several metres above the meadows. They are very significant works of civil engineering. The major Anglo-Saxon settlement in the Hull valley in East Yorkshire was at Beverley on higher ground just to the west of the flood plain. Subsequently, a new port was established at Hull at the mouth of the river where it joins the Humber. Roads had to be constructed to the town across the very broad valley. Leland noted: 'From Cotingham to Kingeston [Kingston-upon-Hull] about a 4. miles by low ground, wherof 2. miles be causey way, dikid on booth sides.'[28] Causeways were a vital part of many bridge, and ferry, crossings. Those at Chesford Bridge, Warwickshire, across the River Avon, were described as annexed to the bridge ('de ponte de Chesterford et calcetis eidem ponti anexis').[29] Their maintenance and repair could require as much attention as the bridges themselves.

Even more remarkable than those on the flood plains were the structures which stretched over the fens of East Anglia or the Somerset levels. The eighth-century *Life of St Guthlac* tells us of the obstacles there areas posed: 'There is in the midland district of Britain a fen of immense size, which begins at the banks of the River Granta, not far from the camp which is called Cambridge, and stretches from the south as far north as the sea. It is a very long tract now consisting of marshes, now of bogs, sometimes of black waters, overhung by fog, sometimes studded with wooded islands and traversed by tortuous streams.'[30] Across this unpromising land a series of long causeways were constructed creating road links to centres such as Boston, the Isle of Ely, Ramsey, Spalding, and Wisbech.[31]

OPTIONS

Structures suitable for these varying conditions could be built in several ways. All involved the use of timber or stone, and occasionally brick, or a

---

[27] Brooks, 'Rochester Bridge', 5. [28] Leland, i. 48. [29] Flower, *Works*, ii. 221.
[30] *Felix's Life of Guthlac*, ed. B. Colgrave (Cambridge, 1956), 87.
[31] Darby, *Medieval Fenland*, 106–18.

combination of them. The three most common types were timber girder (also known as trestle) bridges, stone and timber bridges, and stone vaulted bridges. The timber girder bridges were formed from posts which projected from the river bed to support a timber roadway. Stone and timber bridges were made up of stone piers on which a timber roadway rested. The vaulted or arched bridges invariably consisted of stone barrel vaults, but they were of very varying designs with arches of very different shapes and spans.

The Literature on Bridge Design

Each option had its pros and cons. The advantages and disadvantages of timber and of stone bridges, as well as a discussion of how bridges should be designed and constructed, have been considered in a long literature, beginning in the fifteenth century. Although there were major differences between literary accounts and practice, through this literature we can see the key principles of bridge design. We can probably also get some idea of what medieval masons thought they were doing and the rules they applied to the construction of bridges. The earliest work to refer to bridges is Alberti's architectural treatise, *De Re Aedificatoria*. Copies were circulating in the 1450s and it was printed in 1485. In the sixteenth century other treatises followed, including Serlio's and Palladio's. Bridges are not the main focus of these books, but all contain some material on key aspects of bridge construction, even though the very influential treatise *De architectura*, written by the Roman architect Vitruvius, had not mentioned bridges.[32] From the eighteenth century there are specialist works on bridge building. The first, the *Traité des ponts*, was written in 1714 by Henri Gautier, an experienced French government engineer, who described himself as 'Architect, Engineer, and Inspector of Bridges and Roads of the Realm'.[33] Three years later he published his *Dissertation sur l'epaisseur des culées des ponts . . . sur la largeur des piles, sur la porteée des voussoirs, etc.* The earliest English book was Charles Hutton's *Principles of Bridges* of 1772, although plans to build the new bridge (constructed 1735–50) across the Thames at Westminster generated a considerable literature, if less based on experience than Gautier's study.[34]

[32] L. B. Alberti, *De re aedificatoria* (Florence, 1485); A. Palladio, *I quattro libri dell architettura* (Venice, 1570); S. Serlio, *Tutte l'opere d'architettura e prospettiva* (Venice, 1566).

[33] H. Gautier, *Traité des ponts* (Paris, 1714). He later published *Dissertation sur l'epaisseur des culées des ponts . . . sur la largeur des piles, sur la porteée des voussoirs, etc.* (Paris, 1717). For a brief account of bridge-building in France in the late 17th and 18th centuries, see Hopkins, *A Span of Bridges*, 59.

[34] C. Hutton, *The Principles of Bridges* (Newcastle-upon-Tyne, 1772). The debate about how to construct Westminster Bridge is discussed in Ruddock, *Arch Bridges*, 3–7, and R. J. B. Walker, *Old Westminster Bridge* (Newton Abbot, 1979), 44–63.

The fifteenth- and sixteenth-century architectural treatises inevitably only had space for brief comments about bridge design.[35] They tend to concentrate on how to build a first-rate bridge and have less to say about cheap, utilitarian practices. As might be expected, they were more impressed by Roman than recent bridges: it is worth noting that Alberti, though a Florentine, does not mention and does not seem to have recognized the importance of the remarkable bridge in the town, the Pontevecchio, notable for its wide, flat spans and thin piers, which had been built 100 years before he wrote.[36] Nevertheless, it is likely that the treatises provide some evidence of the traditions of the preceding medieval centuries. They include sensible, practical advice which their authors must have learnt from their contemporaries, who were the inheritors of long-standing traditions; for example, Alberti advises that bridges should not be built on the bends of rivers, and he recommends that arches be constructed on the river banks so that abutments were not undermined. Most importantly, they enunciate the key and universal rules of bridge design.[37]

Gautier's *Traite des ponts* is a yet more valuable source. It has been described as the first textbook on bridge-building.[38] He considers practicalities, describing the often cheap and easy methods which were used. It is the work of someone who had spent a lifetime building all types of bridges. Through him we are able to gain a very significant insight into the work of a long tradition of bridge-building. Many of the practices he describes would have been known to medieval masons and carpenters.

Timber Bridges

The treatises concentrated on arched, stone structures. Nevertheless, timber bridges were not entirely ignored. Alberti does little more than attempt a description of Caesar's bridge over the Rhine, but Palladio (who also describes Caesar's bridge) has rather more to say. He provides a number of ingenious truss structures which demonstrate how 'wooden bridges can be built without putting piles in the river'.[39] Nothing like this in England was erected until the eighteenth century.[40] He also describes a major covered bridge he designed over the River Brenta, which up to road level was a traditional timber girder bridge. An important feature was the great size of the timbers: many were over 30 feet long. The vertical posts were 1½ feet thick. Palladio points out that because the distance between the rows is so great it would be difficult for the beams making up the length of the bridge to support the load placed on them.

---

[35] Alberti has one chapter on bridges out of 136; Palladio more, 12 from 98 chapters.
[36] Hopkins, *A Span of Bridges*, 59. [37] Alberti, 77–8. [38] Hopkins, *A Span of Bridges*, 59
[39] Palladio, 171–9. [40] Ruddock, *Arch Bridges*, 28.

Therefore various ways were found to support the weight, including the use of large struts to provide diagonal bracing.[41]

Very large timber bridges like this were erected in England in the middle ages and later. To construct such structures, powerful pile-drivers were necessary to drive the timbers into the river, or large sole plates had to be laid on a river bed prepared to take them. For any large bridge with a timber deck, as Palladio's account shows, the key question was deciding what section of timber was necessary for a given span. He fails to say how this was decided, but in practice a relatively simple set of ratios of span to the thickness of the beam would have been applied. For instance, modern calculations suggest that a carriageway 6 metres yards wide with planking *c.*2 inches thick would require 12-inch square beams to support a 30-foot span, 15-inch square beams for a 40-foot span, and 18-inch square beams for a 50-foot span.[42] The present *Building Regulations* contain simple tables of advice about the size of timber joist for a given span.

Major timber bridges had advantages: they were cheap; vertical posts took up little of the waterway and, with the right pile-driver, they could be very firmly driven into the river bed so the problem of laying stone foundations was avoided. Unfortunately, there were also many disadvantages. Wood is far more perishable than good stone. Gautier had little time for timber bridges, arguing that while the design, construction, and maintenance of stone bridges was fraught with difficulties, timber bridges were even more troublesome. A masonry bridge should be built, even if it was ten times as expensive as a wooden structure, because the difference in maintenance costs would justify the initial outlay.[43] Timber bridges needed constant repair. There were various problems: they caught fire, joints deteriorated because of the moisture, and piles driven into the river bed worked loose.[44]

Despite these disadvantages, a few major timber bridges lasted well into the eighteenth century, and major new timber structures were being built in the 1790s.[45] The choice of option depended on local conditions and the money available. Timber bridges were preferred where the river bed was muddy or porous and foundations were difficult to lay, or where stone was scarce or good timber was readily available. These factors may explain why there were so many wooden bridges on the middle Thames up to the eighteenth century, and on the downstream sections of other large rivers (plate 7).

At a few sites, however, there were wooden bridges even where building stone was available, foundations were relatively easy to lay, and the neighbour-

[41] Palladio, 180–1.   [42] Brooks, 'Rochester Bridge', 25.
[43] For a discussion of this point, see Boyer, *French Bridges*, 145.
[44] Hopkins, *A Span of Bridges*, 119.   [45] e.g. Selby Bridge (*North*, 85).

ing bridges were stone. One such was Castle Mills Bridge, Bedford, over the Great Ouse, which was short distance downstream of Bedford Bridge. It carried mainly local traffic, and was one of the few timber bridges over the river in the early sixteenth century.[46] Cheapness must be the explanation for its construction: presumably there was no money to pay for the higher capital cost of a stone bridge. The need to opt for the cheapest initial outlay regardless of the lifetime costs was doubtless a powerful influence five centuries ago, as it is today.

The low costs also explain why simple, small timber bridges have always been common in some upland locations. A weak timber bridge designed to fail during a flood can be, and always has been, an attractive and cost-effective alternative in these areas to a high stone arched bridge. A number were built to replace the bridges destroyed near Lynmouth in 1952.[47]

Vaulted Stone Bridges

Much more attention has been paid in the literature to stone bridges. Although preferred to timber bridges in most locations, they were not without their problems. Building stable arches over a river, which requires the construction of piers on the river bed where they are constantly threatened by scour, is not easy. The basic problems have been addressed by all the writers from Alberti onwards. The disciplines of structural engineering and hydraulics have provided ever greater understanding of the issues involved.

The modern study of structural engineering goes back to the seventeenth century.[48] An examination of structural analysis as it has developed since then, comparing it with the work of Gothic architect/engineers, is contained in a most important work, *The Stone Skeleton: Structural Engineering of Masonry Architecture*, which was published in 1995 by Jacques Heyman, Professor of Engineering at Cambridge University, who has specialized in the study of arches in medieval cathedrals and other ancient structures.[49] What he shows is remarkable: much of the analysis developed over the last 350 years is of little help in finding out how to build stable masonry structures. He argues that Gothic builders, and classical ones before them, understood that geometry is the key to building stable arches. The rules of proportion will lead, when correctly applied, to a masonry structure that will stand up. An understanding of the complex stresses involved is unnecessary for building arches.

[46] Leland, i. 102.   [47] Keene and Elsom, *Lyn in Flood*, 16.
[48] The development of the analysis of arches is discussed in J. Page, *Masonry Arch Bridges* (London, 1993), 16–46.
[49] J. Heyman, *The Stone Skeleton: Structural Engineering of Masonry Architecture* (Cambridge, 1995).

Heyman concludes his study in the following way:

[In 1638] Galileo was laying the foundations of modern structural analysis. His first 'new science' was based on rational mechanics rather than empirical geometrical rules of ancient and medieval times. Once this science had been developed, the way was open to use structural materials to the limits of their strength, and to abandon design rules based upon geometry . . .

These are not the design criteria of the masonry structure. Correspondingly, modern structural calculations and modern codes of practice find only a marginal place in the assessment of a masonry bridge or a cathedral. The key to the understanding of masonry is to be found in a correct understanding of geometry.[50]

Geometry, rules for the relationship between different parts of the bridge, is, as we shall see, a constant theme of early works, from Alberti to Gautier.

The modern academic study of bridge hydraulics goes back to the eighteenth century at least. Labelye calculated the fall (that is, the difference in the level of the water surface upstream and downstream of the bridge), which would be generated by his proposed bridge at Westminster. Smeaton made similar calculations when designing a new bridge at Hexham, following the destruction of its predecessor in the innundation of 1771.[51] Calculations since then have become ever more sophisticated. By 1840 d'Aubuisson had devised equations to predict the obstruction of bridge piers to the flow of water. Today, as works such as Hamill's *Bridge Hydraulics* indicate, a host of factors, which govern the interaction of bridge, river, and river bank, are taken into account in bridge construction.[52]

The works from Alberti to the modern studies by Hamill and Heyman provide straightforward practical advice for successfully constructing masonry bridges. The main points are: reduce the effects of scour, reduce scour, and build stable arches. This is done by building the bridge in the right part of the river and by ensuring that there are firm foundations, sufficiently wide waterways, sufficiently thick arch rings in relation to the arch span (i.e. getting the geometry right), and sufficiently large abutments.

Foundations are especially important, not only for supporting the superstructure but also for mitigating the consequences of scour. Alberti and Palladio made various recommendations for ensuring they were firm: piers and

---

[50] Ibid. 154. A number of relatively recent works have considered ancient bridges in the context of modern engineering knowledge of both structures and hydraulics. O'Keeffe and Simington, *Irish Stone Bridges*, stress that the major threat to bridges comes from the river, from floods and scour. O'Connor, *Roman Bridges*, concentrates on questions of structural engineering.

[51] For Labelye, see Ruddock, *Arch Bridges*, 4–6; Unfortunately Smeaton's calculations were based on faulty premises, and his bridge, like its predecessors, was also destroyed (ibid. 100).

[52] Hamill, *Bridge Hydraulics*, 199–226.

abutments should be founded on rock if possible; if they were not, the river bed should be excavated until a solid foundation was found; otherwise the bed should be piled. Alberti claimed that scour was worse on the downstream side of piers. Because of this, special care should be taken with the foundations there. The piers should have angular cutwaters both upstream and down. Piled foundations should also be provided for the abutments if they could not be founded on rock.[53]

The literature also stresses the importance of an adequate waterway. Hamill explains what happens when the river approaches the bridge: 'Because the openings of a bridge are usually less than the full width of the river, the water accelerates as it approaches and passes through the waterways. Consequently the velocity is higher than it would otherwise be, and this can cause scour and undermining of the foundations of the bridge. The narrower the openings the larger the velocity.'[54]

A narrow opening also makes it more likely that water-borne debris will damage the superstructure, especially the piers, or, more likely, will be trapped beneath the arch or lodged near the piers. The effective width of the waterway can be increased by finding ways of easing the passage of water through a bridge. Various ways to achieve this were recommended, for example, by making sure that the bridge is not askew to the waterway (i.e. by ensuring that the river does not approach the bridge at an angle). More recent work has shown how, in addition, abutments, piers, arches, and wingwalls can be designed to improve the flow of water.[55]

The height of arches is also extremely important, not just to ease the passage of large objects. In particular, water levels should remain below the crowns of bridges because the consequences of flooding are far worse when arches are submerged (i.e. when the water completely fills the arch). As this happens there is extreme turbulence, and the safety of the bridge is threatened.[56] To ensure that the arches are not overtopped, most bridges are designed so that their crowns will be higher than the water level experienced in a severe flood. Usually the arches are higher than the surrounding land, so that the river bursts its banks before the openings are submerged. It is quite common to see a bridge standing proud of the surrounding flooded land. Modern authorities recommend that the height of the opening should be 0.6 to 1 metres above the design flood level.[57] The decision in 1565 to replace the two collapsed central arches of

[53] Alberti, 78.   [54] Hamill, *Bridge Hydraulics*, 15.   [55] Ibid. 199–226.   [56] Ibid. 48.
[57] Ibid. 13. Modern bridges are designed to withstand floods of a certain frequency; e.g. a bridge in a town might be designed to cope with the type of flood predicted to occur once every 500 years; elsewhere a bridge might be designed for a 100-year flood.

Ouse Bridge, York, with a single, much taller arch which had a rise of 27½ feet must have been made with such considerations in mind (plate 3). As a result, the bridge was able to cope with all subsequent floods, until it was replaced in 1818 because the roadway was too narrow.[58]

In some locations it is not possible to build a high enough arch to deal with extreme floods. Problems occur where the flood plain is blocked by buildings or is narrow and itself fills with water, which is what happened in the Lyn valley in 1952. In a few places medieval masons may have neglected to build adequate arches. Those of Teston Bridge, Kent, are usually completely submerged at times of flood.[59] Later changes to the environs can cause such problems. Most of the medieval bridges over the Loire were built between 1000 and 1250. They lasted for 500 years, but did not long survive the raising of the levees on its banks in the eighteenth century. The new levees raised the flood level to a height of 7 metres above mean water level; as Professor Boyer has pointed out, this was 'fatal to bridges built to accommodate a crest of 5–5.5 m., and one after another the giants at Blois, Jargeau, and Tours succumbed'.[60]

The treatise writers offer a straightforward measurement of the adequacy of a waterway: the ratio of the width of the pier to the arch span. Alberti and Palladio advised that the piers must be no thinner than one-sixth the arch span and should not normally be thicker than one-quarter; Gautier proposed one-fifth for spans of 20 feet and more.[61]

They also gave advice about how to build stable arches. The abutments 'must be made extremely strong and thick so that they serve not only to support the load of the arches, as the other piers do, but, particularly, hold together the whole bridge and prevent the arches from springing open'.[62] If the arches are segmental the abutments need to be even 'stronger and thicker'.[63] For the arches themselves, the key ratio is that of the thickness of the arch ring to the arch span. Alberti warned that there should not be a single stone in the arches of thickness less than one-tenth the span. Gautier stated that the ratio depended on the span of the arch and the quality of the stone. Thus he recommended a ratio of 1:5 for small spans, but 1:15 for spans of over 40 feet if constructed with strong stone.[64] As Heyman has shown, such ratios remain of vital impor-

[58] Palliser, *Tudor York*, 267; Ruddock, *Arch Bridges*, 85.

[59] J. Heyman, N. B. Hobbs, and B. S. Jermy, 'The Rehabilitation of Teston Bridge', *Proc. Inst. Civ. Engrs.*, 68 (1980), 489–97.

[60] Boyer *French Bridges*, 88, 140.

[61] Alberti, 78; Palladio, 182; Ruddock, *Arch Bridges*, 201–2.

[62] Palladio, 182.   [63] Alberti, 78.

[64] Ibid. Alberti's and Palladio's recommendations are conveniently brought together in *Irish Stone Bridges*, 303–5, and Ruddock, *Arch Bridges*, 201–2.

tance: if the arch ring is too thin, the arch will collapse. Alberti also stressed the importance of good infill and precisely cut joints in the arch ring.[65]

This, then, is what studies from the fifteenth century to the present day recommended should be done. Much of the advice was important and sensible, but some of it was over-prescriptive. The relationships between span and pier and span and arch ring are essential to bridge design, but the values the treatise writers ascribed to them were arbitrary.[66] They were certainly not always followed. There were limits to how thin the arch rings could be for a given span, but within these limits a great deal of leeway. Many medieval arches were constructed to a very conservative standard with very thick arch rings; others, in contrast, had a radical ratio of arch thickness to span.

Similarly the ratio of pier width to arch opening has varied considerably. The treatise writers were more conservative than is necessary: in eighteenth–century France the ratio of pier to arch could be as low as 1:10. This required the arches of a bridge to be built simultaneously to provide the self-equilibrating thrust from the arches. Furthermore, the bridges Palladio admired, including his favourite bridge at Rimini, had considerably smaller spans and wider piers than he recommended.[67] Modern work, though favouring very wide openings, recognizes that 'there is no universally applicable definition of what constitutes an adequate opening'.[68] Medieval stone bridges demonstrate this very clearly. Masons of the period often built bridges with shallow foundations, thick piers, narrow spans, and a restricted waterway. On the other hand, they also built structures with firm foundations, comparatively narrow piers, and huge spans.

SOURCES

By the sixteenth century there is a huge amount of information about the options chosen. We know whether major bridges were constructed of stone or timber; if stone, how many arches they had and whether they were large or

---

[65] See the analysis of Clare College Bridge, Cambridge (Chap. 7 below) and Page, *Masonry Bridges*, 9–11, 79–81. Neither Alberti nor Palladio realized that segmental arches are stronger, seemingly ignoring this major advance in late-medieval design. They preferred semicircular arches on the grounds that they do not thrust against each other, although they recognized that semicircular arches might produce too steep a gradient (Alberti, 78; Palladio,182).

[66] In this context, see Harvey's comments on the advice of the French architect, Jean Mignot, to the Milan authorities (who were building a new cathedral) about rules of construction: J. Harvey, *The Medieval Architect* (London, 1972), 163. Harvey notes that Mignot had learnt a set of rules but this did not mean that he himself understood them; nor do they seem to have been based on empirical evidence.

[67] Palladio, 183–5.   [68] Hamill, *Bridge Hydraulics*, 11–12

small; if timber, there is also often evidence about the superstructure. Many medieval bridges have been demolished, but a large number of them are known from illustrations, descriptions, observations made when bridges were taken down or repaired, and a few modern archaeological investigations. In addition, over 200 bridges built before 1600 survive.

Illustrations

Bridges were depicted with some accuracy from an early date. A manuscript of *c*.1480 of the poems of Charles, duke of Orleans, contains a view of the Tower of London with London Bridge in the background.[69] In the following centuries there are an increasing number of illustrations. Picturesque views of ancient bridges were a popular subject for distinguished artists, including Richard Wilson, whose *Holt Bridge* is in the National Gallery, and Cotman, who painted an early watercolour of Bishop's Bridge, Norwich, which is in the city's Castle Museum. Many amateur painters produced paintings of bridges, and their pictures are often to be found in local collections. Monmow Bridge, Monmouth (plate 6), which possessed the added attraction of a medieval tower, was drawn or painted by Samuel Prout, A. V. C. and T. H. Fielding, David Cox, Francis Grose, the Varleys, Cotman and Turner and numerous lesser artists.[70] A recent study of the pictorial evidence for Old Ouse Bridge, York, lists almost fifty images of the old bridge made before the 1820.[71] Many views of bridges were engraved: a particularly useful collection for those interested in bridges are the panoramic views of towns which Nathaniel and Samuel Buck published in the first half of the eighteenth century, often with the town bridge as a prominent element in the foreground.[72]

By the second half of the eighteenth century there are accurate representations. Scale drawings of the new bridge at Putney and the long medieval bridges at Bideford and Burton-on-Trent appeared in the *Gentleman's Magazine* for 1751. The *Book of Bridges belonging to the West Riding of the County of York* of the following year contains architectural records of all the bridges maintained by the county.

Fortunately, a very large number of major English bridges survived until the late eighteenth century. The eighteenth-century Englishman's antiquarian interests and love of topographical drawings, paintings, and engravings have

[69] BM, Royal MS. 16 F.II, fol. 73; it is reproduced in *London Bridge*, 98.

[70] M. L. J. Rowlands, *Monmow Bridge and Gate* (Stroud, 1994), 30.

[71] B. Wilson and F. Mee, 'The Fairest Arch in England', *Old Ouse Bridge, York, and its Buildings: The Pictorial Evidence* (York, 2002), 83–92.

[72] They are reproduced in Hyde, *A Prospect of Britain*.

ensured that there are illustrations of many of them. The increasing threat of demolition encouraged artists, publishers, and clients. Henry Cave, who produced sketches of Old Ouse Bridge for his *Antiquities of York* (1813), noted that: 'The destroying hand of time, and a predominant spirit of improvement, are lessening the number as well as the figure of the remaining antiquities of York; and the forms of many of them will be shortly known only in their engraved representations.'[73]

We have a remarkable pictorial record of even the Severn bridges, although just one of the present bridges over it contains medieval material. This consists of a ribbed arch at the west end of Bridgnorth Bridge, and parts of the piers of the bridge, which was subsequently remodelled in 1670 and c.1810.[74] Illustrations show that most of the other medieval bridges over the river were of similar design. The two bridges at Shrewsbury had semicircular, ribbed arches like the surviving Bridgnorth arch. The stout ribs of the arches and the bulky piers are a particularly prominent feature of Paul Sandby's image of old Welsh Bridge (plate 10). Images of Bewdley Bridge, which has a medieval chapel on one of the piers, depict a similar structure with rounded arches. Old Worcester Bridge and Buildwas Bridge had pointed arches, but they were of similar spans to the other bridges. They all had massive piers and spanned the river in about five or six arches, the largest with a width of about 10 metres.[75] There is a surviving bridge at Ludlow across the neighbouring River Teme which provides a good idea of what these bridges were like (plate 25). Although of shorter overall length (three arches), it has similar individual spans and its massive piers are particularly prominent. Finally, on the lower Severn, where the flood plain is very broad, there was the crossing at Gloucester. A splendid engraving published in the *Complete English Traveller* shows it as a long causeway with bridges over the several channels of the river (plate 1).

Descriptions

The road from Gloucester to the Severn was also described by Leland:

The bridge that is on chefe arme of Severne, that renethe hard by the towne, is of 7. great arches of stone. There is anothar a litle more west of it, that hathe an arche or 2, and servythe at a tyme for a diche or dreane of the meads. A little way farthar is anothar bridge, hard witheout the weste gate, and this bridge hathe 5. greate archis.

---

[73] Quoted by Wilson and Mee in *Old Ouse Bridge*, 66–8.

[74] A. Blackwall, *Historic Bridges of Shropshire* (Shrewsbury, 1985), 7–9.

[75] The illustrations are to be found in Morriss, *Shropshire Severn*; Ward, *Bridges of Shrewsbury*; T. R. Nash, *Collections for the History and Antiquities of Worcestershire*, 2 vols. (London, 1781–99), ii. 274; *Worc. Hist. Soc.*, 31 (1915–20).

From this bridge there goithe a greate causey of stone, forcyd up thrughe the low meds of Severn by the lengthe of a quartar of a myle. In this cawsey be dyvers doble arched bridges, to drene the medows at flods. At the end of this causey is a bridge of 8. arches not yet finished.[76]

Leland's typical descriptions are not so detailed, but they do often indicate whether bridges were of stone or timber, and often how many arches they had. They provide evidence of relatively minor bridges which we have no images of, and of major bridges which collapsed at an early date. For instance, he saw a three-arched bridge at Bridge Hewick, near Ripon. It must have had giant spans similar to those of Piercebridge since the River Ure is wide at Ripon, and there is currently a bridge of six arches at the site (plate 22). Leland's bridge had disappeared by 1675, and his account is the only record of its existence.[77] Many other documentary sources, before and after Leland, provide information about the design of bridges. They include place-name evidence, descriptions of battles at bridges, and expenditure accounts and surveys, as well as journals, such as those of Celia Fiennes and Daniel Defoe, and Ogilby's road maps, which often indicate whether the bridges on his descriptions of roads were of stone or timber.

Archaeology

Illustrations and descriptions of bridges can be supplemented by accounts of detailed investigation of the fabric. By the mid-eighteenth century there are descriptions of the condition of bridges, including the quality of foundations and infill: we have a number of detailed reports of this kind, such as those by Labelye and Dance the Elder on London Bridge.[78] These were primarily practical studies, concerned with the condition of the bridge with a view to its repair or justifying its demolition. Smeaton's notebooks are slightly different: he was interested in learning from the study of ancient bridges, making observations about the depth of the arch ring, noting the use of counter arches and where and why there was distortion.[79]

In the next century there is increasing evidence of a historical interest in ancient bridges. As more and more famous medieval bridges were pulled down, observations made during their demolition were published, some in early volumes of *Archaeologia*. These reports contain interesting, even surprising, material about otherwise invisible parts of bridges: the most unusual were the

---

[76] Leland, ii. 57–8.
[77] Ibid. v. 139; Ogilby shows a wooden bridge at the site (plate 95).
[78] The reports are printed in W. Maitland, *History of London*, 3rd edn. (London, 1760), ii. 827–33.
[79] They are discussed in Ruddock, *Arch Bridges*, 80–102.

discoveries made when Teign Bridge, where the Plymouth–Exeter road crosses the River Teign, was reconstructed in 1815. A series of earlier bridges was revealed, one on top of the other. Under the old two-arched bridge in use in 1814 was found an older bridge, constructed of red stone; it consisted of five arches, three of which were under the abutment and approach road of the newer bridge. Even more surprisingly, under some of the piers of the red stone bridge were discovered piers of a third, earlier bridge constructed of white ashlar stone.[80]

Although the demolition of medieval bridges largely ceased in the twentieth century, they continued to be widened and reconstructed. Observations and analysis of the fifteenth-century Burford Bridge, Abingdon, were published by the historian H. E. Salter and the engineer in charge, J. J. Leeming.[81] Unfortunately, studies of this kind were all too rare. Few archaeologists took an interest in even major repairs, and thorough archaeological investigation of ancient bridge sites was uncommon. Most engineers showed a similar lack of concern. In many counties records of repairs were not kept by Highways Departments. For instance, in Bedfordshire 'few detailed records [of repairs] survive from the late 19th and early 20th century . . . written documentation is largely missing until the 1950s'.[82] Nevertheless, engineers seem to have been more interested in ancient bridges than historians or archaeologists. The borough or county bridge engineer was more likely than the local historian to publish local histories of bridges.[83] When the medieval bridge at Teston in Kent was assessed in 1973, prior to repair and strengthening, the findings were written up by a team consisting of a professor of engineering, a soil specialist, and the county's bridge engineer.[84]

The situation has begun to change: there are a few good examples of liaison between the professions. In Bedfordshire the Conservation Section of the Planning Department has established a thorough programme of recording and research carried out by archaeologists, linked to a comprehensive programme of repairs to the county's historic bridges which the county surveyor began in 1982.[85] In 1988 excavations were carried out below the piers and abutments of Monmow Bridge, Monmouth, as part of a flood alleviation scheme.[86] Such efforts remain, however, exceptional.

---

[80] P. T. Taylor, 'An Account of some Discoveries made in Taking Down the Old Bridge over the River Teign', *Archeologia*, 19 (1821), 308–13.
[81] J. J. Leeming and H. E. Salter, 'Burford Bridge, Abingdon', *Oxoniensia*, 3 (1937).
[82] Ibid. 12.   [83] e.g. Wallis, *Dorset Bridges*; Ward, *Bridges of Shrewsbury*.
[84] Heyman et al., *Teston Bridge*, 490.   [85] 'Bridges of Bedfordshire', 7.
[86] Rowlands, *Monmow Bridge*.

Since systematic investigation has been scant, most major discoveries have been made by chance. Ancient piles and other parts of bridges have been revealed during works carried out by utilities, gravel extraction, or road building. A few finds have been spectacular, including a series of bridges dating from the eleventh to the thirteenth century across a disused channel of the Trent.[87] These structures were found because they and the roads leading to them fell into disuse long ago; the remains of most ancient bridges and causeways, however, are likely to lie under existing roads and bridges. If the opportunity to examine them is taken when it arises, it is likely that major discoveries will be made.

The Surviving Bridges

The most important and impressive source of information about design and construction is the surviving ancient bridges. There are many of them: at least 200 extant English bridges contain some material which dates from before *c.*1600. They enable us to answer questions about detailed aspects of bridges which descriptions rarely mention and illustrations often do not show. Were the bridges constructed of ashlar? Were there cutwaters upstream and downstream? How were the arches constructed? A significant number of the surviving bridges were already very old in 1600. A few have an arch or arches which can probably be dated to the eleventh century, and there are examples of bridges from every century thereafter.

Some bridges can be dated with relative accuracy, but by no means all. A number can be at least roughly dated on architectural grounds, such as Exe Bridge, Exeter, with its Norman arches, or the four-centred arches of the bridges at Abingdon (plates 2 and 15). Some can be precisely dated from documentary references. The county quarter sessions order and minute books provide a detailed record of many of the structures built after 1600. Medieval sources can also be a reliable guide to the date of construction, and the preference for patching and mending before the late eighteenth century, at least in lowland England, means that once built in stone some of the original structure often survived.[88] The problem usually lies in determining the original construction date. For instance, major repairs or rebuilding were undertaken at Huntingdon Bridge in 1300, 1340, and 1370. Jervoise, Pevsner, and the Royal Commission on Historic Monuments each chose a different one of these dates for the current bridge.[89] The expenditure of large sums does not necessarily

---

[87] See Chap. 6.   [88] Chalkin, *Public Building,* 113.
[89] *Mid and Eastern,* 102; Pevsner, *Beds., Hunts., etc.,* 273, *RCHM Hunts.,* 151.

imply reconstruction but might have involved repairs to an earlier bridge. Shoring up the foundations of the piers of a stone and timber bridge could be very expensive.

Although it can be difficult to date bridges precisely, in most cases bridges built before the mid- to late sixteenth century can be distinguished from those of later centuries. First, we can often tell whether a bridge which is standing today had been built when Leland visited the site. For instance, he saw a three-arched structure at Piercebridge which survives to this day: without this evidence we might doubt whether the bridge had been built before 1550, despite its series of arch rings which are typical of the northern bridges of the fifteenth and sixteenth centuries.[90] Secondly, many bridges built between c.1200 and c.1600 have one or more of the following which are rare in later centuries: pointed arches, ribs, and chamfered arch rings, often in two orders (plate 26).[91] Equally, later bridges often have distinctive features which mark them out from earlier ones; for instance, many Yorkshire bridges, both great and small, of the late seventeenth and eighteenth centuries contain an unchamfered, ashlar arch ring surmounted by a narrow archivolt.[92]

Major and clearly medieval bridges, many of which can only be very roughly dated, are to be found in all parts of the country and in almost every location. A few of the more impressive include: East Farleigh Bridge across the Medway in the south-east; the bridge at St Ives with its medieval chapel on the Great Ouse in East Anglia (plate 17); Croft Bridge across the Tees joining Durham and North Yorkshire in the north (plate 8); Wye Bridge in Hereford in the west; and Wadebridge over the Camel in the south-west. They survive in a variety of locations. Some, like Huntingdon Bridge, were on a national highway (plate 12). Others are in the centre of towns and cities, including Dee Bridge in Chester, and Elvet Bridge as well as Framwellgate Bridge in Durham (plates 13 and 5). Yet others are in the country on roads which join local towns: on the Upper Thames, Radcot Bridge links Bampton, Burford, and the Cotwolds with Faringdon to the south. Thornborough Bridge, much patched but with elaborate hood moulds and ribs, formerly carried the Buckingham–Bedford road across Claydon Brook, a tributary of the Great Ouse. Almost the only type of location where no major examples have survived is on the main rivers in big cities, including Bristol, Leeds, London, Manchester, and Newcastle; many survived until the last century, but all had been demolished by 1900.

---

[90] Leland, i. 77.

[91] Although these features are not altogether unknown later, see e.g. *East*, 26.

[92] Typical examples are Town End Bridge, Sowerby, probably of 1672 (4 arches each with a span of c.10 m.) (*North*, 50–1, 74) and Greta Bridge of 1789 (a single span c.25 m.).

While it is highly unlikely that new, splendid medieval bridges like these will be found in future, it is probable that more medieval work will be identified. My estimate of 200 pre-1600 bridges is conservative. For many areas Jervoise is the main, sometimes the only, source. His principal aim was to uncover ancient bridges rather than date them precisely. More recent detailed local surveys, of Northamptonshire and Bedforshire for instance, have usually taken a more bullish approach. Contributors to the National Monuments Record since Jervoise have been more inclined to judge bridges, or parts of them, medieval than he was.[93]

The remains of medieval structures are likely to be discovered in two main ways. First, there are probably bridges with a medieval arch, or other feature, which has not yet been recognized hidden under later arches. They are not always easily detected. Jervoise knew there had been a medieval bridge at Banbury in Oxfordshire, and he had seen illustrations of it, but he appears not to have spotted the two original arches embedded in later reconstructions in brick with iron girders.[94] This is not altogether surprising: as the Oxfordshire Museums Information Sheet observes, 'you really have to peer underneath to see the medieval arches'.[95]

Secondly, there are a number of bridges which have stonework of post-medieval date but may contain a medieval core or foundations. As an example, Tadcaster Bridge has rounded arches and arch rings dating from its reconstruction in 1698–9.[96] The arches' spans and height, which are similar to those of the nearby medieval bridge at Wetherby, suggest a much earlier date. It is likely that the arches at Tadcaster are reconstructions, with perhaps a refacing of the medieval piers. If timber under the piers survives it could be dated by carbon dating or dendrochronology, techniques used on timbers found at Sutton Bridge, Bedfordshire, and Monmow Bridge, Monmouth.[97]

Fortunately, even without further discoveries the evidence we have about the surviving medieval bridges and the information from illustrations, descriptions, and inspections mean that we know a good deal about the options chosen from the twelfth century on. From this period we can trace important developments in bridge design. By the sixteenth century there is a wealth of information about fabric and design and some about construction techniques. Something, thanks largely to chance discoveries, is known too of pre-twelfth–century structures. It is to them we now turn.

---

[93] e.g. Goodfellow (*Northants Bridges*) found medieval work at Thorpe Waterville and possibly Thrapston, which Jervoise did not refer to.
[94] *Mid and Eastern*, 153.   [95] *Bridges in Oxfordshire.*   [96] Chalkin, *Public Building*, 111.
[97] 'Bridges of Bedfordshire', 74; Rowlands, *Monmow Bridge*, 81.

6

Early Solutions:
Timber Deck Bridges and Causeways

THE ROMAN INHERITANCE

In his 1961 article D. P. Dymond identified the two main types of Roman bridge in Britain which have left traces. The smaller were timber girder bridges, the larger ones were stone and timber. He noted that a striking feature in Roman Britain was the lack of evidence for stone arched bridges. Neither of the two major survivals in Britain, at Corbridge and Chesters, have produced voussoirs, which one might have expected to find near the bridge, for example, in the river bed.[1] While more recent studies have found a small number of arched bridges, in general they have confirmed Dymond's conclusion.[2]

This may seem strange, since arched bridges are a well-known characteristic of Roman engineering. Several superb examples still survive from many parts of the Empire, including the Puente de Alcantara in Spain, the Pont de Trajan in Tunisia, and the Severus Bridge at Kahta, on the flanks of the Taurus Mountains in Turkey, which has a huge single span.[3] It is notable, however, that all the extant Roman arched bridges are in the Mediterranean world or in the East. Such structures were rare in any part of northern Europe. Differences in rivers and climate seem to explain the differences between practice in the south and the north: in the former region 'tides are slight, and river flows are slow and water levels low in summer; and accordingly foundations are easy to establish'. Further north, substantial river flows throughout the year and muddy river beds made the construction of bridges so much more difficult.[4]

The timber bridges Dymond found traces of were smaller (under c.20 metres). Since any signs of wood are rarely preserved, these bridges are

---

[1] Dymond, *Roman Bridges*, 146.

[2] O'Connor, *Roman Bridges*, 148–9. Voussoirs have been found reused in the remains of abutments at Chesters and at the bridge which carries Hadrian's Wall across the River Irthing near Willowford.

[3] Ibid. 109–11, 121, 127–9.   [4] Brooks, 'Medieval Bridges', 12–14.

identified by the survival of abutments, which were usually constructed of earth, and by the absence of stone at the site.[5] Often all the archaeologist finds when a Roman road comes to a stream are the remains of an earthen ramp, once the support of a wooden bridge. At Stockley Gill in Durham, Dere Street ran up both sides of the valley on a considerable ramp or causeway which stopped abruptly at the edges of the stream to form abutments 8–9 feet high: they were constructed of earth and cobbles, the southern 36 feet, the northern 40 feet wide.[6]

The Romans also built more substantial timber bridges of the type depicted on Trajan's column.[7] In the 1960s the remains of such a bridge were found at Aldwincle, Northamptonshire, across the Nene. It was about 25 metres long and the largest timbers were *c.*5 metres in length and between 0.4 and 0.5 metres in section. Trestles or piles supported horizontal girders, and on this structure the cross planking of the timber deck was laid. This supported a metalled road which was possibly laid on sand, matting, or clay rather than directly onto the planks.[8]

Causeways were constructed across marshy land. On the Somerset levels a well-made structure was found with vertical piles and wooden sleepers. Over this was a 'thin layer of concrete on which were laid side timbers forming a trough almost 12 ft. wide and 30–33 inches deep filled with stones to form the roadway, and, on each side of this, sloping banks of brushwood and stones for a width of 30 feet'. Another causeway at Strood, near Rochester in Kent, con-sisted of 'layers of flints, chalk, pebble-gravel and Kentish Rag which rested on piles and a framework of timber "cells"; the width was 14 ft.'.[9]

THE FIFTH TO THE TWELFTH CENTURIES

The Survival of Roman Bridges

The new road system, which evolved in Anglo-Saxon England, made use of a few Roman bridges, as we have seen.[10] The best evidence for survival comes from Rochester. Here, what appears to have been a massive Roman pier foun-

---

[5] Dymond, *Roman Bridges*, 146–9; the abutments of timber bridges were, however, sometimes revetted with stone.

[6] Ibid. 141–2.

[7] O'Connor, *Roman Bridges*, 138–9. Trajan's column depicts bridges built by the army on campaign, but O'Connor considers it probable that other major timber bridges were of a similar construction.

[8] Jackson and Ambrose, *Aldwincle*, 39–72.

[9] Dymond, *Roman Bridges*, 150, and see Margary, *Roman Roads*, 125.

[10] Chap. 3.

dation was discovered in 1851, when a new bridge was built on the site of the Roman bridge and a short distance from the medieval structure.[11] Using the eleventh-century Rochester Bridge document, which lists the piers that groups of estates were obliged to repair and the amount of timber decking they were liable for, N. P. Brooks has produced an ingenious reconstruction of the bridge. It consisted of nine unequally spaced stone piers with a timber roadway. The longest span was 66 feet from the centre of the piers. These were probably *c*.6–7 metres wide.[12] Brooks has calculated that if they were 7 metres wide, the longest beams would have had an unsupported span of 43 feet; an oak trunk of this length sawn to a square section of *c*.0.5 metres would weigh an enormous 4 tons;[13] if the piers were 6 metres in width then the unsupported span would have been even longer. The massive foundations consisted of: 'piles mainly of oak, driven into the gravel that overlies the chalk bedrock and packed around with ragstone rubble to a depth of at least thirteen feet. Some of this rubble may have comprised the core of the pier from which masonry facing had been subsequently robbed. But most of it must have been the foundation that the Romans had constructed beneath the bed of the river.'[14] Some timber framing was found, which may have been the remains of a coffer dam, which was left *in situ* after the bridge had been constructed to protect the piers from scour.

More about this type of construction is known from the one north European Roman bridge which is still in use. Although the present arches replaced the timber superstructure of Trier Bridge in the nineteenth century, the survival of the huge Roman piers has enabled archaeologists to examine them and their foundations closely. Seven cofferdams were constructed in the river and, once the water had been removed, the alluvium of the river bed was excavated until the gravel terrace was reached; massive piles of oak up to 50 centimetres in diameter and shod in iron were then driven into the gravel subsoil and a rubble foundation of ballast was tipped in and rammed down around the piles to form a secure foundation on which the masonry piers were built.[15]

There is some evidence that other Roman bridges in England with stone piers and timber decks survived for several centuries, including those at Piercebridge and Corbridge. The names themselves may indicate survival. The remains of massive stone piers of the former were visible until the flood of 1771, and detached stones and timber piles have been found downstream. At Corbridge, about half-a-mile upstream of the present bridge, Dere Street

---

[11] Brooks, 'Rochester Bridge', 22.

[12] One pier was found in 1851; it was *c*.6 m. wide, the same as the piers at Corbridge; on the other hand, the width of the piers of the major Roman bridge to survive at Trier is 7 m. (ibid.).

[13] Ibid. 24–5.   [14] Ibid. 9–10.   [15] Brooks, 'Rochester Bridge', 8–9.

crossed the River Tyne. Here 'the masonry substructure of the [Roman] bridge
. . . is partly visible at low water; there are between five and ten stone piers and
two stone abutments; the piers have cutwaters at the upstream ends and are 7.5
metres long, 5.9 to 6.0 metres wide'.[16] Lower down the Tyne, when the areas
around the piers of the old bridge at Newcastle were explored during its demolition, foundations of earlier stone bridges were revealed. They possibly included the remains of the *Pons Aelius*, built by the Emperor Hadrian. Coffer
dams similar to those at Trier were found. It has been claimed that, as at
Rochester, the piers of the Roman bridge remained in use for more than a
millennium, that is, until the thirteenth century when a new arched bridge was
built.[17]

Anglo-Saxon Bridges

Most of the major bridges which existed by the time of the Norman Conquest,
however, were not Roman survivals, but had been newly built between the
eighth and eleventh centuries. Their erection was a formidable undertaking,
but most of them are a mystery to us, even the most important, like the bridge
over the Trent at Nottingham. On the other hand, we do have some information about a few timber bridges, and we can at least identify the main types.

Timber Girder Bridges

Anglo-Saxon timber bridges were of two utterly different designs. One was the
timber girder bridge, constructed with vertical posts supporting the roadway;
the other, a bridge constructed with piers taking the form of huge wooden boxes
filled with rubble. The remains of a girder bridge were found on the upper reaches of the River Hull, near the significantly named hamlet of Brigham, at Skerne
in East Yorkshire. In 1982 rows of substantial oak piles, which probably formed
the vertical trestles of a series of abutments of a bridge, were uncovered in conjunction with a Viking sword of the ninth or tenth century, and were assumed
to be of that date. The piles had rotted tops which had been sealed by a thick
layer of alluvial clay. They had been sharpened and embedded in the river bed
and bank by their own weight. To ensure that they did not sink too deep, cross
pieces were inserted through holes drilled in the uprights.[18]

In 1989 a fragment of a collapsed eleventh-century bridge was uncovered on
the site of the River Fleet in London. In contrast to the regular spacing of the
timber trestles found at Skerne and elsewhere, the Fleet bridge consisted of a

---

[16] O'Connor, *Roman Bridges*, 146–7.
[17] J. Bruce, 'The Three Bridges over the Tyne at Newcastle', *Archaeologica Aeliana*, NS 10 (1885), 1–11; his
interpretation is challenged in T. Brigham, 'Roman London Bridge', in *London Bridge*, 41–2.
[18] J. Dent, 'Skerne', *Current Arch.*, 91 (1984).

series of piles, apparently irregularly spaced, which supported a number of horizontal parallel beams, lying edge to edge and forming a roadway.[19] A bridge of similar structure was found almost a hundred years earlier in Norwich, buried under the streets leading to Fye Bridge and in the bed of the River Wensum. Here too, there were many irregularly spaced old piles of oak of 4 to 5 feet in length. W. Hudson, who observed the excavations, considered that they had supported a plankway road and bridge. Two horizontal planks were found *in situ*. As we have seen, Hudson thought the bridge and causeway Roman, but they may provide a remarkable and unique example of a structure used to obstruct the passage of hostile Danish boats: wide, piled abutments restricted the waterway and were clearly designed to obstruct the passage of ships.[20]

'Laftwork Caisson' Construction

The best example of the other, 'wooden box pier' type of construction was found in 1993, while a quarry company was stripping the soil above an old river channel at Hemington about 200 metres from the present course of the River Trent. Dr Salisbury, a retired local GP, spotted the oak timbers and worked stone of a bridge. Subsequent excavation uncovered two more bridges.[21] The oldest, dating from the eleventh century, was of a most unusual design. It consisted of huge wooden piers in the form of immense diamond-shaped boxes of the size of stone piers. The excavators described it in the following way:

The remains consisted of two diamond shaped pier bases laid onto the river bed, each made out of four massive squared beams with internal horizontal braces to form a base frame . . . In the four corners of the frames were braced upright posts, holding together planked revetments—essentially forming wooden boxes, 8 by 5 metres across, looking not unlike log cabins. The bases had been filled with several tonnes of sandstone rubble to provide ballast and stability.[22]

No remains of other bridges of this construction have been found in England, but it is most unlikely that Hemington Bridge was unique. Interestingly, in an article written several years before this bridge was unearthed, S. E. Rigold had argued that just such a timber bridge might have been a natural choice for Saxon and Norman builders.[23] He pointed out that the medieval seal of Innsbruck shows in plan a bridge which had large, boat-shaped piers, cased with intersecting beams and apparently filled with rubble.[24] It is very like

[19] B. Watson, 'The Saxo-Norman Timber Bridge', in *London Bridge*, 80–1.

[20] W. Hudson, 'On an Ancient Timber Roadway across the River Wensum at Fye Bridge, Norwich', *Norfolk Arch.*, 13 (1898), 217–32.

[21] Cooper et al., *Hemington Bridges*, 319.   [22] Ibid.

[23] Rigold, 'Structural Aspects', 53.   [24] Ibid.

Hemington Bridge. B. Watson notes other examples in Scandinavia, which he describes as 'laftwork caissons', for instance at Brogepollen near Vestvagoy in Norway, where they formed the piers of an eleventh- or twelfth-century bridge.[25]

As a result of years of investigation by the Museum of London Archaeology Service (MOLAS), a picture has emerged of one giant bridge of this period. Two *ex situ* timbers of c.1000 have been interpreted as a baseplate and beam from the abutment of a bridge across the Thames at London.[26] These timbers were reused as part of the foundations for a twelfth-century bridge caisson, similar to the piers of the Hemington Bridge, constructed at the south end of the bridge. B. Watson of MOLAS thinks caissons were probably not used for the rest of the bridge in deeper water. He puts forward two possible reconstructions of the bridge: one is that there were caissons in the shallower water and trestles (of a timber girder bridge) in the deep water; the other is that the caissons formed the abutments of a timber girder bridge. The presence of posts of a bridge of this type is suggested by the accounts of St Olaf's naval attack on London. The admittedly later legendary saga says that there 'were poles [presumably posts] below down in the river which held up the bridge'. Olaf's aim was to loosen these posts.[27]

Timber Causeways

There were also large piled causeways, which were being built from an early date. One very substantial structure has been found, which linked Mersea Island to the Essex mainland. Uncovered in 1978 when a water main was being laid, it provides a vivid impression of the causeways built across the shallow estuaries in this part of England. Two rows of oak piles, 2–2.6 metres long, were found; the piles in each row were between 0.4 and 2.8 metres apart and the rows were 0.7 metres apart. The archaeologists who examined the site considered that it may have consisted of as many as 3,000 to 5,000 oak piles in fifteen to twenty rows, each 400 to 500 metres long. The earliest roadway was made of sand and grit. It was a major undertaking, which was dated by dendrochronology to c.AD 700.[28] Place-names may indicate other Anglo-Saxon causeways of a similar scale in the area. An impressive structure must have connected North and South Fambridge (meaning 'fen bridge'), Essex, on the Rochford and Dengie peninsulas across the wide, tidal Crouch Estuary. It could have been a bridge, but a causeway of the Mersea Island type is perhaps more likely. Neither

[25] Watson, *Saxo-Norman Bridge*, 77. Exactly how the piers carried the superstructure of these bridges is unclear (Rigold, *Structural Aspects*, 53).

[26] Watson, *Late Saxon Bridgehead*, 57.   [27] Watson, *Saxo-Norman Bridge*, 73–82.

[28] J. Hillam, 'An English Tree-Ring Chronology', *Med. Arch.*, 25 (1981), 37; P. Crummy, J. Hillam, and C. Crossan, 'Mersea Island: The Anglo-Saxon Causeway', *Essex Arch. and Hist.*, 14 (1982), 77–86.

this structure nor Hullbridge above it could be maintained at a later date, possibly because of rising water levels. The lowest crossing at present is 5 miles upstream.[29]

There are also several place-names, which contain the suffix bridge preceded by a first element which has the sense of 'brushwood' or 'made of brushwood', for example, in Ricebridge (Surrey), Risebridge (Durham, Essex), and Rising Bridge (Notts.).[30] Since it is hard to conceive of a brushwood bridge, these names may denote brushwood timber causeways. It is possible that they bore some resemblance to the prehistoric structures across the Somerset levels which were built between 3000 and 2000 BC. These were constructed of bundles of twigs or brushwood, usually birch, which were laid across the marshy land and held in place by pegs driven into the ground on each side.[31]

A number of place-names mean 'plank bridge' or 'plank causeway', including Elbridge (Sussex), Felbrigg (Norfolk), Fell Briggs (North Riding), Shide Bridge (Isle of Wight), and Thelbridge (Devon).[32] There were not major rivers at any of these sites, and so the names also appear to refer to major causeways. Possibly they resembled the causeways of planks like those constructed in prehistory by laying planks of wood or split logs along the line of the road, held in place with pegs driven into the ground,[33] but it is more likely that their design was similar to the roughly contemporary 'causeway-bridge' found at Ravning Enge. This consisted of over 1,600 oak posts, each 1 foot square, which had been felled in AD 979–80. These heavy posts had been driven into the ground and formed an orderly series of trestles, which supported a planked carriageway 5.5 metres wide. The whole structure spanned the wide valley of the River Vejle, near Jelling in central Jutland.[34]

FROM THE TWELFTH CENTURY

Causeways

Saxon causeways were also constructed of earth and other material dug up on the site; for instance, an artificial causeway, constructed of gravel excavated from its south side, was found adjacent to the Viking Age bridge at Skerne in East Yorkshire.[35] Such structures are frequently recorded from the twelfth century. Some of the great fenland causeways were of this construction.

[29] Rackham, *Countryside*, 261–3.   [30] Cameron, *Place Names*, 178.
[31] Taylor, *Roads*, 13.   [32] Cameron, *Place Names*, 177.   [33] Taylor, *Roads*, 13.
[34] E. Roesdahl, *Viking Age Denmark* (London, 1982), 147–55.   [35] Dent, *Skerne*, 252.

Throughout the middle ages carts went to gravel pits near Soham to obtain new ballast for the causeway from Soham and Stuntney to Ely.[36] These causeways were usually ditched on either side and pierced by timber bridges, as at Holland causeway, the very long embanked road from Donnington to Bridge End on the route from Nottingham and Grantham to Boston. It was almost 4 miles long and contained thirty bridges, each 10 feet broad and 8 feet high.[37] There were smaller structures of similar design, for instance, at Steyning in Sussex.[38] Earth embankments might be contained by stone retaining walls. This is presumably what was meant by the 'cawsey of stone' with many small bridges of planks from Osney to Hinksey Ferry, to the west of Oxford.[39]

Stone and Timber Bridges

Bridges with stone piers and timber roadways may have been constructed in Anglo-Saxon England, but it is only from the thirteenth century that new structures of this type are recorded. During the excavations at Hemington, the final bridge to be built on the site was found upstream of the other two. It dated from the thirteenth century and consisted not only of the foundations and lower courses of a number of masonry piers, but also of the remains of the timber superstructure; no voussoirs were found at the site. Similar bridges were still in use centuries later. At a few bridges the original timber roadway was replaced by stone arches. In 1491 a bequest was made 'to the making of the arches of the bridge of Sherington now not vawted with stone with a perpoynt wall upon the said arches'.[40] Some examples of this development may survive. Mordiford Bridge, Herefordshire, may be a case in point; likewise Powick Bridge, Worcestershire, which has huge piers from which spring rather incongruous flat arches.[41]

Bridges were also constructed with stone abutments but timber trestles. A fifteenth-century contract specified a bridge of this type at Newark.[42] Other bridges were a curious hybrid of timber supports and stone piers, including Caversham Bridge, Reading (River Thames). Leland described it as 'a great mayne bridge of tymbre over the Tamise, wher I markid that it restid most apon foundation of tymbre, and yn sum places of stone'.[43]

Timber Bridges

In contrast to the survival of stone and timber designs, after 1200 there is no further evidence of the great, cabin-like wooden caisson piers of the first

[36] Darby, *Medieval Fenland*, 109.   [37] Ibid. 116.   [38] See Chap. 2.
[39] Leland, v. 72.   [40] Chibnall, *Sherington*, 9.
[41] Crook, *Medieval Bridges*, 21–2; *Wales and Western*, 150–1.
[42] Salzman, *Building*, 546–7.   [43] Leland, i. 111.

Hemington Bridge. All timber bridges were girder bridges. The key work on the subject is S. E. Rigold's 1975 article. He distinguishes two main types of girder construction. On the one hand there were 'earth-fast' bridges, where the vertical posts of the timber trestles were driven straight into the river bed. The other type of design was the 'sole-plate' bridge, constructed not by driving in vertical posts but by tenoning them into horizontal beams of wood (known as sole-plates) which were laid on or pinned into the river bed.

The Earth-Fast Design

Earth-fast timber bridges were, according to Dr Rigold, the norm in the middle ages on the Thames from Reading to Kingston. They are known from illustrations made from the seventeenth century onwards: by Jan Silbrechts of Henley Bridge; by Farington of Windsor Bridge (plate 7); and by Elizabeth Ranyard of Kingston Bridge.[44] Rigold describes them in the following way:

Their trestles are closely but irregularly spaced, having two to five unsquared but accurately driven 'projecting piles', rising straight from the bed to a lintel; they have absolutely no longitudinal bracing but sometimes a rough transverse bracing of 'scissors' or single oblique members, rudely trenched, or even bolted, across the piles. Simple, ungraceful, yet evidently effective, they are the complete antithesis of the precisely squared and jointed, but over-reinforced, technique of the great early medieval roofs and belfries. Their crudity goes beyond any explanation by the common late-medieval tendency to simplify framing or by a persistence of building with earth-fast posts, which was certainly recessive by the 13th century.[45]

Rigold argued that the key to the construction of these great timber bridges of the Thames lay 'in the mastery of deep and accurate pile-driving', and notes that a large driver was certainly in existence from the late thirteenth century, when it was frequently mentioned in royal accounts. In contrast, earlier bridges, like the Ravning Bridge, used earth-fast piles, which were adhesive; that is, they were relatively short and able to find their own level under their own weight in suitable soft ground; others employed piles which were short enough to be driven without large machinery.

There are reasons for doubting his dating. Substantial earth-fast timber bridges were constructed before 1250. One of the timber bridges discovered at Hemington, dating from the early thirteenth century, was also of this design, consisting of a 'double row of earthfast posts, some 56 metres long'. Moreover, most of the timber Thames bridges had been constructed by 1250, and several

---

[44] Jan Silbrechts, *Henley Bridge* (in the Tate Gallery); Elizabeth Ranyard, *Kingston Bridge* (in Kingston Central Library).

[45] Rigold, 'Structural Aspects', 51.

were probably considerably older. They therefore pre-date the references to the large pile-driver. There seem to be two possibilities: if Dr Rigold is right about the date of the large pile-driver, we must assume that the Thames bridges were originally built to a different design, but were reconstructed in the late thir-teenth century; the alternative is that machines capable of driving large piles existed before 1250. This seems possible: a considerable machine must have been necessary to drive the piles for the starlings of Old London Bridge, which was begun in 1176.

The Sole-plate Design

Dr Rigold also observed that, in contrast to the limited knowledge of large medieval timber bridges of all types, rather more than forty smaller bridges at castles and moated sites had been examined by the 1970s. He noted that: 'Nearly all the moat-bridges, from the late 11th to the 16th centuries, are struc-turally similar in that their posts are not earth-fast but tenoned into transverse sole-plates.'[46] He considered that these bridges were essentially 'box frames', and among the earliest examples of this type of construction. The same design was used for small bridges in all types of locations, including steep 'v'-shaped ditches and shallow ones. Smaller timber bridges over streams are likely to have been of a similar construction. Rigold concluded that, 'from soon after the Conquest until the sixteenth century this, and no alternative, was the normal conception of a light bridge'.[47]

The 'sole-plate' design was also used for larger bridges. During the exca-vations carried out below the piers and abutments of Monmow Bridge, Monmouth, in 1988, the remains of a large sole-plate were found. Under the lowest part of the ashlar pier:

a stout vertical timber runs down to, and is jointed into, an horizontal timber (the sole plate) which runs in beneath the pie . . . the arrangement is typical of medieval trestle-type wooden bridges . . .

Only days after the initial discoveries, even better evidence of the previous wooden bridge was found. In the midst of the river bed a further complete bridge sole plate was revealed. Eight metres long, the sole plate was orientated, as was the first one, for a bridge almost exactly on the same site as the existing one . . . The timber had been felled sometime between AD 1123 and 1169.[48]

Bridges of this design and scale were still being constructed 300 years later. A contract of 1485/6 for a bridge with timber piers and stone abutments at Newark specifies that it should have twelve spans with wooden sills under the

---

⁴⁶ Rigold, 'Structural Aspects', 48.   ⁴⁷ Ibid. 90.   ⁴⁸ Rowlands, *Monmow Bridge*, 78–81.

water into which would be set huge 14-by-12 inch vertical posts.[49] A third large bridge with a sole-plate, but of a different design, the 'English' half of Chepstow Bridge on the Wye, was recorded by Archdeacon Coxe *c.*1800 under exceptionally low-water conditions. From the topmost transverse sole-plates, as Rigold describes them, 'accurately worked trestles rose . . . Each trestle had three massive and well-squared posts 12 m tall'. The tops of these posts were fastened into lintels on which the timber superstructure and road-way was laid.[50]

Presumably the sole-plate design was preferred wherever it was relatively easy to lay a sole-plate on the river bed, which is why it was invariably employed for small bridges where the bridge could be constructed in dry conditions. The design avoided some of the disadvantages of earth-fast bridges: in particular, since their vertical posts were firmly attached to the timber base, they did not so easily become loose. The earth-fast design is likely to have been preferred where it was difficult to lay sole-plates, and hence easier to drive piles into the river bed. Thus, bridges founded in relatively deep water on a muddy river bed were presumably constructed to this design.

Large timber bridges of both the sole-plate and the earth-fast design de-pended on massive timbers, which came from very large trees. What was required is provided by the evidence of the Close Rolls, which record gifts of royal oaks for the repair of bridges from the thirteenth century. Amongst the bridges which benefited from the royal forests were those at Durham, Topcliffe, Windsor, Wichnor (River Trent), Ickford (Bucks.) Nottingham, Rockingham, Lancaster, 'Smalebrok', Brignorth, Combe (near Stonesfield, Oxon), Worcester, Gloucester, 'Ellebridge' near Dymock (Glos.), Ditchford, and Huntingdon.[51] Timbers were supplied for vaulted stone bridges, presumably for centring or piles, but most were used for the huge vertical posts and lintels of timber bridges and for the beams which supported timber roadways. Today, when these bridges have gone, perhaps the best way to appreciate the scale of their massive timbers is to look at those which survive in the great churches of the age, like the roof of the nave of Wells Cathedral, erected in the years around 1200, or the high roof of Exeter Cathedral nave, built between *c.*1325 and 1342, using forty-eight great oaks.[52]

---

[49] Salzman, *Building*, 546–7.

[50] It differed from the Newark and Monmouth bridges, in that its vertical posts rose from sole plates built into low piers made of a keel-shaped enclosure of horizontal timber beams (three laid on top of each other) laid on the river bed, which were filled with stonework (Rigold, 'Structural Aspects', 53–4).

[51] *CCR* (*1227–31*), 8; (*1231–4*), 515; (*1234–7*), 141, 475; (*1242–7*), 209, 225; (*1251–3*), 128, 341; (*1256–9*), 96, 271; (*1264–8*), 8, 9, 27, 211; (*1268–72*), 200, 382.

[52] C. A. Hewett, *English Cathedral and Monastic Carpentry* (Chichester, 1985), 6, 46–7.

7

Vaulted Stone Bridges: From the Eleventh Century to the Late Middle Ages

In 1884, a diplomat at the French embassy in London, J. J. Jusserand, published *Les Anglais au moyen age: la vie nomade et des routes de Angleterre au xiv siède*, a study of travel in the fourteenth century, full of vivid details. It was one of the first works on medieval transport to make use of the evidence of administrative documents relating to bridge construction and repair. In it he claimed that Dark Age bridges were timber, but that from the twelfth century onwards most new bridges were built, and many old bridges rebuilt, in stone.[1] It is likely that he was in essentials right. The earliest surviving stone arched bridge in England probably dates from the late eleventh century, and it seems that at that date they were rare. Over the following centuries a huge number were erected. Before 1200 very large estuarine bridges were being built in deep, tidal waters. By the thirteenth century large arches were constructed in the north, and by the fourteenth century huge segmental arches. These developments must be related to the ability to erect stone vaults with great precision, to establish foundations in a variety of locations, and to undertake very complex construction projects.

THE SPREAD OF STONE BRIDGES

The remains of perhaps the oldest extant vaulted stone bridge in England survive encased in later widenings and under the road to the south of Grandpont (Folly Bridge) in Oxford. They are considered part of the massive stone bridge and causeway which Robert d'Oilly caused to be constructed in the late eleventh century across the many channels of the Thames and its flood plain in Oxford. Possibly the ancient arches visible under later spans are also d'Oilly's work. In the sixteenth century the causeway was 700 metres long and con-

---

[1] Published in English as *English Wayfaring Life in the Middle Ages* in 1889; *Wayfaring Life*, 19.

tained more than forty flood arches.[2] Of about the same date may be an arch of
Ock Bridge, Abingdon, with a rubble barrel vault which has survived in a later
medieval reconstruction.[3]

Grandpont may have been one of the first major vaulted bridges built in
England. There is just one possible pre-eleventh-century reference to a bridge
of this type. This is to a structure which existed by the eleventh century at
Winchester but may have been older.[4] It is likely that such bridges were uncommon in northern Europe much before Grandpont was constructed. The information is slight—we know nothing of the fabric of most bridges—and the
difficulties in proving a negative are well known. However, apart from the
absence of references to arched bridges, there are the following suggestive pieces
of evidence. Those place-names which indicate the type of construction point
to the existence of timber, but not arched, bridges before 1100. Many of those
places which denote a wooden bridge (for example, with the meaning 'plank
bridge', 'causeway of brushwood', or 'bridge of logs') are first referred to in
Domesday Book or earlier.[5] A few bridges were described as stone bridges before
1086, but that does not mean that they were vaulted: they might be bridges
with stone piers and a timber roadway, or even a stone ford.[6] There are a small
number of place-names which explicitly refer to an arched bridge, but none is
recorded before the twelfth century. They include Bow in Devon, which was
called *Limet* in 1086 but *Nymetboghe* in 1270, and Bow in Middlesex, named
after the bridge which Queen Mathilda, who died in 1118, caused to have built
over the River Lea. They are derived from the Old English *boga*, meaning a
bow.[7] It is worth noting that major stone vaults in large churches only begin to
appear at about this time. They remained rare throughout the twelfth century.[8]

Bridges with stone arches as well as stone piers were first recorded in
other European countries at about the same time. Between 1000 and 1250 the
multi-arched stone bridges were erected across the River Loire: according to
M. Boyer, bridges at Blois and Tours may have been built before 1100, and the
river was spanned in stone at Saumur before 1162, Orleans before 1176, and
Beaugency before 1160–82.[9] The situation seems to have been the same in
several other countries.[10]

---

[2] Durham et al., *The Thames Crossing at Oxford*; Blair, *Anglo-Saxon Oxfordshire*, 173–7; J. M. Steane, *The Archaeology of Medieval England and Wales* (London, 1985), 110.

[3] *Bridges in Oxfordshire*.

[4] M. Biddle and D. J. Keane, 'Winchester in the Eleventh and Twelfth Centuries', in M. Biddle (ed.), *Winchester in the Early Middle Ages* (Oxford, 1976), 241–448.

[5] See Chap. 3.   [6] See Chap. 2.   [7] Ekwall, *Dictionary*, 56.

[8] E. Fernie, *The Architecture of Norman England* (Oxford, 2000), 264–7.

[9] Boyer, *French Bridges*, 88, 84–6, 36.   [10] Brooks, 'Medieval Bridges', 12.

In England after 1100 there is an increasing amount of evidence of arched bridges. Ranulf Flambard, bishop of Durham from 1099 to 1128, caused the first stone bridge across the Wear in the city to be constructed: Simeon of Durham clearly thought that Flambard had built something very special, commenting that he 'joined the two banks of the River Wear with a stone bridge, a major construction supported on arches'.[11] The bridge was rebuilt in the late middle ages, but a smaller, rounded arch, which may have been part of the original structure, is shown in a series of watercolours by Thomas Girtin, and may survive hidden by later buildings.[12] One of Flambard's successors, Bishop Hugh de Puiset (1153–95), erected a second stone bridge in the town, Elvet Bridge.[13] Excavations have revealed the remains of another twelfth-century stone bridge at Gloucester.[14]

By the late twelfth century major stone bridges were being constructed all over the country. A major undertaking, Ouse Bridge, York, was rebuilt in stone at about this time, since in the Yorkshire Museum, York, are some parts of the 'richly decorated' late twelfth-century chapel, dedicated to St William, which stood at the south end of the bridge (plate 3).[15] At the other end of the country, Exeter Bridge was built in the some period. It was originally 750 feet long, consisting of a section across the main stream of the river and many flood arches across the surrounding marshland in the river valley, which was subject to frequent flooding. The main arches were demolished in 1778 when a new bridge was built, and the remaining arches of the medieval bridge were buried for almost 200 years. Then, in 1968–72, eight of them were exposed and restored. Because they had been covered up, the arches were in remarkably good condition: several can clearly be dated to the years around 1200, being ribbed arches 'of simple Norman semi-circular type' (plate 2).[16]

Thereafter the examples of new stone bridges multiply. There is not space to describe them all here, but the following gives a indication of their spread. In the 1230s the men of Doncaster were given permission to take a toll on carts crossing the bridge of their town to rebuild it of stone.[17] Harnham Bridge, Salisbury, with its several stone arches, belongs to the next decade.[18] Old

[11] Symeon, 276–7.

[12] *North*, 44. One of the paintings is reproduced in G. Smith (ed.), *Thomas Girtin: The Art of Watercolour* (London, 2002).

[13] Geoffrey of Coldingham, *Liber de statu ecclesiae Dunhelmensis*, 7, ed. J. Raine, *Historiae Dunhelmensis scriptores tres*, Surtees Soc., 9 (1839), 12.

[14] H. Hurst, 'Excavations at Gloucester 1971–73', *Antiq. Jnl.*, 54 (1974), 46–50.

[15] C. Wilson, *The Shrines of St William of York* (York, 1977), 23; *VCH City of York*, 516.

[16] J. Brierley, 'The Medieval Exe Bridge', *Proc. Instn. Civ. Engrs*, 1: 66 (1979), 127–39.

[17] *CPR (1232–47)*, 498.   [18] *VCH Wilts.*, iii. 344.

Bristol Bridge is thought to have been built at the same time.[19] Also probably of the thirteenth century is the present Monmow Bridge (plate 6).[20]

By the start of the fifteenth century we can get a glimpse of the scale of bridge building. It is clear that at any time several major projects were being undertaken. In around 1400 the existing bridge across the Tees at Yarm and another over the Wear at Shincliffe were paid for by Bishop Skirlaw.[21] Preston Bridge over the Ribble was reconstructed in stone.[22] In 1416 work began on the bridges at Abingdon.[23] In the 1420s and 1430s bridges were built in Yorkshire at Catterick, Kexby, Skipbridge, and Thornton.[24] In 1425 indulgences were granted to those contributing to rebuilding Eamont Bridge, Cumberland, in stone. In the next year, the surviving bridge chapel at St Ives in Huntingdonshire was consecrated following the reconstruction of the bridge (plate 17).[25] The bridge Sir Gerard Braybrooke left his goods to complete at Great Barford was being built a few years later. The bridge, although widened, survives to this day (plate 18).[26]

Some of the new stone bridges, like those at Abingdon, Barford, and Kexby, replaced a ford or a ferry.[27] So did Wadebridge. Leland recounted: 'Wher as now Wadebridge is ther was a fery a 80. Yeres syns, and menne sumtyme passing over by horse stoode often in great jeopardie. Then one Lovebone, vicar of Wadebridge, movid with pitie began the bridge, and with great paine and studie, good people putting their help therto finishid it with xvii. Fair and great uniforme arches of stone.'[28] The bridge is still standing, 320 feet long, still with seventeen arches.[29] Elsewhere stone bridges replaced timber bridges, as at Stratford-upon-Avon.[30] The change was not always all one way, and occasionally timber bridges replaced stone ones: in 1421 the new stone bridge was to be built at Catterick 'be twix ye olde stane brigg' and 'ye Newbrigg' of tree [wood]'.[31] Nevertheless, at Catterick, as elsewhere, the trend to all-stone bridges is clear.

Stone arches were also widely used in causeways. These now tended to be constructed as earth embankments interspersed with flood arches. Often, as at Gloucester, the embankment was retained by a stone wall (plate 1). A few miles downstream, Leland observed what must have been a similar structure at Newbridge: 'the ground ther al about lyethe in low medowes often ovarflowne by rage of reyne. Ther is a long cawyse of stone at eche end of the bridge.'[32]

[19] Ruddock, *Arch Bridges*, 57.   [20] Rowland, *Monmow Bridge*, 3.   [21] *DNB*, xviii. 357–8.
[22] *CPR* (*1401–5*), 236.   [23] See below.   [24] *Test. Ebor.*, ii. 20.
[25] *The Register of Thomas Langley, Bishop of Durham, 1406–1457*, ed. R. L. Storey, 6 vols., Surtees Soc. (1956–70) iii. 41; Pevsner, *Beds., Hunts. etc*, 338.
[26] *Register of Henry Chichele*, 412; 'Bridges of Bedfordshire', 26–30.
[27] Leland, v. 113–8; ii. 48–50; *CCR* (*1422–9*), 140, 410; *North*, 73–4.   [28] Leland, i. 178.
[29] *Cornish Bridges*, 115–9.   [30] Leland, ii. 49–50.
[31] Salzman, *Building*, 497; and see Leland, v. 71.   [32] Leland, v. 73.

As an alternative, there were very long bridges with numerous arches. Several survive, including Barford Bridge, and Irthlingborough Bridge which, although widened in 1922 by building additional arches out on the top of upstream cutwaters, is a good surviving example of this type of structure. It is 90 metres long and has nineteen arches which span the Nene valley.[33] While bridges of this type did not attain the same length as the great earth causeways, which was unsurprising given their greater cost, they could still be immense. The largest extended for about 500 metres.

Over the 400 years which separated Grandpont from the bridges at Great Barford and Stratford-upon-Avon the bridge network was being transformed. Whereas Grandpont had been the exception, Barford Bridge was the norm for new bridges. At some point the bridge network came to consist largely of stone bridges, but it is unclear when this happened. S. E. Rigold argued that 'the cumulative tenor of documents is that most major bridges were entirely of timber until the fourteenth century and that over some rivers, not least the Thames, this was true until the eighteenth century'.[34] In view of the evidence for a substantial body of stone bridges by 1300, this is unlikely; it probably reflects Dr Rigold's interest in the bridges over the middle Thames. In contrast, it has been claimed that in western Europe the major bridges 'seem likely to have mostly been built in stone between c.1050 and 1300'.[35] This may have been the situation in England, but the truth is that the evidence does not allow us to be certain. Undoubtedly many stone bridges had been built by 1300, but equally, many major timber or stone-and-timber structures were not replaced until the fourteenth and fifteenth centuries.

DEVELOPMENTS IN DESIGN: FOUNDATIONS AND ARCHES

The chief characteristics of the medieval bridges constructed in lowland England are undoubtedly the width of the piers and the relative narrowness of the arch spans. Some bridges, especially those across smaller rivers, like Ock Bridge, Abingdon, or Lower Heyford Bridge over the River Cherwell, consist of a stone causeway pierced by a series of arched openings; there is little which can be described as a pier as such.[36] Most major bridges were constructed with piers, but they were wide in relation to the arch spans, which were usually under 6 metres. Bridges of great length and short bridges were constructed in

---

33 *Mid and Eastern*, 75.   34 Rigold, 'Structural Aspects', 49.
35 Brooks, 'Medieval Bridges', 12.   36 *Bridges in Oxfordshire*, 2–4.

much the same way for many centuries. This design of bridge was still effective in the fifteenth century, when the main arches of Barford Bridge and Clopton Bridge, Stratford-upon-Avon, were constructed (plate 21). The spans of their main arches are about 5 and 6 metres respectively, about twice the width of the piers.[37]

It is one thing to build stone arches on the upper reaches of the Thames at Oxford, where the river was broad and relatively shallow, quite another to construct them downstream in deep, tidal waters. Yet less than a century after Grandpont this is just what happened. The leading example is Old London Bridge. Work here, beginning in 1176, was recorded in a number of contemporary chronicles. The Annals of Waverley noted laconically: 'Hoc anno pons lapideus Londoniae inceptus est a Petro Capellano de Colechurch.'[38] The bridge had nineteen piers, which supported arches with average spans of *c.*8 metres[39] Throughout the middle ages and beyond the bridge was seen as a prodigious structure. It inspired many works of art: from the medieval depiction, through the evocation of it at low tide by de Jongh in the seventeenth century, to engravings of its last years in the nineteenth century.

Subsequently other large arched bridges were constructed in deep water. Tyne Bridge, Newcastle, over 700 feet long, is traditionally thought to have been built in the 1250s after its predecessor burnt down in 1248.[40] In the early fourteenth century the long stone bridge over the River Trent at Nottingham was begun by John le Palmer, a prominent citizen, and his wife Alice. After her husband's death Alice continued to oversee work on the bridge for several decades. The completed structure was almost 650 feet long.[41] The Trent is very deep there. Defoe made the following observations about the bridge, which was probably the structure built by the le Palmers: 'Over the Trent there is a stately stone-bridge of nineteen arches, and the river being there join'd into one united stream, is very large and deep; having, as is said, but lately received the addition of the Dove, the Derwent, the Irwash, and the Soar, three of them very great rivers of themselves, and all coming into the Trent since its passing by Burton in Staffordshire.'[42] Later in the century major timber bridges were replaced by stone vaulted bridges at Rochester (560 feet long) and Chester (420 feet).[43] Two very long bridges survive: at Barnstaple and Bideford (plate 19).

[37] *CEH: Eastern and Central*, 256–7.   [38] *Annals of Waverley, Ann. Mon.*, ii. 240.

[39] B. Watson, 'The Construction of the Colechurch Bridge', in *London Bridge*, 85–9.

[40] Bruce, *Three Bridges*, 5.

[41] T. Foulds, 'Trade and Manufacture', in J. Beckett and P. Dixon (eds.), *A Centenary History of Nottingham* (Manchester, 1997), 73–4; M. O. Tarbotton, *History of Old and New Trent Bridges* (Nottingham, 1871); *Mid and Eastern*, 9–13.

[42] Defoe, *Tour*, ii. 142.   [43] Britnell, 'Rochester Bridge', 47–8; *Wales and Western*, 26–9.

With their many arches (the former has sixteen, the latter twenty-four) and length (*c.*700 feet), they give a good impression of the other, now demolished great bridges.[44]

The other major developments in bridge design occurred in the English uplands. Narrow stone arches were unsuitable for the huge surges experienced in flash floods in these areas; therefore arches with wider and higher spans were necessary if stone bridges were to be constructed. It is likely that such arches had been built by the first half of the thirteenth century, if not earlier. The main river arches of Elvet Bridge, Durham, which survive to this day, probably date from the 1220s, when indulgences were granted to those contributing to 'the building of the new bridge of Elvet'. They have three striking features: the quality of the ashlar masonry; their height; and their spans, which were each of about 10 metres, that is, roughly double that of bridges in the south of England.[45] The wide arches are designed to provide a large waterway and to take the rise in water when the river is in full spate. Bridges of similar design were built throughout the north, for example, at Yarm, Croft, and Wetherby, and as far south as Cromford and Matlock in Derbyshire (plates 8 and 9).

It is possible that soon even larger spans were being constructed. The earliest may have been the central spans of Old Tyne Bridge, Newcastle.[46] The largest arch had a span of about 60 feet, almost twice the spans of Elvet Bridge or Matlock Bridge, and the two openings on either side were over 50 feet.[47] These, if the traditional mid-thirteenth-century dating is correct, would have been among the largest vaults of any structure in England at the time. An illustration of the ruined bridge made shortly after its collapse in 1771 shows the large, solitary, semicircular central arch with its wide powerful ribs, together with the remaining smaller arches on the Newcastle side of the river. Bridges with similar rounded arches do survive in the north; perhaps the finest is Devil's Bridge, Kirby Lonsdale, which has two large arches, much like those of Old Tyne Bridge, and one smaller one (plate 27).

Single-arch bridges particularly lend themselves to very large spans, since the arch rests on abutments which can be constructed on dry land. In France in the fourteenth century a massive bridge was constructed at Vielle-Brioude with

---

[44] *Devon Bridges*, 85–7, 92–3.

[45] In 1225 and 1228 indulgences were issued to those contributing to the 'building of the new bridge of Elvet' (*The register, or rolls, of Walter Gray, Lord Archbishop of York*, ed. J. Raine, Surtees Soc., 56 (1872), 4).

[46] Horsley, *Eighteenth Century Newcastle*, 2; it is, however, possible that much of the bridge was rebuilt in the 14th cent., when £1,500 was needed for its repair (*Cal. Inq. Misc.* (1348–77), 718).

[47] The measurements are taken from a plan of the ruined bridge by Ralph Beilby drawn soon after its collapse in 1771; it is reproduced in Horsley, *Eighteenth Century Newcastle*, 10.

one span of 50 metres. It survived until 1822.[48] For 400 years it was the largest arch in the world. In the middle ages in England, large single-span bridges were built, although none on this scale. The largest is Twizel Bridge in the steep valley of the River Till. Its *c*.30 metres span is huge, although no greater than the individual spans of some other northern medieval bridges with two arches. Leland was clearly impressed, describing it as 'of stone one bow but greate and stronge'.[49]

Another late medieval development of great importance was the use of segmental arches. The arches of Tyne Bridge, Newcastle, Devil's Bridge, and Twizel Bridge were semicircular; the latter has a rise of 40 feet, which is appropriate for a long bridge or a narrow steep valley, but not for every location. By the fourteenth century, however, in the north of England, as in Italy and southern France, bridges were being constructed with much flatter arches which were normally the shape of the segment of a circle or were segmental-pointed rather than semicircular.[50] These arches offer several advantages. They enabled large spans to be erected without creating the steep gradients which are associated with semicircular arches. They are also much stronger, in the sense that an arch ring of given thickness would support a segmental arch of almost twice the span of a semicircular arch; or, to look at it another way, smaller, thinner arch-rings could be used for the construction of segmental arches.[51]

Possibly at first the spans, as at Kildwick (*c*.1300), were relatively modest, but soon in England, as elsewhere, they began to increase. By the mid-fourteenth century large arches were constructed. The Pontevecchio in Florence was rebuilt in 1345, with three very flat segmental arches. The central one has a span of 86 feet and a rise of only 11 feet 6 inches.[52] The earliest English evidence for large segmental arches may also come from the fourteenth century. This is Dee Bridge, with spans of up to 60 feet (plate 13). In 1378 a bequest was made for the construction of Warkworth Bridge, which may be the date of the existing bridge of two segmental ribbed spans, each *c*.20 metres wide (plate 14).[53] Thereafter segmental arches were relatively common in the north. Framwellgate Bridge, Durham, probably built in 1400, has two spans of almost 30 metres each, exceeding those of the Pontevecchio (plate 5).[54]

In the north for the next 200 years bridges of the Elvet Bridge design of *c*.10–12 metres span were replaced by bridges with very large arches. On his way

[48] Boyer, *French Bridges*, 156.   [49] Leland, v. 66.
[50] Although some arches were segmental-pointed (i.e. they were very flat pointed arches).
[51] See O'Connor, *Roman Bridges*, 179.   [52] Hopkins, *A Span of Bridges*, 40–1.
[53] J. Wallis, *Natural History and Antiquities of Northumberland*, 2 vols. (London, 1769), ii. 355.
[54] *North*, 44.

to the Tees, Leland observed: 'then to Perse brid[g]e sumtime of 5 arches, but a
lat made new of 3 arches.'[55] The central arch of this new bridge, which is still
standing, is 72 feet wide (plate 22). Barnard Castle Bridge was probably rebuilt
about fifty years later: it had three arches when Leland saw it, but now has two
ribbed arches.[56]

Thus, during the period from the eleventh to the fifteenth centuries there
were opposing tendencies in different parts of the country. Most lowland
bridges in the south and Midlands remained of similar design and construction
for centuries. Elsewhere medieval masons made significant advances: the principal were the ability, first, to devise foundations for even the most difficult
conditions; and secondly, to erect very big arches, and to recognize the value of
and to construct large segmental arches.

Foundations

Types of Foundations: The Lowlands

The foundations employed depended on a wide range of factors: the nature of
the river bed, the size of the arches, whether the site was particularly subject to
flash floods, the depth of water, and of course the budget and the skills of the
masons. A great variety of types were described by Henri Gautier in the early
eighteenth century: the masonry of the piers could be laid on planks, on joists,
or on a grille of square timbers with openings into which piles were driven.
Another option was to rest the masonry on piles surrounded by a pen of piles
to compress the ground and prevent scour. Finally the pier could be founded
on material dumped in the water.[57]

The foundations of many surviving bridges are now lost because concrete
platforms have been constructed under the piers or across the entire river bed.
Nevertheless, there is ample evidence about the types of foundations
employed. Piers and abutments of typical medieval lowland bridges were often
adequately supported on shallow foundations because their broad piers spread
the load over a relatively wide area.[58] Bearing piles seem to have been considered unnecessary provided the river bed was firm, for instance, if it consisted of
firm gravel or well-compacted clay. In this they were right: bridges founded on
these types of river bed have survived to the present day. When Teston Bridge
was examined in 1976, all except the east abutment was found to rest on a 'firm
to stiff clay overlain with a stratum of variable thickness of assorted gravel'.
Despite the heavy loads they carried, the foundations were considered ade-

---

[55] Leland, i. 77.   [56] Ibid.   [57] Ruddock, *Arch Bridges*, 201.
[58] This point is well made in 'Bridges of Bedfordshire', 110–11.

quate except for the abutment, where the gravel was overlain with alluvial clays.[59]

In constructing bridges on shallow foundations it is probable that the builders normally excavated the river bed, removing surface mud and silt and loose gravel until firmer gravel or clay was found. Such work may be implied by a late medieval contract for Sheffield Bridge which refers to the 'clensying of the ground work'.[60] The piers and abutments were commonly built either directly onto the river bed or, as Gautier described, on a wooden frame or on joists and planks on the river bed. The excavators of Burford Bridge, Abingdon, in the 1930s noted that the foundations of the abutments 'were very shallow and it was almost impossible to tell where the abutments ended and the subsoil began'.[61] The masonry piers of Monmow Bridge rest on a rubble and cement core, under which is a timber sole plate. This sits on gravel; the masons had not excavated down to the marl bedrock, even though it is quite close to the surface (plate 6).[62]

Piled foundations were often employed, however, where the river bed was soft. There could be serious consequences of not using them, as the eighteenth-century builders of Westminster Bridge discovered to their cost: they thought piles unnecessary and, as a result, one of its piers sank under the weight of the superstructure.[63] Piles were used both for bridges over small watercourses, such as the one excavated near Waltham Abbey, and over significant rivers such as Whitemill Bridge, Sturminster Marshall (plate 23). The engineer who inspected the bridge described the classic piled foundations as follows: 'Apparently the original builders had driven oak piles into the river bed and then built oak rafts on top of them of the size of the required piers. Off these rafts the masonry structure was built.' During the demolition of Bedford Bridge in 1811 it was observed that 'the Foundations of all the Piers which have hitherto been taken down were built upon Piles, about 3 feet long, driven through a stratum of Clay, lying on a Rock of solid Stone'.[64]

Regardless of whether the foundations rested on piles or a relatively firm river bed, there were a variety of ways in which they could be given additional

[59] Heyman et al., *Teston Bridge*, 490. Mabes Bridge, one of the few ancient Irish bridges to have survived, was founded on very stiff boulder clay (*Irish Stone Bridges*, 90–1). See also 'Bridges of Bedfordshire', 111.

[60] The contract is published in J. Hunter, *History and Topography of the Parish of Sheffield* (Sheffield, 1869), 339.

[61] Leeming and Salter, *Burford Bridge, Abingdon*, 137.

[62] Rowlands, *Monmow Bridge*, 95–6.

[63] R. J. B. Walker, *Old Westminster Bridge* (Newton Abbot, 1979), 267.

[64] P. J. Huggins, 'Excavation of a Medieval Bridge at Waltham, Essex', *Med. Arch.*, 14 (1970), 133–5; Wallis, *Dorset Bridges*, 26; *Bridges of Bedfordshire*, 111.

protection from scour. The bridge piers and abutments could be surrounded
by piles. The excavators of the mid-thirteenth-century bridge at Hemington
across the Trent, which had stone piers and a timber roadway, found in the old
river channel a six-sided enclosure of oak piles . . . driven deep into the river
bed. 'The structure was not a coffer dam, as such, but the protective timber cas-
ing for a masonry pier.'[65] Similarly at the site of Great Bridge, Burton-on-Trent,
masonry from the piers was brought up protected by a double row of piles.[66]
Piers and abutments could also be protected by loose stones, sometimes contained within an enclosure of piles, a form of structure which could be
described as a starling. These are best known for their use in constructing piers
in deep water, but could be used to give added protection to any bridge: those
at York were added in the seventeenth century.[67]

Cutwaters too protected bridge piers from scour. Pointed cutwaters are best,
and they were invariably used on the upstream side of cart bridges. The situation on the downstream face was more variable. They were constructed where
they were most necessary, where rivers were most turbulent. Pointed cutwaters
were the norm in the north and much of the Welsh borders, and for large
bridges as early as the twelfth century. On the other hand, in parts of the
Midlands, bridges such as Clopton Bridge were built without downstream
cutwaters as late as the end of the fifteenth century (plate 21). Some bridges
employ square buttresses as downstream cutwaters.

There were other options, first described in post-medieval sources but
probably in use earlier. Piles can be driven into the river bed upstream of the
bridge piers to catch debris and possibly relocate scour away from the bridge.
Another simple and cheap method was known as 'framing and setting'. The
technique: 'consisted of frames of timber balks laid flat on the river-bed and
usually fixed to short piles driven into the bed, the frames then packed with
large squared stones or 'setts' which would not be easily moved by the current
and so defended the river-bed against the violence of floods. It was a method
used throughout the country to prevent scour near piers whose foundations
were at a shallow depth below the surface of the bed.'[68]

Finally, it is clear that medieval bridge builders often ensured that piers were
founded on the firmest parts of the river bed. As Simco and McKeague have
rightly noted, part of the skill of medieval bridge builders was their understanding of the nature of the ground.[69] Whereas later builders tended to aim for

---

[65] Cooper et al., 'Hemington Bridges', 316–7.   [66] Rye, 'Burton-on-Trent Bridge', 5.

[67] Wilson and Mee, *Old Ouse Bridge*, 31.

[68] Ruddock, *Arch Bridges*, 24–5. Another option was the construction of a weir downstream of the bridge
(ibid.).

[69] 'Bridges of Bedfordshire', 111.

symmetry, whatever the cost and whatever the difficulties this led to in laying foundations, medieval masons would space piers irregularly. Nowhere is this seen to better effect than at Dee Bridge, Chester, where arches of about 20 feet are next to those three times the size (plate 13).[70]

Types of Foundations: The Uplands

While shallow foundations were often acceptable for lowland bridges, as far as we can tell they were less common in the uplands.[71] Here, firm and deep foundations were particularly important to support bigger bridges and taller, larger spans, and protect piers from the effects of scour associated with flash floods. A plaque on the medieval Ludford Bridge, Ludlow, records an incident in 1886 when 'the turbulent Teme' washed right over the bridge. Most of the stonework above the arches was removed by the river; the new parapets are built in a grey stone. However, the arches, built in pinkish stone, remained intact because, it is reported, they were firmly founded on the bedrock (plate 25).[72]

Several of the finest bridges in northern England are founded on rock, and the ease of building on rocky foundations must have encouraged the erection of large spans. Some of these bridges are easy to recognize because the rock is above the normal water level, for instance, at Devil's Bridge, Kirby Lonsdale (plate 27), and Stanhope Bridge (River Wear). The West Riding Bridge Book of 1752 describes fifteen bridges, most of them medieval, as founded on rock (including rock below low water level).[73]

Where there was no rock, the foundations of upland bridges were necessarily established in other ways. Warkworth Bridge has two large arch spans: one abutment was founded on rock; the pier and the other abutments were founded on 'timber platforms, protected by sheet piles and a stone apron' (plate 14).[74] Piling could involve a huge amount of work. The construction of a large, single-arched bridge at Kirkstall in 1616 involved driving 340 piles under the abutment areas at a cost of £100.[75] It is unlikely that piling on this scale was new in the north of England in the seventeenth century.

Ways of Laying Foundations: Coffer Dams and Starlings

The foundations of bridges, be they in the uplands or lowlands, are best laid dry. The water has to be removed from the area where the piers or abutments are to be built. Those who wrote about it, from Alberti onwards, thought that

---

[70] *Wales and Western*, 31.

[71] For possible examples of shallow foundations, see Wakefield Bridge (Ruddock, *Arch Bridges*, 26–7) and J. Weatherill, 'Eighteenth Century Rievaulx Bridge and its Medieval Predecessor', *Yorks. Arch. Jnl.*, 41 (1963–6), 78–9.

[72] Blackwall, *Bridges of Shropshire*, 6.   [73] Ruddock, *Arch Bridges*, 206.

[74] *CEH: Northern*, 18.

[75] W. E. Preston, 'Notes on the Re-building of Some Aire and Calder Bridges', *Bradford Antiquary*, 6 (1913–21), 135–48.

where possible coffer dams should be used for this purpose, and they have been employed for building in water constantly since the late middle ages, and probably earlier.[76] Professor Boyer has described the erection and use of a coffer dam at Albi early in the century.

On Thursday 16 August 1408 work began and carried on over the weekend. 5 metre piles were driven into the riverbed with thinner piles behind them to form two enclosures, one inside the other, the timbers being fastened at the top by crosspieces. On Monday the men threw a clay mortar between the rows of piling to make them watertight. The water was then removed from the dam by bucket. This was the longest task. It took from Tuesday 21 August until Saturday 1 September. Six men stayed on the job around the clock for four days, and two others for five.[77]

Coffer dams were not always used. Dry conditions could be created in other ways. It is argued that in the shallow waters of the Great Ouse in Bedfordshire it would have been a simple matter to divert the flow from part of the river bed. A more extreme approach was to divert the river. This is the stuff of legend. Alberti tells the tale of King Mina, who turned the Nile out of its channel into another when he intended to build the bridge of Memphis. It is hard to believe that this practice was common.[78]

Foundations could be laid in the water. Essentially rubble was thrown onto the river bed until it was at a height (presumably around low water level) at which the piers and abutments could be constructed. The rubble might or might not be encased by a piled pen. Most very large bridges were founded in this way during the middle ages, as well as a number of smaller structures. Observing the demolition of the old bridge at Stratford-le-Bow (possibly dating from Henry I's reign) in the nineteenth century, Alfred Burges noted what seem to have been foundations of this type: 'Rough stones and mortar appear to have been thrown through the water until the surface was raised sufficiently high to allow a more careful method of building to be pursued; but with all this apparent want of care the bridge was without fracture or settlement.'[79] This is the same method that Gautier described.[80]

Three possible explanations have been put forward for laying foundations in wet rather than dry conditions. Watson has argued that coffer dams were not known in England in the twelfth century and, therefore, were not employed in the construction of Old London Bridge. He suggests that they may not have

---

[76] Alberti, 77.   [77] Boyer, *French Bridges*, 156. For a comparison of the costs, see Chap. 10.
[78] Alberti, 77. Ruddock suggested that Bristol Bridge was founded in this way (Ruddock, *Arch Bridges*, 58).
[79] A. Burges, 'Bridge at Stratford-le-Bow', *Archaeologia*, 29 (1842), 379.
[80] As quoted in Ruddock, *Arch Bridges*, 201.

been used in this country until the fifteenth century.[81] Secondly, it was far more expensive to lay foundations in dry conditions, as Boyer has pointed out; she thinks that the builders of large bridges in the eleventh and twelfth centuries may been unaware of the higher maintenance costs of the other options.[82] Finally, it is clear that there were sites where it was impossible until comparatively recently to use coffer dams. The three explanations are not necessarily mutually incompatible.

The facts are as follows. Coffer dams are mentioned in French sources by the fourteenth century,[83] and in English by the fifteenth. They are referred to in the contracts for the bridges at Catterick and Sheffield, which mentions 'the stopping of the watyr'. There seems to be a reference in descriptions of the building of Abingdon Bridge.[84] It is not altogether surprising that documentary references to coffer dams are not found earlier: detailed bridge contracts, which are the first English sources to mention them, do not survive before 1400. The material evidence may take us further back. Most of the medieval bridge foundations which have been examined had been laid dry. Excavations have revealed what the archaeologist in charge judged to be the remains of a coffer dam, employed in the construction of a fourteenth-century bridge near Waltham Abbey, although his interpretation has recently been questioned.[85]

There are strong a priori reasons for thinking coffer dams were regularly used at an early date. They were not difficult to construct, provided the conditions were right. Piles had been driven into river beds throughout the Dark Ages, and making piled enclosures would have been a simple exercise for medieval craftsmen. It was not a large step to realize that such an enclosure could be made watertight. The key task, as the work at Albi showed, was the labour of removing the water by bucket, but this was not beyond the abilities of thirteenth- or even twelfth-century workmen. Indeed, constructing large numbers of stone bridges is likely to have depended on the use of coffer dams.

While coffer dams may have been employed in the construction of many bridges at an early date, it is clear that there were certain locations where they could not be used, in particular where the river bed was not only leaky, but the river deep, fast-flowing, or tidal, like the Thames at London. Similar permeable river beds were found elsewhere.[86] In these locations, in the middle ages and later, a system based on 'starlings' was employed. The term describes the

---

[81] Watson, *Construction of the Colechurch Bridge*, 87.   [82] Boyer, *French Bridges*, 153.
[83] Ibid.   [84] Hunter, *Sheffield*, 337–9; for the bridges at Catterick and Abingdon, see below.
[85] Huggins, *Medieval Bridge at Waltham*, 133; Watson, *Construction of the Colechurch Bridge*, 87.
[86] e.g. Smeaton discovered quicksand below a thin layer of gravel on the bed of the Tyne at Hexham: Ruddock, *Arch Bridges*, 98–9.

wooden pens which surrounded the base of the piers of large medieval bridges, but is also applied to the method of founding large, old bridges. In England the earliest bridge we know to have been founded on starlings is Old London Bridge, but the method may have been employed a little earlier in France to build bridges over the Loire.[87]

There are excellent descriptions of the starlings of Old London Bridge, which were observed at its demolition: '. . . the probable mode adopted in founding . . . the piers appears to have been first to form an inclosure by driving piles around the outside line of the width of the pier, into which a quantity of loose rubble stones with chalk and gravel were thrown; upon this they commenced their foundation sills, of oak and ashlar masonry, at such periods as the tide would permit.' As the circle of piles containing rubble was not stable, it was made more secure by building around it starlings, which consisted of another, outer shell of poles which was also infilled with rubble. The writer thought the starlings were built, '. . . in order to prevent the rubble work from shifting by the operation of the tide, and running out from under the pier'. The total area enclosed by the two piled enclosures was 90 feet by 40 feet.[88]

Later bridges were slightly different, in that piles were driven into the river bed at the places where the piers where to be built. Charles Hutton, in the *Principles of Bridges* (1772), described such foundations:

[A set of piles, known as stilts, is] driven into the space intended for the pier, whose tops being sawed off about low-water mark, the pier is then raised on them. This method was formerly used, when the bottom of the river could not be laid dry; and these stilts were surrounded, at a few feet distance, by a row of piles and planks, &c, close to them like a coffer dam and called a sterling or jettee; after which, loose stones, &c, are thrown or poured down into the space, till it be filled up to the top, by that means forming a kind of pier of rubble or loose work, which is kept together by the sides of the starlings: this is then paved level at the top, and the arches turned upon it. This method was formerly much used, most of the large old bridges in England being erected in that way.[89]

The essence of this method of laying foundations was that piles were driven into the river bed and left proud, sticking out of it to the height of low water. This meant that the arches constructed on top of the piles were not very stable and had to be supported by the starlings which surrounded them.

Hutton's description seems to have been based chiefly on Rochester Bridge. It is certainly an accurate account of it. When the bridge was destroyed in the last century it was discovered that the piers were supported by piles of elm tim-

[87] Boyer, *French Bridges*, 84–6.

[88] W. Knight, 'Observations on the Construction of Old London Bridge', *Archaeologia*, 23 (1831–2), 119.

[89] Quoted in D. Ormrod, 'Rochester Bridge, 1660–1825', in Yates and Gibson, *Traffic and Politics*, 190.

ber driven into the bed of the river, at this point mostly chalk. The piles were about 20 feet long, driven closely together and forming large platforms about 45 feet in length and 20 feet wide.[90] Surrounding this piled platform, more piles were driven to form another larger pen, enclosing an even bigger space *c.*95 feet long by 40 feet wide.[91] Less is known about other large bridges, but Old Trent may have been founded in much the same way, although the starlings were narrower.[92]

Others differed in detail. At Bideford (plate 19) the starlings have a slightly different function:

The piers have no special foundations as we know foundations, but were built directly on the sand bed as deep as the tidal water would allow. (Waterlogged sand while it is held in place is a good foundation) . . . To prevent the flow of the river from scouring out the sand from under the piers, they were protected and surrounded at the base by loose stones which had the appearance of a spreading foundation and are known as Sterlings. These loose stones were supported and held against the piers by a platting of holly or hazel forming a kind of basket round and held in place with stakes driven into the river bed.[93]

Large bridges were built in this way because there was no alternative in deep, tidal waters. Over 700 years after Peter of Colechurch started work on his great project, coffer dams still could not be used in the construction of new bridges in London. The technology would not be available to find a significantly more satisfactory solution for founding bridges in difficult conditions until the nineteenth century.[94]

Arches

Although inadequate foundations were the main cause of severe problems, constructing arches, even of relatively small spans, required careful craftsmanship. Mistakes were made. A detailed survey of the seventeenth-century bridge at Clare College, Cambridge, undertaken by Heyman and Padfield, shows what could go wrong. The bridge is severely distorted, the central arch sags, the west arch is deformed to the west, the west pier leans in the same direction, and the abutment at the river bank shows considerable displacement. They concluded that the bridge had been poorly built by masons who lacked the necessary skills. The main settlement occurred at the time of construction, which led

---

[90] M. J. Becker, *Rochester Bridge, 1387–1856* (London, 1930), 7–8.
[91] Britnell, 'Rochester Bridge', 49.   [92] Tarbotton, *Trent Bridges*, 8–9.
[93] F. E. Whiting, *The Long Bridge of Bideford Through the Centuries* (Bideford, 1997), 9; the baskets, known as windlasses, were last purchased in 1856; thereafter the stonework of the starlings was held together with mortar.
[94] See Chap. 8.

to the tilting of the west pier and distress of the west abutment; the fill had been placed without due care, being dumped first on the east and central arches, producing a large, out-of-balance force on the west pier. Moreover, the construction of the arch had been skimped. The voussoirs were too thin, especially given the inadequacies of construction; twice the thickness would have been appropriate for the central arch. They were also poorly cut with too small a wedge angle, so that they were tight on the intrados (the inner face of the arch) and there were gaps on the extrados (its outer face). Nevertheless, despite all these mistakes, the bridge was not in danger provided it was not used by vehicles. The bridge had stood for 300 years and was still safe to use as a footbridge.[95]

As the treatise writers stressed, the key to the construction of stable arches is to ensure that the arch rings are sufficiently thick for the arch span and that the abutments are able to resist the horizontal thrust of the arches.[96] Strength is enhanced by good-quality construction, including well-bonded infill above the arch springings, well-cut voussoirs of the right shape, and accurately shaped centring.

We know little about some of these factors: the infill of ancient bridges is hidden from view. Relatively few of the many internal inspections, which have been undertaken, have been recorded. In the twentieth century many arches were strengthened with reinforced concrete, which means we will never know what the fill was like. About all that can be said at present is that it was variable, sometimes of fairly loose stones and sometimes of relatively solid rubble and mortar. For instance, the fill behind the abutment of the small fourteenth-century bridge at Waltham Abbey consisted of a layer of loose flints underneath well-coursed flints with mortar; a survey of Old London Bridge in 1746 found that behind the ashlar facing of the piers was rubble laid with good mortar.[97] These materials, if well bonded, can be very strong; in 1856 explosives had to be used to destroy old Rochester Bridge.[98]

There is more information about the thickness of arch rings because so many ancient bridges survive, but there is a problem: that 'the arch rings seen in the elevations are no guide to the true thickness of the barrels'.[99] The elevations may suggest a wide arch ring or rings, but the arch itself may be made of much thinner stones. It is difficult to know how widespread this practice was.

[95] J. Heyman and C. J. Padfield, 'Two Masonry Bridges: I. Clare College Bridge', *Proc. Inst. Civ. Engrs.*, 52 (1972), 305–18.

[96] See Chap. 5.   [97] Huggins, *Medieval Bridge at Waltham*, 135; Ruddock, *Arch Bridges*, 55.

[98] J. Preston, 'Rochester Bridge, 1825–1950', in Yates and Gibson, *Traffic and Politics*, 243. The aims were to loosen both the superstructure and the foundations. See also Page, *Masonry Bridges*, 10.

[99] Heyman et al., *Teston Bridge*, 491.

The situation may have differed from region to region. The Dorset bridge engineer A. J. Wallis does not refer to it. At Harrold Bridge in Bedfordshire the arch stones visible in elevation continue throughout the soffit.[100]

Many lowland arches seem to have been adequate. The 'single order limestone arch rings' of most medieval Bedfordshire bridges, like Harrold Bridge, 'were of very strong proportions'.[101] In addition, the bridges in the county were built with a second 'counter arch' above the main arch ring. Elsewhere strength was added by ribbed arches which supported the soffit (plate 23). In much of lowland England the ratio of arch ring thickness to span was very conservative. If this is the case, it would have allowed for many other inadequacies, such as rough-and-ready stones pitched round the arch 'with little attempt at regularity' rather than accurately cut voussoirs.

Arches were constructed in a variety of ways from a range of different stones. Three main factors seem to have been involved: the available funds, the local building stone, and the arch span. The narrow arches of several Wey bridges were cheaply made, using a local stone. Alec Clifton-Taylor described the stone used at one of them, Tilford Bridge, as a 'very hard ferruginous sandstone', noting that 'it can only be employed as a coarse random rubble, but it is very resistant to the weather', and in this respect ideal for bridges. Where appropriately employed and constructed, this hard stone, well bonded with mortar, has produced a series of very durable bridges.[102] Similar materials were also used elsewhere, for example, in the small two-arched bridge at Fifehead Neville (plate 24). A slabby shale was used in the relatively narrow arches of several surviving medieval bridges in Devon: at Horrabridge and Staverton, as well as in the long bridges at Bideford and Barnstaple (plate 19).

Many medieval bridges in the south were mostly constructed of rubble, but with high-quality ashlar voussoirs and, where the vault is ribbed, ashlar ribs: at Stanton Drew Bridge the beautifully carved, chamfered, ashlar arch rings and ribs stand out from the coursed rubble of the spandrel walls (the spandrels are this space between the roadway and the arches and piers). The most significant bridges, including those at Huntingdon and London, were entirely built of ashlar. This was probably largely a matter of prestige, but there may also have been practical advantages; for instance, ashlar blocks were less easily detached from piers or abutments.

In the north, ashlar construction was common: it was regularly used for all the facing stonework, for instance, at Warkworth Bridge and Devils Bridge,

---

[100] *Bridges of Bedfordshire*, 114.   [101] Ibid.
[102] Pevsner, *Surrey*, 80; the manner of construction is described in Renn, 'Wey Bridges', 81.

Kirby Lonsdale (plates 14 and 27). Here huge, powerful ribs constructed with large ashlar voussoirs support a soffit consisting of stone flags which look very like paving slabs (plate 5). The arches of major bridges were almost always ashlar, even if, like Framwellgate Bridge, the rest of the stonework—the spandrel walls, piers, and abutments—was rubble. While many large northern bridges were also of ribbed construction, some, including Piercebridge, have arches built without ribs: there voussoirs form a soffit which has the appearance of a vast, smooth masonry wall.

A striking feature of many of these northern structures is that there are at least three arch rings. These arch rings very probably do reflect the fact that each span consisted of several arches, one above the other, known as counter arches, a term in use at least since Smeaton's day. He noted that the thickness of the middle arch of Ouse bridge, York, arch was 2 feet 1½ inches, but he added that it had 'two counter arches of 19½ and 14 ins., the thickness through all [was] 6 ft.'.[103] Bridges with counter arches of this type, like Devil's Bridge, were the norm in England well into the eighteenth century. This was different from Roman and medieval French custom, where the use of one ring of very large voussoirs was usual; English practice had disadvantages, but also some advantages: for example, it was much easier to lift the smaller voussoirs into position.

While the arches of these great bridges look immensely powerful, the ratio of total arch thickness (including counter arches) to span is very radical.[104] They were very daring but assured constructions, as if the masons had a clear grasp of what they were doing. Framwellgate has arches of similar construction (three arch rings and ribs) and thickness to its neighbour, Elvet Bridge, but its spans are almost three times as big. The central opening of Ouse Bridge, York, was, according to Smeaton's measurements, more than fifteen times the total thickness of the arch; the spans of the bridges at Warkworth and Piercebridge seem to be about twenty times the thickness of the arch and counter arches combined. This meant that the voussoirs of these arches had to be very precisely cut, and there is not only visual evidence that they were. The seventeenth-century contract for Kirkstall Bridge, a very large single-span bridge, indicates that more was paid for the voussoirs of the lower arch than for those of the higher arch: 1,700 arch stones at 3½ *d.* per foot were used to make the bottom arch-ring. A coarser top arch-ring was laid on top at the lower price of 3 *d.* per foot. The carpenters also had a vital role. Centring for arches of 20 to 30 metres also had to be very accurately shaped; making it was a difficult and expensive task (plate 11). The timber for the centring of the Kirkstall Bridge arch cost £45, over 10 per cent of the total cost.[105]

---

[103] Ruddock, *Arch Bridges*, 85.   [104] This ratio is discussed in Chap. 5.
[105] Preston, *Aire and Calder Bridges*, 146–7.

Some surviving northern bridges do show signs of distress. Wensley Bridge on the River Ure consists of three arches, each of the relatively large span of 36 feet. One arch is segmental and has been rebuilt since the eighteenth century. The other two medieval arches are segmental-pointed in shape, but one of them has a sagging arch. One of the four segmental arches of Catterick Bridge on the neighbouring Swale is also distorted (plate 16). The cause of the distortion is hard to establish, as it always is, especially without the kind of very careful internal inspection undertaken on the Clare College Bridge. The movement of the abutments or piers (possibly caused by feeble foundations) can be a cause of sagging arches.[106] Alternatively, the problem may be that the voussoirs of the sagging arches of both bridges were too thin: it is notable that some of the other arches of Catterick Bridge have been rebuilt with broader voussoirs.

That much could go wrong throws into relief what impressive structures so many of the medieval bridges are. Remarkably, many of the great surviving bridges in the north, including those at Piercebridge, Warkworth, Twizel, and Kirby Lonsdale, still appear to be in superb condition, their huge arches showing few signs of distress. It is possible that in some cases this is because of later repair or reconstruction, using the original stones, but it may also be because the bridges were extremely well designed and constructed. They demonstrate that often medieval masons in the north, though bold, knew what they were doing.

Reasons for the Developments in Bridge Design

The construction of major stone bridges from the eleventh century was a European phenomenon. The interplay of influences between England and continental countries is, however, obscure. There are few snippets of information about possible links. London Bridge was built at about the same time as French bridges over the Loire of similar construction. Although Peter of Colechurch, an Englishman, began the bridge, after his death and towards the end of the project the Crown called in a French engineer to help with its completion. Later, large segmental arched bridges appeared in southern France, Italy, and northern England, possibly at about the same time, in the fourteenth century. There is, however, no evidence of direct influence. It is possible that a mason had seen large flat arches when travelling abroad and decided to copy them, but it is clear from their characteristic ribs and counter arches that the northern bridges were constructed, using traditional methods of arch construction, by northern masons.[107]

---

[106] Ormrod, 'Rochester Bridge, 1660–1825', in *Traffic and Politics*, 194.
[107] The different traditions of arch construction are discussed in D. F. Harrison, 'Medieval Bridges', *Current Arch.*, 11 (1990), 73–6.

While it is hard to demonstrate direct foreign influence, it is evident that the ability to build impressive masonry bridges is related to developments in ecclesiastical architecture. Stone vaulted bridges appear at about the same time as major stone vaults in large churches.[108] General improvements in the quality of masonry construction in the twelfth century may have stimulated bridge building. The relationship between the building types could be very close. Bridges and churches were commissioned by the same clients and designed and constructed by the same masons. Ranulf Flambard's stone bridge at Durham, which so impressed Simeon of Durham, was built at the same time as the nave of Durham Cathedral. While the bridge was one of the earliest vaulted stone bridges, the church possesses the earliest major ribbed stone vaults in England (*c.*8 metre span), as well as showing significant improvements in stone cutting, including 'fineness of joints, smoothness of finish, and accuracy of angles', which may have affected the ability to build vaulted bridges.[109] We find a similar situation at Salisbury. In about 1240, while he was overseeing the construction of the new cathedral, Bishop Bingham commissioned the new bridge across the Avon just to the south of the cathedral precinct.[110]

The most distinguished masons designed both bridges and major churches: in the late fourteenth century Henry of Yevele was involved both in the remodelling of the nave of Canterbury Cathedral in the Perpendicular style and in the construction of the stone arched bridge at neighbouring Rochester (*c.*1383–*c.*1391). He designed the nave of Westminster Abbey and other major buildings in the capital, was bridge warden at London Bridge and responsible for the new chapel on the bridge. He also contracted with Westminster Abbey to construct Moulsham Bridge, Chelmsford. Yevele's younger associate, Stephen Lote, who was in charge of the works at Canterbury Cathedral from 1400 to 1418, was consulted about the large cracks which had appeared in the stonework of Rochester Bridge twenty years after its construction, in 1409–10.[111]

By the later middle ages some large stone church vaults were being constructed. The width of the nave of Girona Cathedral in Spain was 22 metres.[112] However, none compared with the almost 30 metres of Framwellgate Bridge (plate 5), or Twizel Bridge, or the even greater spans of Newton Cap Bridge, one of which is 100 feet. No bridge with an arch of greater span was built in

---

[108] Fernie, *Architecture of Norman England*, 267, suggests that the influence may have been from bridges to churches.

[109] Ibid. 34–6, 134–6, 264–8.   [110] Pevsner, *Wilts.*, 390, 458–9.

[111] Harvey, *Henry Yevele* (London, 1944), 80, 54–5; Britnell, 'Rochester Bridge', 70; D. Ingram Hill, *Canterbury Cathedral*, (London, 1986), 54–5.

[112] N. Coldstream, *Masons and Sculptors* (London, 1991), 60–1.

England until the eighteenth century, and no significantly larger arch until the nineteenth century. Their scale can only be explained by the existence of a school of bridge builders—perhaps we should say a lodge or lodges of masons—who had grown confident in the construction of large bridges and probably sought to rival one another in erecting giant spans.

HOW STONE BRIDGES WERE CONSTRUCTED

Building major bridges was a complex and difficult task. Fortunately, we know a good deal about it. Archaeologists have been able to work out the process of construction from observations made during demolition or from the evidence of surviving structures. Watson has shown the probable means of constructing Old London Bridge,[113] Renn the crude rubble bridges over the River Wey. The latter were built in the following way:

The rubble voussoirs of the arches would have been supported on timber falsework until the mortar set . . . Medieval mortar took a long time to set, and it was essential that the falsework should be taken down at the right moment. Too early, and the 'green' mortar would not prevent radial slippage; too late, and the arch might be partly over-stressed and brittle, and unable to ease by slight movement . . . the irregular profiles . . . suggest that the falsework was not elaborately carpentered . . . A simple frame of poles lashed together and covered with brushwood and earth would suffice . . .[114]

There are also contemporary sources, two of which are of great interest. One relates to the construction of a great northern bridge: this is the contract of 1421 for building a bridge at Catterick (plate 16). The other is the poem about the bridges and causeway built in the lowlands, in and near Abingdon.

The Catterick contract was made between Nicholas de Blakburne, the wealthy York merchant, several other clients, and three masons, Thomas Ampilforde, John Garrett, and Robert Maunsell. It provides very specific information and is worth discussing at some length.[115] The contract's concerns are: the specifications of the bridge; the logistics of the operation, indicating, in particular, which tasks should be undertaken by the masons and which by the clients; the order and timing of construction; and the method and timing of payment. Interestingly, the contract provides more details of the obligations of the clients than of the masons, which suggests that Blackburn and his agents were managing the project, hiring carpenters, and contacting for materials to

[113] Watson, *Construction of the Colechurch Bridge*, 87–9. [114] Renn, 'Wey Bridges', 80–1.
[115] The contract is printed in Salzman, *Building*, 497–9.

be carried to the site. It may also suggest that Ampilforde and his colleague were held in high regard.

The bridge was to be of stone and to be well constructed in a similar manner to Barnard Castle Bridge (some 10 miles away), with two piers (of the same dimensions as Barnard Castle Bridge), two abutments, three arches, and five courses of 'egeoves' of the same thickness as Barnard Castle Bridge. Salzman translates 'egeoves' as parapets, but the term may refer to the ribs of the bridge, indicating that it was to have five ribs.[116] The bridge was also to have a 'tabill of hewyn stane undir ye Allurying oure watir', possibly meaning a hewn stone soffit, or that the parapet walls would be built on top of a course of flat stones; 'allurying' meant parapet. Other features are mentioned in the contract or implied by it. The bridge was to be constructed both of free stone, presumably to be used for the outer skin of the piers, abutments, spandrel walls, parapets, and soffits, and of 'fillynge' stone, presumably to be utilized for the infill. The masonry of the piers and abutments was built on 'branderiths' which seem to have been wooden frameworks or platforms, consisting of wood laid out in a criss-cross manner, on which the masonry of the piers and abutments were laid.[117] The use of coffer dams is implied by the phrase 'kepe ye wat' wer' And defend itte fro ye saides [masons] . . . to ye tyme ye branderath be laid and yair werke of masoncraft be passed ye danger'. There is no reference to the use of piles, but it is just possible that piling could have been part of the work undertaken by the clients.

The logistics of the operation, who is responsible for what and when they are to do it, are listed in particular detail. Nicholas Blackburn and the other clients were to construct a lodge for the masons to work in. They ensured that the stone was quarried and conveyed to the bridge at their expense. They provided wood and coal for the limekiln and, in addition, three hundredweight of iron and steel. Presumably the iron was used to clamp the stone blocks together; it would be sunk into the blocks and kept in place with lead. The clients also supplied the necessary timber for the bridge, and (it is implied) employed carpenters to undertake a very substantial amount of work, constructing centring (see plate 11), scaffolding, and the wooden platforms under the piers and abutments. They were also to erect coffer dams in which the masons laid the lower

---

[116] Kurath gives as a meaning 'a diagonal rib of an arch or vault, an ogive'; Part E1, p. 25; parapet is very unlikely interpretation because the contract also refers to an alluryng, alouring, which means a parapet; Kurath, Part A, 220–1: H. Kurath and S. M. Kuhn (eds.), *Middle English Dictionary* (Michigan, 1954–). It is possible that the 'egoves' refers to the number of arch rings, but 5 is unlikely.

[117] Salzman considers that branderiths referred to coffer dams, but this is at variance with Kurath. The term was more commonly used to mean a gridiron on which pans, for example, were placed; here it seems to mean a timber version of a gridiron, i.e. a wooden framework of the type described by Gautier.

masonry courses. The masons largely restricted their part of the work to masoncraft, working the stone at the quarry and on site and constructing the stonework of the bridge.

The work was to be done to strict deadlines: the 'branderith' for one abutment was to be laid by the Feast of the Discovery of the Holy Cross, 3 May 1422, and the other by the Feast of the Nativity of St John the Baptist, 24 June. The abutments were then constructed. At the same dates in the following year the 'branderiths' of the piers were to be laid. After this the piers would have been constructed. The centres of the arches were to be erected by the same dates in the third year, 1424. The masons were to have finished the bridge by Michaelmas 1425. They were to be paid 260 marks in installments, mainly of £20 to £40, together with gifts of gowns.

The bridge was to built in the following way: a coffer dam was set up round the area of one of the abutments and then the other, while the clients ensured that the wooden platforms were laid on the river bed. The second platform was to be in place by midsummer 1422. This presumably had to be done so the masons could construct the abutments before the end of the building season. The next year, again using a coffer dam, the platforms of the two piers were laid by the same date and the masons then raised the stonework of the piers to a safe height. Between spring of the third year, 1424, and autumn of the following year, 1425, the centring for the arches was put in place and the arches and the rest of the stonework, presumably including the spandrel walls and the parapets, were constructed. The timetable suggests that the three arches were constructed at the same time and their centring removed simultaneously.

The work seems to have been carried out according to plan, since in September 1427 new bridges were being constructed 'in workmanlike manner after the fashion of Cateryk bridge'. The bridge was still standing in April 1432, since Nicholas Blackburn's will of that month instructed his executors to take appropriate action if the bridge were to fall through any failing in the workmanship. Further provision about the upkeep of the bridge was made in his wife's will of 1435. Subsequently, major repairs were undertaken in 1446; possibly it was reconstructed.[118] The present bridge on the site is ancient but differs significantly from the bridge proposed in the contract. It has four (rather than three) segmental arches, which are constructed without ribs. The arches are built in different ways and must have been constructed at different periods. It is possible that part of the bridge is fifteenth century, but the northern arch was probably constructed or reconstructed in the late sixteenth or seventeenth century,

---

[118] *Test. Ebor.*, ii. 20, 50.

when the 'north pillar [abutment]' was a continual expense. The river may have been eroding its north bank, which could have made it necessary to construct an additional arch.

The second detailed source is a delightful poem which relates the story of the building of a series of typical lowland bridges and causeways across the several streams of the Thames in and near Abingdon in the early fifteenth century. In the town the main channel of the river is divided into two by a small island, and both streams were bridged. Jervoise knew the bridge across the stream nearest the town as Abingdon Bridge and the other as Burford Bridge; in the fifteenth century the whole structure seems to have been called Burford Bridge. A long causeway was constructed across Andersey Island to Culham where Culham Bridge (plate 15) was built over another channel of the Thames, called the Back Water. These works were undertaken between 1416 and 1422. In about 1430 three flood arches known as Maude Hailes Bridge were built to the south of Burford Bridge, possibly because the bridge had blocked the river and caused flooding. A few years later, in the middle of the fifteenth century, the poem was inscribed on a memorial tablet in St Helen's Hospital, which had been founded by John of St Helens, who had played a prominent role in building the bridges, and endowed them and the hospital.[119]

The poem makes clear the great difficulty in laying foundations in a river and the scale of the project. It was a major piece of civil engineering. The whole town was involved: wives brought food out to their husbands as they worked. The first lines point out the religious nature of the work and stress that it will save lives. Attention is drawn to the leading figures who made very large contributions to the bridge. Several elements of the work are then emphasized, in particular laying the foundations, making the centring, and building the arches. Creating dry areas in which to lay the foundations proved very difficult, and this seems to have been achieved largely through the skill and energy of one man:

> Then the strengthe of the streme astoned hem stronge,
> In labor and lavyng moche money was lore.
> Ther loved hem a ladde was a water man longe,
> he helpe stop the streme til the werke were a fore.

Constructing the arches required a surprising number of men. Eleven labourers had to work together:

---

[119] The verses were appended by Hearne to Leland's *Itinerary* (Leland, v. 113–18).

> Then must they have mooldes to make on the bowys . . .
> They founde oute the fundement and layde in large stones
> They reysid up the archeys be geometre in rysyng.

The last line is particularly interesting in the light of J. Heyman's work.[120] Each arch was constructed independently. Each had to be capable of standing independently and was not supported by its neighbours. The piers were sufficiently wide to take the thrust of the arch when the centring was removed.

The construction of the bridges and causeways created a very large building site, with 300 men working there during the summer. Craftsmen were hired from afar, attracted by the high wages. The construction of the long causeway over Andersey Island involved a lot of effort. Many labourers seem to have been employed digging ditches in the hard ground and building up the earth to carry the road with spades, shovels, and mattocks.

The poem also recounts buying out the ferry, paying for a right of way for the new causeway from Culham Bridge across Andersey Island to the bridge at Abingdon, and ensuring that no tolls were charged for its use. Finally, it records the passing of an Act of Parliament:

> That al the brekynges of the brige the towne bere schulde,
> This was preved acte also in Perlement,
> In perpetual pees to have and to holde.

The bridges were widened in 1828 and a navigation arch was inserted in Burford Bridge in 1790. In 1927–8 a new bridge was built at Culham, bypassing the old bridge. The causeway across Andersey Island was rebuilt the following year. Maud Hales Bridge and a large part of Burford Bridge were demolished and the bridges widened. Fortunately, much of the medieval work of these famous structures survive. Two of the old arches of Burford Bridge were kept and stones of the old bridge were reused in the new. Abingdon Bridge and Culham Bridge remain, remarkably little changed after over 500 years.[121]

These two remarkable sources, which provide such vivid detail about the construction of the bridges at Abingdon and Catterick in the early fifteenth century, demonstrate the difficulties, complexity, and organization involved in building a stone bridge. They tell a story which was repeated from the eleventh century on at countless sites, as the network of English bridges was transformed.

---

[120] See Chap. 5.   [121] *South*, 6–7.

8

The Golden Age of Stone Bridges: From the Late Middle Ages to the Nineteenth Century

In 1300 there were many bridges. Some were stone, others timber, others a combination of the two. We do not, however, know how many there were of each type. The situation was the same in 1400. By the 1540s, when Leland had finished his travels, the position was completely different. Now there is an abundance of information about the fabric, width, and design of major bridges. Thereafter, there is ever more detailed evidence.

THE STATE OF THE BRIDGE NETWORK IN 1540

A Country of Stone Bridges

The most striking characteristic of major bridges in the early sixteenth century is that the great majority were vaulted and constructed of stone. A signifi-cant minority were of timber trestle construction. The remaining structures either brick bridges or bridges with stone piers and a timber deck. The latter were becoming rare when Leland set off on his travels. He noticed a few: Crowlington Bridge, Shropshire, across the Teme, was of 'stone and tymbar';[1] near Chislehampton he saw a bridge on the main stream of the River Thame which consisted of '5 great pillers of stone, upon the which was layid a timbre bridge.'[2] The five medieval piers survive, but, as commonly happened, the tim-ber deck has been replaced by stone arches.

Brick bridges, like most brick buildings, were confined to the south and east of the limestone belt and, in particular, to the east-coast counties.[3] Some sur-viving pre-1550 bridges are constructed entirely of brick, for example, Mayton Bridge, Norfolk. Others employ brick with other materials: Moulton Bridge in

---

[1] Leland, ii. 83.

[2] Ibid. i. 116. When Leland refers to a stone bridge he seems to have meant a bridge with stone vaults.

[3] A. Clifton-Taylor, *The Pattern of English Building* (London, 1972), 211–18.

Suffolk is constructed from brick, flint, and stone.[4] However, there were not many brick bridges even in East Anglia. There are few pre-1550 examples elsewhere; among them is the sixteenth-century brick bridge at Hampton Court, revealed when the moat was re-excavated.[5] There is no evidence that very substantial brick bridges were built in England: Toppesfield Bridge, which is the longest surviving English medieval bridge to employ brick (with stone), has three arches and is a mere 16 metres long; by contrast, in France there are some superb brick examples, including the massive bridge at Montauban over 200 metres in length.[6]

The effects of centuries of constructing bridges with stone vaults can readily be seen by looking at the situation on the River Nene, which rises in the Northamptonshire hills where there is access to good building stone. As the laconic descriptions in the Pevsner volume for Northamptonshire indicate, a number of stone bridges survive, at least in part, on this river.

Ditchford: BRIDGE. Probably C 14. 14 ft wide. Massive cutwaters.
Irthlingborough: BRIDGE across the river Nene. Of ten arches, mostly pointed; C 14. Several arches with chamfered ribs. Cut-waters. Widened in 1922.
Thrapston: BRIDGE. Of nine arches, largely medieval, widened later. The arches rebuilt in brick. Some stone cutwaters remain. The bridge is threatened with demolition.[7]

Other stone bridges on the Nene, now demolished, are known from illustrations. Views of Northampton depict South Bridge with its pointed medieval arches.[8] A Tillemans watercolour of Oundle depicts the bridge outside the town with several small, irregular pointed arches and a long causeway.[9] Leland described this and another bridge in the town. At Thrapston he observed by the bridge of stone 'a very large Heremitage and principally welle buildid but a late discoverid and suppressid'. There were significantly fewer timber bridges. Leland saw one at Fotheringay, Ogilby recorded another near Wellingborough, and a third, probably the latest of a series of similar bridges on the site, is shown in a panorama of Peterborough with the great medieval abbey behind it.[10]

The Nene was typical of the situation both in the Midlands and in many other parts of England. Tables 8.1–3 summarize our knowledge of the bridges over twenty-two rivers. They are therefore representative of a high proportion of major and middling rivers.[11]

---

[4] *Mid and Eastern*, 116.
[5] C. R. Pears, 'On the Stone Bridge at Hampton Court', *Archaeologia*, 62 (1910), 309–16.
[6] *Mid and Eastern*, 128; M. Prade, *Les Ponts monuments historiques* (Poitiers, 1986), 373.
[7] Pevsner, *Northants*, 187, 268, 430.   [8] Hyde, *Prospect of Britain.*
[9] *Country Life*, 12 Nov. 1987, p. 231.   [10] Leland, i. 3–6; Hyde, *Prospect of Britain.*
[11] The rivers in this sample are the same as those examined in Tables 2.1–3.

TABLE 8.1. *Fabric of bridges over the great rivers, c.1540*

Rivers	Total number of known bridges	Stone	Timber	Fabric unknown
Avon (Midlands) (downstream from Finford Bridge)	17*	13	3	1
Great Ouse (from Claydon Brook to Ely)	17	8	2	7
Severn (from Montford Bridge)	10	9	1	0
Thames (from Lechlade)	17	7	9	1
Trent (from Stoke-on-Trent)	16	5	1	10
Ure and Ouse (from Bainbridge)	10	6	2	2

Note: *c.1580.

TABLE 8.2. *Fabric of bridges over Yorkshire rivers, c.1540*

Rivers	Total number of known bridges	Stone unknown	Timber	Fabric
Aire (downstream from Coniston)	16*	3	0	13
Calder (from Sowerby Bridge)	7	1	0	6
Derwent (from Ayton Bridge)	9	3	0	6
Nidd (from Ramsgill)	13	5	4	4
Wharfe (from Kettlewell)	11*	4	0	7
Swale (from Grinton)	7	3	3	1
Tees (from Egglestaone)	5	5	0	0

Note: *The situation in 1600.

The tables demonstrate very clearly the preponderance of stone construction. Across eleven of the twenty-two rivers listed in these figures more than half of the bridges were built of stone. Across another six rivers in the sample more stone bridges are recorded than wooden ones.[12] Roughly equal numbers of timber and stone bridges are recorded for only two of the rivers. One was the

[12] But the material from which more than half of the bridges on each of these six rivers were built is not known.

TABLE 8.3. *Fabric of bridges over other major rivers, c.1540*

Rivers	Total number of known bridges	Stone	Timber	Fabric unknown
Avon (Bristol) (downstream from Malmesbury)	13	9	0	4
Avon (Hants.) (from Salisbury)	7	6	0	1
Medway (from Tonbridge)	8	7	0	1
Stour (Dorset) (from Blandford)	6	6	0	5
Tame (Staffs.) (from Water Orton)	6	4	0	2
Wear (from Stanhope)	9	6	0	3

Sources: See Table 2.1.

Nidd, the other the Swale, where there were timber bridges on the lower reaches in the Vale of York. Only across the Thames was there a majority of timber bridges. From Reading to Kingston all bridges were timber, although upstream of Reading all were stone.

Admittedly, nothing is known about the fabric of a considerable number of the bridges in the survey, but it is unlikely that a high proportion of them were timber: many were over the middle and upper reaches of the Trent, the Derwent, the Aire, and the Wharfe, and therefore probably of stone like the other bridges on those stretches of the rivers. The available evidence suggests that in many parts of the country timber bridges tended to be located, not upstream but on the lower reaches of major rivers, as on the Thames and the Swale. When Leland saw them, the three lowest bridges over the Wye (the river was not included in the survey) were timber.[13]

The bridges analysed in Tables 8.1 and 8.3 provide the fullest evidence. They show a very high proportion of stone bridges. At least three-quarters of all of the bridges across seven rivers described in Table 8.3 (the Bristol Avon, the Hampshire Avon, the Medway, the Dorset Stour, the Tamar, the Tame, and the Wear) were built of stone, and few timber bridges are recorded on these rivers. There were also many stone bridges across some of the largest rivers listed in Table 8.1; for example, on the Severn all were of stone except for that at Upton. Across the Great Ouse there were many stone but few timber bridges. There was one at St Neots and another at Castle Mills near Bedford. Leland

[13] Leland, ii. 69.

commented: 'I passid first by a bridge of wood over this arme [at Castle Mills near Bedford]; and by and by over the mayne streame of Use-ryver by a timber bridg. And I heare lernid of the millar that there was but another bridge of tymbre on Use at . . . betwixt the mylle and S. Neots.'[14]

Regional Variations

Fabric

Each of the rivers examined in the survey was typical of its region. Just as the bridges over the Wear and Tees were stone, so were those on other rivers in the north-east. The Tamar bridges were stone as were the others in Devon and Cornwall. While there were a number of timber bridges on the lower Wye, most of the bridges across rivers on the Welsh border, such as the Lugg and the Teme, were, like the bridges across the Severn, stone. Timber bridges, although rare elsewhere, were not only common on the middle Thames, but also on its northern tributaries near London, such as the River Colne and the River Lea.[15]

There is relatively little information about one area, East Anglia. Leland only visited part of the region, and therefore has few comments to make about the bridges there. The limited evidence points to the presence both of stone and of timber bridges. In Norwich by the mid-sixteenth century three of the five bridges across the Wensum were constructed of masonry.[16] What we know about the wider region is as follows. There was a lack of good building stone in many parts of the region, and there were several major wooden bridges, including those at Cambridge, Boston, and Wisbech. On the other hand, there were navigable rivers on which stone could be transported, and masonry bridges were built before the mid-sixteenth century in the area. In addition to the brick bridges which survive, there are several stone arched bridges, for instance, at Cringleford (River Yare, near Norwich), and Wiveton (River Glaven) near the north Norfolk coast.[17] A number of other medieval masonry bridges in Norfolk, which have subsequently been demolished, were illustrated by Francis Stone, including Trowse Bridge (River Yare) and a bridge with three pointed arches at Attlebridge. Even in 1830, however, his collection also contains many timber bridges, several with a single timber span between stone abutments.[18] Ogilby also presents a mixed picture, recording a wooden bridge in the fens at Spalding (River Welland), but also stone bridges in or near the Fens,

[14] Ibid. i. 102.   [15] Ibid. 107–8; ii. 69–70; *Cornish Bridges*, 39–55; *South*, 53–6.
[16] S. Cocke and L. Hall, *Norwich Bridges Past and Present* (Norwich, 1994).
[17] *Mid and Eastern*, 117, 115.
[18] F. Stone, *Picturesque Views of all the Bridges belonging to the County of Norfolk* (Norwich, 1830–1).

1. Perspective view of the City of Gloucester engraved for the *Complete English Traveller*. Roads across broad river valleys, like the Severn at Gloucester, were carried by causeways sometimes a mile or more long. The causeways were commonly made of earth retained by a stone wall. There were bridges over the many channels of the river.

2. The surviving arches of Old Exe Bridge, Exeter. The medieval arches were uncovered during works from 1968–72. Some appear to date from the 12th century when the bridge was built at great expense. The bridge was 15' wide in places which would have enabled two carts to pass. Most bridges were cart bridges but few were more than 12' in width until the late 18th century.

3. Old Ouse Bridge, York, engraving for the *Beauties of England and Wales*. The huge central arch with an 82' span was built in 1566 in place of two older central arches which were swept away in a flood. The original stone arches and the chapel (hidden by the buildings on the left) were constructed in the late twelfth century.

4. T. Hearne, *View of Harrold from Chillington Church Yard*, published in 1803. Like many other bridges across the Great Ouse, the repair of each arch was the responsibility of a different landholder or village. This was possible because the bridge was designed so that each arch was supported by broad piers and could survive the collapse of one of its neighbours. When an arch fell it could be readily patched up with a temporary repair in wood. Here, however, the wooden span was erected in the 1530s but survived until the 1840s.

5. Framwellgate Bridge and Durham Cathedral. Each arch spans almost 90'; nothing significantly larger was built until the reign of Queen Victoria. The present bridge dates from *c*.1400. Its predecessor which was also of stone was built by Ranulf Flambard in the early 12th century at the same time as the vaulted nave of his cathedral was being completed. Major stone vaults were rare in both bridges and churches at this time.

6. Monmow Bridge, Monmouth, probably 13th century Many town bridges were built with towers. This is a rare survival. Excavation under the piers of the bridge revealed the sole-plate of an earlier 12th century timber bridge

7. J. Farington, 'Windsor Bridge' (the old timber bridge), published in 1798. In 1500 the middle Thames was one of the few parts of England where timber bridges were common Until the late 18th and 19th centuries all the bridges from Reading to Kingston were wooden. Old Windsor Bridge was demolished in 1824.

8. Croft Bridge, River Tees. The bridge which carried the Great North Road is typical of major northern bridges of the 13th and 14th centuries. They consist of tall arches with individual spans of 10–12m. There are, or were, structures of similar design over the lower stretches of several northern rivers including the Aire, Wharfe, and Wear, and as far south as Derbyshire.

9. Matlock Bridge, Derbyshire. The bridge was at the southern limit of the Croft-style bridges. The arch mouldings are particularly elaborate: such distinct architectural features are rarely found in bridges. The bridge has been widened by building what is effectively another bridge next to the medieval structure.

10. P. Sandby, 'The Bridge at Shrewsbury' (Old Welsh Bridge), published in 1776. Note the ribbed arches and stout cutwaters, typical of the medieval bridges over the Severn. The bridge was demolished shortly after the engraving was published.

11. S. Ireland, 'Bildewas Bridge'. Until the late eighteenth century it was rare for bridges to be demolished; arches would be rebuilt when necessary. It was vital that the timber centring on which the arch stones rested during construction was accurately-worked.

12. Huntingdon Bridge, probably fourteenth century. The bridge has survived, but the setting has been spoilt by building a modern footbridge too close to it. Like many ancient bridges it is difficult to know precisely when it was built. Jervoise, Pevsner, and the RCHM all suggest a different date.

13. Dee Bridge, Chester, probably mid-fourteenth century. These may be the earliest large flat segmental arches built in England. Some of the spans are *c*.60'. The bridge appears to be contemporary with the Ponte-vecchio in Florence. Medieval masons sought to found bridge piers on the firmest parts of the river bed. This may explain the asymmetrical siting of the piers.

14. Warkworth Bridge, probably *c*.1380. Giant segmental arches of *c*.20m. span. The ashlar ribs are constructed to a very high standard.

15. Culham Bridge, near Abingdon, early 15th century. One of a series of bridges built to form a new crossing of the Thames near Abingdon. The project is commemorated by a remarkable poem inscribed on a 15th century monument in Christ's Hospital in the town.

16. Catterick Bridge, R. Swale. Sixteenth century, but possibly containing some remains of the three-arched bridge built in 1421. One of the arches is distorted, possibly because the arch rings are too thin for the span.

17. St Ives Bridge, Great Ouse, with its 15th century chapel. Chapels built on a pier of, or at the end of, were common. This is one of the few which survives

18. Barford Bridge, Great Ouse, *c*.1430. Sir Gerard Braybrooke, left his goods for its completion *c*.1430. Like many bridges it has been widened. The original stone arches are visible behind the later brick work. The arches on the flood plain allowed the movement of water along the flood plain when the river burst its banks. Solid embankments would have forced the flood waters back through the bridge, increasing the risk of damage.

19. The Long Bridge, Bideford, late 15th century. One of two surviving medieval estuarine bridges. It is 700' long. At low water the starlings on which the piers are founded are visible. The arches are built of hard, rubbly, voussoirs—a common feature in Devon bridges.

20. Horse Bridge, Tamar, 15th century. One of a series of very similar fifteenth century bridges over the River Tamar. The individual arch spans of the bridges range from 20–25'. Each of the arches of the bridges has three arch rings. They differ noticeably from the cruder arches of Bideford Bridge. Note the debris which has accumulated under the arch.

21. Clopton Bridge, Stratford, late 15th century. Built by Sir Hugh Clopton, a Stratford boy who became Lord Mayor of London. The design differs little from Old Exe Bridge, which had been built 300 years earlier. Like many bridges in this part of the country there are no downstream cutwaters. Leland commented: Afore the tyme of Hughe Clopton there was a but a poore bridge of tymber, and no causey to come to it; whereby many poore folkys [and] othar refusyd cum to Stratford, when Avon was up, or cominge thithar stoode in jeoperdy of lyfe.

22. Piercebridge, c.1500. The climax of medieval bridge design. Three arches with a central span of 72', notable for its counter arches and precisely-cut voussoirs. The bridge replaced a five-arched structure of the Croft-style.

23. Whitemill Bridge, Dorset. A lowland bridge found on piles. It was at serious risk about 40 years ago: in a routine inspection the County Bridge Engineer found that foundations of one of the piers had been scoured away and the tops of the piles had rotted.

24. The bridge at Fifehead Neville. A good example of a crudely built rubble packhorse bridge. Note the timber railings which were common even on larger bridges. These have often been replaced by stone parapet walls.

25. Ludford Bridge, Ludlow. During the flood of 1886 the river washed away the parapet walls (note the different stonework), but the bridge survived because it was firmly founded on rock below the water level.

26. Trotton Bridge, Sussex. The bridge cannot be precisely dated but like many others its chamfered arch rings and ribs suggest a date before 1600. A concrete apron has been built under the piers to protect them from scour

27. Devil's Bridge, Kirby Lonsdale. An excellent place to build a bridge where the piers can be founded on rock. The huge arches (45' above the normal water level) seem unnecessary when the river is low, but in flood the Lune, like other upland rivers, can rise to a great height. The arch is built not from large voussoirs forming a single arch (as Roman arches were) but from arch ribs, an arch and a counter arch.

for instance at Crowland. He shows several small wooden, stone, and brick bridges across drains and dykes in the vicinity.

Although the situation in East Anglia is unclear, in the rest of the country there is little doubt about the balance of stone and timber bridges. In most of the south and midlands, except for a stretch of the Thames valley, the great majority of bridges were stone. Throughout the north of England stone bridges were the norm, with a few timber bridges, usually on the lower reaches of rivers. In Devon and Cornwall, where the timber bridge at Bideford was rebuilt in stone in the late fifteenth century, there may have been no major wooden bridges in 1550.[19]

The Design of Stone Bridges

By 1550 the very distinct regional variations in the design of stone bridges which we have glimpses of before can be clearly demonstrated. The medieval bridges still standing enable us to get a very good impression of them. The arch spans of bridges were very similar in each region, but varied enormously from region to region.

We can identify three broad groups of English bridges according to span. First, over half the extant bridges have no span greater than 6 metres, with some no more than 3 metres (although 6 metres is not all that small— it is, for instance, wider than the arches built in most parish churches). The majority of the bridges in the south of England and the Midlands are of this type.

Secondly, there are bridges with wider spans, from over 6 metres to 12 metres. About thirty of these have individual arch spans of 9–12 metres, that is, a little more than the span of the nave of most major churches. Most, but not all, are north of the Humber. Some have segmental arches, others have tall pointed arches, like Elvet Bridge or Croft Bridge, and there are bridges of similar design in the Midlands across rivers rising in high ground: in Derbyshire, Staffordshire, Herefordshire, and Shropshire (plates 8 and 9). There are also a few bridges which stand in low-lying land in the east of England, notably Huntingdon Bridge (largest span 33 feet). Bridges with spans of over 6 metres but under 9 metres, almost thirty in number, are mostly found in the same counties or in Devon and Cornwall. Four magnificent medieval bridges, Higher New Bridge, Greystone Bridge, Horse Bridge (probably derived from Hautes, 'high'), and New Bridge still stand across the River Tamar, their individual spans ranging from 20 to 25 feet (plate 20).[20] There is also a series of medieval bridges across the Medway with spans up to 26½ feet.[21]

---

[19] *Devon Bridges*, 92–3.   [20] *Cornish Bridges*, 44, 49–53.   [21] *CEH: Southern*, 226–8.

Thirdly, about ten bridges have very large arch spans of over 15 metres, and several are enormous, with individual spans in excess of 20 metres; with the exception of Dee Bridge, Chester, all are in North Yorkshire or further north (plate 13). A few of these bridges, such as Twizel Bridge, are in steep-sided valleys, but others, including Piercebridge, are not. In France there were also distinct regional differences, between the large spans of southern France and the smaller spans of the north.[22]

Chance survival cannot explain the larger arch spans of bridges in the north than in the south and midlands. This is not a matter of coincidence, reflecting the differential survival of evidence. The extant bridges are characteristic of the stone bridges standing in 1500 which have not survived.[23] Leland's evidence makes this very clear. Consider, for example, the midlands Avon: all but a few of the bridges over the river from the environs of Coventry to the confluence of the Avon and the Severn were arched stone bridges. Leland describes several of them, some of which are now demolished, including Finford Bridge, which had eight arches of stone, Barford Bridge, with 'eight fare arches', and Evesham Bridge, with '8 goodly large arches.'[24] Surviving bridges on the river are similar. Stare Bridge, Stoneleigh, has nine arches, Bidford-on-Avon Bridge, eight. The medieval arches of the bridges at Tewkesbury, Warwick, and Stratford are of very similar span to the other bridges on the river.[25]

By the sixteenth century, where roads had to cross flood plains, causeways were the norm on smaller and larger rivers. We find several in the Cherwell valley: at Banbury and at Lower Heyford. The lowest crossing of the river, Magdalen Bridge, Oxford, was approached by a stone causeway 1,500 feet long with twenty arches.[26] Across the broader valleys there were massive causeways. Several carried roads over the Trent valley: for example, at Burton-on-Trent, Swarkeston, Harrington Bridge, Nottingham, and at Muskham, where Haybridge was linked to Newark by a causeway.[27] Many were demolished in the last century, including the Great Bridge at Burton-on-Trent, which was constructed with a continuous arcade of thirty-six arches of spans of between 33 and 36 feet in the western section and averaging 21 feet in the eastern. The length of the structure was c.500 metres, that is, over half as long again as London Bridge. An engraving of 1760 shows it curving across the flood plain, looking rather like a railway viaduct.[28]

---

[22] Prade, *Ponts monuments*.
[23] This is not to say that all the bridges in a region were as well constructed or well founded. The better-built bridges are more likely to have survived, but they were built to similar designs.
[24] Leland, ii. 47, 108; v. 9, 155.   [25] *Eastern and Central*, 255–7.
[26] *VCH Oxon*, iv. 284; *Bridges in Oxfordshire*.   [27] *CPR* (1374–7), 298; (1343–5), 568; Leland, i. 96.
[28] Rye, 'Burton-on-Trent Bridge', 18–20.

Fortunately, one good example of a very large Trent causeway remains. This is Swarkestone Bridge, the mile-long series of bridges and embankments which carries the main road to Derby. William Woolley in the early eighteenth century observed that 'at Swarkeston is a curious stone bridge near upon a mile in length, reaching to Stanton, but the river passeth but through the first six arches; the others may be compared to a causey'.[29] Although the arches across the main channel have been replaced, the earth causeway still rises above the Trent flood plain, with groups of small, pointed medieval arches where it crosses some of the many channels. It gives a powerful impression of the length and narrowness, here emphasized by the walls on the side of the roadway, of these great medieval structures.

Width

By 1550 all but a few major bridges were cart bridges. Over smaller rivers and streams there were large numbers of footbridges and horsebridges as well bridges for carts. We know this because of the evidence of pontage grants, occasional references in other documents, and the structures themselves.

Pontage grants were authorizations of the right to levy tolls on goods and vehicles passing over a named bridge for the repair of the bridge. They contain long lists of what rates may be charged on what commodities. They all mention carts, for instance a grant in aid of St John's Bridge, Lechlade, of 1387 lists the tolls to be taken on many goods, which includes one halfpenny on every *cart-load* of grass for sale.[30] Each grant has a slightly different list of items and charges, which suggests that they were not repetitions of empty formulae, but were related to the likely goods carried across the bridge. The grants were issued on behalf of many bridges over the great rivers: the Severn, Thames, Trent, Great Ouse, and Nene.[31]

There is also information, although it is inevitably sporadic, about carts and width in other documentary sources. For instance, the Coroners Rolls record in 1312: 'In the vill of Oundle . . . a bridge . . . which is built of stone and mortar, and crosses the river Nen.' The width of the bridge was '12 ft between the two crosses which stand upon it'.[32] It is, however, unusual to be informed of dimensions; we are more commonly told that a bridge was constructed for carts or horses or pedestrians. Several of the legal cases included in Flower's *Public*

[29] 'William Woolley's History of Derbyshire', ed. C. Glover and P. Riden, *Derbyshire Rec. Soc.*, 6 (1981).
[30] 'Account of Lechlade Bridge, Gloucestershire', *Collectanea Topographica et Genealogica*, 1 (18–34).
[31] See Chap. 11.
[32] *Select Cases from the Coroners' Rolls A.D. 1265–1413, with a brief account of the history of the Office of Coroner*, ed. C. Gross, Selden Soc., 9 (1896), 64.

Works in Medieval Law contain such information. We have this evidence about four bridges over major rivers. All four were bridges for carts—at Biddenham over the Great Ouse and Brand bridges over the Medway, Myton-on-Swale, and Pershore across the Avon. Here 'the abbot of Westminster ought to repair the bridge for carts, waggons, horsemen and footmen'.[33] In contrast, where we hear about a bridge for horses and pedestrians it is invariably over a smaller river or stream.[34]

The evidence of the physical structure of bridges confirms the ubiquity of cart bridges on major rivers. Illustrations of now-lost bridges sometimes show carts and other vehicles crossing ancient bridges: for instance, the Tillemans drawing of the bridge at Oundle, which dates from the early eighteenth century, and therefore before the period when bridges were commonly widened, shows a carriage rising above the parapets on its way to the town. The evidence of the surviving medieval bridges completes the picture. All the many extant medieval bridges across major rivers were built as cart bridges.[35] The longest extant medieval packhorse bridge, at Hampton-on-Arden in Warwickshire, has five arches with a total span of under 25 metres over the upper reaches of the small River Blythe.[36] Using the combination of evidence we can demonstrate that in the early sixteenth century bridges over major rivers, such as the Thames and Severn, were cart bridges.

There were a very few narrow bridges across major rivers. Leland described one such bridge at Offenham, Worcestershire, as a 'narrow stone bridge for foot men . . . over Avon'.[37] Another was on the upper Trent where there is a relatively long bridge by a ford on a minor road to Shugborough Hall (Staffordshire); the present, fine stone bridge replaced an earlier timber structure. These few examples, however, must be the exceptions which prove the rule.

How wide were cart bridges and how narrow horse bridges? The dividing line must necessarily be hazy, but a rough guide is that cart bridges were usually more than 6 feet wide, and major bridges were considerably wider.[38] Some horse bridges were relatively narrow. Bruton Bridge in Somerset is under 4 feet wide. To compensate for their width, most had low parapets which permitted the passage of heavily laden horses. Others were wider. A bridge to be built at Weybridge, Surrey, in the sixteenth century was described as a horse bridge and was to be 5 feet 3 inches wide. The surviving packhorse bridge at Fifehead

---

[33] Flower, *Works*, ii. 362.   [34] Ibid. 270–5, 362; i. 1–2, p. xxxv.

[35] It should be noted that, although many surviving medieval cart bridges have been widened, the widening is normally clearly visible. None was originally a horse bridge.

[36] J. A. Cossins, 'Ancient Bridges, Fords and Ferries', *Trans. Birmingham Arch. Soc.*, 42 (1916), 1–15.

[37] Leland, ii. 47.

[38] E. Hinchliffe, *A Guide to the Packhorse Bridges of England* (Milnthorpe, 1994), 6.

Neville is of about the same dimensions (plate 24). Presumably, small carts could, if necessary, have used the larger horse bridges: according to one eighteenth-century commentator, there were carts in the Rotherham and Sheffield Region which were as little as 3 feet 6 inches wide.[39]

There were narrow cart bridges. In 1572 the proposed bridge at Polweverell in Cornwall was to be 7 feet wide for horses and carriages.[40] At least one long, important bridge in the county was of a similar width. Descriptions of Looe Old Bridge estimated that at its narrowest point it was between 6 and 7 feet wide.[41]

Most major bridges, however, were considerably wider. We can measure the original width of most of the surviving medieval bridges. Even where they have been widened it is possible to detect the original measurements. The main problem is estimating the width where the parapet has been rebuilt: the width of the roadway would depend on whether there was originally a stone parapet or wooden railings. Despite the difficulty, rough estimates can be made. The great majority of the existing bridges were originally 9 to 15 feet wide (plate 2).

Thus, many bridges were sufficiently wide to allow the passage of two carts side by side. The minimum necessary width was probably about 12 feet, the width of London Bridge between the buildings on either side.[42] Almost two-thirds of surviving bridges were probably this wide. Several were considerably wider. About fifteen extant bridges, usually important bridges on major roads in towns, were 15 feet wide or more.

FROM THE SIXTEENTH TO THE EIGHTEENTH CENTURY

Between the early sixteenth century and the early eighteenth century, changes in the design of bridges, fabric, techniques of construction, and notably width were negligible. Timber bridges were a small proportion of major and middling bridges in 1500 and a smaller percentage in 1750. By the late seventeenth century in much of England timber bridges over rivers were a most unusual sight In most of the south, west, and Midlands, stone bridges were common as they had been in 1500. In the west Midlands Ogilby shows a handful of timber bridges on post roads, for instance at Pembridge across the Arrow, but there were an astonishingly small number.[43] By 1750 the few major wooden bridges

[39] D. Hey, *Packmen, Carriers and Packhorse Roads* (Leicester, 1980), 98.   [40] *Cornish Bridges*, 24.
[41] Ibid. 68–9.
[42] Watson et al., 'The Buildings and Spaces on the Medieval Bridge and Their Use', in *London Bridge*, 102.
[43] See Ogilby, plates 59, 72, 57, 44, and 2.

in the north had been replaced. The three timber bridges over the lower Swale, at Morton, Skipton, and Topcliffe, were reconstructed in stone in the early seventeenth century.[44] Fifty years later Defoe commented: 'no part can shew such noble, large, lofty, and long stone bridges as this part of England, nor so many of them; nor do I remember to have seen any such thing as a timber bridge in all the northern part of England, no not from the Trent to the Tweed.'[45]

The Thames valley downstream of Reading remained an exception. Bridges were timber into the late eighteenth century; moreover, new bridges constructed over the river, including Datchet Bridge in 1706 and Putney Bridge in 1729, were of wood.[46] Ogilby depicted timber bridges over the Thames's tributaries at Uxbridge, High Wycombe, and Ware.[47]

Major bridges were of a similar width in 1750 and 1500. In the 'Book of bridges belonging to the West Riding' of 1752, 115 bridges are described, built at various times from the middle ages, of which fewer than ten exceeded 16 feet in width and many measured about 12 feet. There is little evidence that in other areas medieval bridges were widened before 1750.[48] In keeping with bridges of this width, new bridges, such as Wilton Bridge, Ross-on-Wye (c.1600), were still built with pedestrian refuges above the cutwaters; so was Eckington Bridge (Midlands Avon), constructed in 1728.[49]

The techniques of laying foundations also changed little. As in the middle ages, piers were laid on rock when it was convenient, sometimes on piles, but shallow foundations continued to be employed, even for major bridges. As late as the 1770s John Gwynn considered piles unnecessary for his major bridges in Shrewsbury, Oxford, and Worcester. When the piers of English Bridge, Shrewsbury, were inspected in 1925–6, they were discovered to be founded without any piles on oak platforms, some of which were only 'just below the gravel bed of the river'; however, they were in perfect condition and the superstructure showed no sign of foundation movement.[50] Coffer dams were the norm in the eighteenth century, but there remained situations where they could not be employed, notably on the Thames at London. In the first half of the century a different technique was tried for founding bridges, in preference to starlings. At Westminster Bridge (1738–50) and at Blackfriars Bridge (1760–9) caissons, which were watertight, open-topped wooden boxes containing the lower courses of masonry, were sunk in place on the river bed.[51]

[44] *North Riding Quarter Sessions Records, 1605–1791*, ed. J. C. Atkinson, 9 vols., North Riding Rec. Soc., (1884–92), iii. 118–9; iv. 3, 9.

[45] Defoe, *Tour*, ii. 211.   [46] *South*, 9 and 16.   [47] Ogilby, plates 1, 5.

[48] Ruddock, *Arch Bridges*, 207.   [49] *Wales and Western*, 120–1, 169–70.

[50] Ruddock, *Arch Bridges*, 111–12.   [51] Ibid. 9, 73.

Starlings, however, remained at London Bridge and elsewhere. The age-old annual routine of renewing their piles continued. New starlings were being constructed as late as the 1770s.[52]

There were changes in the design of stone bridges during the sixteenth century, but they were essentially superficial. New bridges were rarely constructed with pointed arches. In contrast to churches, rounded arches had been employed in bridges throughout the middle ages, but they became more common in accordance with new Renaissance fashions. Under the influence of Palladio, semicircular arches were considered both the most beautiful and the strongest. Palladio preferred them because they had less horizontal thrust than segmental arches.[53] Arch shape was the subject of discussion in coffee houses. Dr Johnson published in support of the semicircular arch on behalf of his friend John Gwynn.[54]

Large spans in the south, however, remained in the future. Before 1750 arch spans showed the same regional distinctions as they had in 1500. In the south and midlands bridges with small arches remained the norm until 1750 and in many cases later: Eckington Bridge of 1728 has six segmental arches spanning only 43 metres in total.[55] Hawksmoor in 1736 noted that there was only one bridge in the south with a long span, that built by him *c.*1716 in the grounds of Blenheim Palace (span 101½ feet).[56] On the Welsh borders new bridges continued to be built to a similar design to that of medieval bridges in the region; the size of arch spans in particular remained the same. Wilton Bridge, Ross-on-Wye, of *c.*1600 was constructed in a similar way to the neighbouring medieval bridges, for instance at Hereford, consisting of wide piers and six arches. In the north new, large arched bridges were built. Several survive from the seventeenth century, but no public road bridges built between 1600 and 1750 surpassed the massive spans of the bridges of the previous two centuries; indeed, if anything, masons seem to have been less adventurous.

POST-1760

After 1760, as the number of bridges increased rapidly, there were also important changes in design and construction techniques. This was the age of famous bridge builders, including Mylne, Smeaton, Rennie, and Telford. Iron bridges were built, the first at Coalbrook in 1779.[57] Their achievements are told by E.

---

[52] Ibid. 98–9.   [53] Palladio, 182.   [54] Ruddock, *Arch Bridges*, 64.
[55] *Wales and Western*, 169–70.   [56] Quoted in Ruddock, *Arch Bridges*, 3–4.
[57] *Wales and Western*, 139.

Ruddock in *Arch Bridges and Their Builders*. Bridges were widened. In the West Riding, Wakefield Bridge was widened from 15 to 23 feet in 1758, Norton Bridge in Ribblesdale from 8 feet 6 inches to 18 feet in 1765. The medieval bridge at Ferrybridge, which had been 15 feet 6 inches wide, was rebuilt in 1765 to a width of 25 feet 6 inches.[58]

Bridges were built to new designs. On the Thames in the 1750s, three bridges, at Walton, Hampton Court, and Kew, were constructed in a most unusual way with stone piers and complicated timber arches, resembling the 'mathematical' bridge at Cambridge. A final traditional timber trestle bridge was built over the river at Shillingford in 1784, but by now the ancient timber bridges over the Thames were beginning to be demolished.[59] The new bridges were stone, brick or iron structures. The bridge at Maidenhead was replaced in 1772–9. Others followed rapidly: Sonning in 1773, Chertsey, 1780–5, Henley, 1782–6, Staines, 1792, Windsor, 1824, Kingston, 1825–8, Marlow, 1832, and Caversham, 1869.[60] Some of the bridges built from the 1760s had large arches: the central span of Kew Bridge (1784–9), was 66 feet, that of Blackfriars Bridge (1760–9), 100 feet.[61] Important bridges were seen as grand architecture and several were decorated with new forms of ornament. Skerton Bridge, Lancaster, completed in 1788, had low rounded cutwaters surmounted by small aedicules, following Palladio's drawing of the Roman bridge at Rimini.[62]

Bridges on smaller rivers in the lowlands were built with many small arches long after 1750. Longham Bridge, Hampreston, Dorset (probably of 1792) has eleven arches spanning 70 metres in total, and Church Cobham Bridge, Surrey (*c.*1780) consists of a large number of small brick arches.[63] Nevertheless, from this time bridges with larger arches became more common in the south on smaller as well as larger rivers. For instance, Moulsham Bridge, Chelmsford, was rebuilt in 1787 with a single arch spanning 14 metres.[64] In the nineteenth century even larger spans were built in the north: Grosvenor Bridge, Chester (1827–33), has a single span of 200 feet, surpassing by a very considerable margin anything built before 1800.[65]

As late as 1812 the engineers building Vauxhall Bridge were still using caissons as foundations. Coffer dams were first employed on the Thames in London for Waterloo Bridge (1811–17). Steam engines were used to pump water out of the coffer dams, but even so the task was not easy. Draining the dam for the north pier, where the river was 17 feet deep even at low water, proved

[58] *YWR Bridge Book.*   [59] *South,* 9.
[60] Ruddock, *Arch Bridges,* 234–42; Phillips, *Thames Crossings,* 146–7, 87, 103, 121, 164.
[61] Ruddock, *Arch Bridges,* 109 and 65.   [62] Ibid. 124.   [63] *South,* 84 and 28.
[64] *Mid and Eastern,* 134.   [65] *Wales and Western,* 31.

especially difficult. Earth had to be thrown round the outside, and another pen of sheet piles driven to retain it.[66]

Bridge builders in early nineteenth century England were influenced by practice in France. Palladio became less influential.[67] The key figure was Jean Rodolphe Perronet, Premier Ingenieur of the Corps des Ingenieurs, sometimes described as the father of modern bridge building, who designed bridges with flat arches of large span, together with thin piers, to achieve very slight gradients and a maximum of free waterway. Perronet's bridges demonstrated that, since the great horizontal thrusts of the flat arches of his bridges were self-equilibrating and were taken by powerful abutments, piers could be much thinner than had been customary or than the likes of Palladio had thought possible. His masterpiece is the bridge at Neuilly (1783), which has arches spanning 128 feet resting on piers 10 feet wide.[68]

CONCLUSIONS: THE QUALITY OF MEDIEVAL STONE BRIDGES

Perronet's contemporaries and later generations of engineers had a low opinion of medieval bridges. Particular criticism was, and has continued to be, directed at the great estuarine bridges. Ruddock describes four large ancient bridges as a background to the achievement of the hundred years from 1735 to 1835, 'a century of great developments in arch bridges'.[69] At three of these bridges the main problem was the starlings. Pictures show Rochester Bridge with its eleven relatively large individual spans of *c*.10 metres. Although the spans were not very different from those of Westminster Bridge, which was completed in 1750, its effective waterway was much reduced because of the 45-foot wide starlings which surrounded each of the ten piers. The bridge was 534 feet long between the abutments, but measured between the starlings the waterway was only 117 feet.[70] Similarly, the narrowness of the openings at high tide made Old London Bridge an immense obstacle to the flow of the river.[71] The water raced through the arches: 'the average fall across the length of the starlings at neap tides was 2 ft. 1 ins., at spring tides 4 ft 4 ins.'[72] At these times the bridge looked like a series of waterfalls. Not only did the turbulent water scour the river bed and undermine the piers, but it also restricted the passage of river traffic. 'Shooting the bridge', as taking a boat through its arches was known, was a risky business.

---

[66] Ruddock, *Arch Bridges*, 179.   [67] Ibid. 175–200.
[68] Hopkins, *Span of Bridges*, 59–66; Ruddock, *Arch Bridges*, 175–7.
[69] Ruddock, *Arch Bridges*, p. xiii.   [70] Ibid. 54, Becker, *Rochester Bridge*, 9.
[71] Ruddock, *Arch Bridges*, 3–5.   [72] Hopkins, *Span of Bridges*, 39.

Emphasizing the contrast between London Bridge and the works of the eighteenth and nineteenth centuries has proved irresistible.[73] The bridge is still regularly presented as the epitome of English medieval bridges, sometimes of all medieval bridges. For example, H. J. Hopkins's historical survey of bridges from earliest times picks out London Bridge and bridges in Florence (the latter are praised for their modernity) as his only examples of medieval structures before going onto discuss the writings of Gautier and the work of Perronet.[74] No bridge has had a greater influence on our idea of the medieval bridge in England. In the 1720s Defoe still saw it as a wonder, but by the end of the century it had come to be viewed as the nadir of arched bridge construction.[75]

The faults of Old London Bridge have been regarded as typical of other medieval bridges. It is implicit in Hopkins's study that other bridges, including ordinary lowland bridges constructed in quite different locations without starlings, had similar problems. The inferiority of medieval to the surviving Roman bridges continues to be repeated, even in important and serious modern technical studies. For instance, L. Hamill, in the introduction to *Bridge Hydraulics*, observed:

Old London Bridge was built because in 1176 a chantry priest . . . decided that there should be a bridge across the Thames. For many centuries there was a tradition of bridge building in the church. Monasteries were active in business and commerce, so good communications were important to them. However, their primary interest was not in the science of bridge construction, which perhaps explains why there was so little advance, or even a regression, from Roman times.[76]

These criticisms of the quality of medieval bridges are misplaced in several respects. First, they seriously underestimate the achievements of medieval bridge builders in spanning wide, deep rivers. The great eleventh- and twelfth-century bridges across the Thames at London and across the Loire were founded on 'starlings' because there was no alternative given the nature of the river bed, the tides, and the depth of the water. Moreover, with heavy, continuous expenditure on maintenance and repair, and, when required, the rebuilding of piers, arches, and abutments, Old London Bridge survived for more than 600 years, the bridges at Newcastle and Bristol lasted over 500 years, and Rochester Bridge over 450 years.[77] Hopkins appreciated why London Bridge lasted so long: 'A repair, when it was needed, consisted of adding another outer skin of starling. In the main this produced a self-equilibrating system: the stream, confined as it were to a mill-race, was a scouring agent, but the starlings

[73] Ruddock, *Arch Bridges*, dustjacket.   [74] Hopkins, *Span of Bridges*, 38–42.
[75] Defoe, *Tour*, i. 105.   [76] Hamill, *Bridge Hydraulics*, 5–6.   [77] Ruddock, *Arch Bridges*, 54.

which were the cause generally proved equal to the self-imposed task of countering the effect.'[78] In the 1430s and 1440s up to 200 elms per year were used for making piles to drive into the river bed around the starlings of Rochester Bridge.[79]

These bridges were finally replaced (London Bridge in 1833 and Rochester Bridge in 1856) in part because they were too narrow, but also because by then technical progress made replacement possible and economic. Ormrod notes: 'The quickening pace of innovation promised long term economies in maintenance as well as the possibility of accommodating much larger flows of traffic.'[80] Until the nineteenth century there had not been the technical progress to enable this to happen. When, in the eighteenth century, Perronet built a new bridge on the Loire where the river bed consisted of leaky gravel, he had to employ a whole regiment of soldiers to empty the water from the coffer dam. One pier was nicknamed 'golden' since it cost so much to build.[81]

Seen in the context of the difficulties of the site, the remarkable feature of London Bridge is that it was built at all. It was a great feat of engineering. Like the cathedrals built in the same decades, including Bourges and Chartres as well as Canterbury, it was a daring, risky business. To contemporaries such as Thomas of Walsingham, who described Rochester Bridge as *sumptuosissimus*, these bridges were very impressive achievements.[82]

The Romans did not attempt to construct arched bridges at Rochester or London or similar locations in northern Europe. They built them where river flows are slow, water levels low in summer, and the river bed is firm, usually rocky, that is, where foundations are easy to establish. Even in the Mediterranean area vaulted bridges were not ubiquitous. O'Connor notes: 'if the locations of surviving masonry bridges are plotted, they are either in rocky mountainous terrain or alternatively in places where rivers run very low or dry at some time during the year . . . there are no traces of [Roman] bridges, for example, at crossings of the River Po . . .'[83]

While the descriptions of the great medieval estuarine bridges made since the eighteenth century are accurate, if lacking in sympathy and understanding for the conditions in which they were constructed, the criticisms of other typical lowland bridges is simply wrong. Old London Bridge was not typical of all bridges; in fact, it was decidedly untypical. It and the handful of other large downstream bridges were quite unlike the hundreds of medieval lowland bridges which were neither built in deep tidal waters nor of the same size.

[78] Hopkins, *Span of Bridges*, 39.   [79] Britnell, 'Rochester Bridge', 63–4.
[80] Ormrod, *Rochester Bridge, 1660–1825*, 218.   [81] Boyer, *French Bridges*, 157.
[82] Britnell, 'Rochester Bridge', 47.   [83] O'Connor, *Roman Bridges*, 145.

These bridges were constructed to a different design philosophy than modern bridges. Their broad piers could be laid on relatively shallow foundations because the load was spread. The combination of broad piers and narrow arches meant that each arch could be constructed independently, since the width of the piers meant that they were able to resist the relatively weak thrust of the small arches when the centring was removed. In addition, the centring could be reused for each arch.[84] Because the arches usually rose above the surrounding flood plain, they were not submerged when the river was in flood; it burst its banks before this happened. Because the embankments and causeways were pierced by arches (which remained dry for so much of the year), the flood water was able to pass down the flood plain and did not back up behind the bridge to the extent it does where the road embankment is solid (plate 18).[85]

This design had several other advantages. Because each arch was independent, if one of the piers of such a bridge was undermined by scour and collapsed, the arches on either side would fall but probably none of the others would. Wide piers and shallow foundations made collapse more likely, but also ensured that the consequence would not be a complete disaster. For example, two of the arches of Rochester Bridge broke in the 1420s but the rest remained.[86] When the arch of a more typical lowland bridge fell, it could readily be patched up with planks. An arch of Harrold Bridge collapsed in 1532. It was replaced by timber, but was not rebuilt in stone until the 1840s (plate 4).[87] In contrast, if one arch of a bridge of large segmental arches of massive lateral thrust fell, all the others might collapse too since the thrusts of adjacent arches counterbalanced each other. The bridge would then have to be completely rebuilt. Independent arches also suited maintenance arrangements, whereby a different landowner or village was often responsible for each arch. Each could carry out his responsibility separately.

While the multi-arched lowland bridge with narrow spans was perfectly adequate for many locations, where necessary and where the site made it possible medieval masons were capable of building stable bridges with very large arches of the highest quality, such as Piercebridge, which might be described as the climax of medieval bridge-building in England (plate 22). Compelled to construct them to avoid the threat of flash floods, and encouraged by the

---

[84] On lateral thrust and stable arches, see Ruddock, *Arch Bridges*, 176; O'Connor, *Roman Bridges*, chaps. 8 and 9; Hopkins, *Span of Bridges*, 18–20.

[85] Hamill, *Bridge Hydraulics*, 38, notes that the water flows along the approach road embankments and has to curve particularly sharply; this can interfere with the main central jet of the river passing through the opening, 'a process which is very troublesome in extreme cases'; and see p. 219: 'the result of flow along the upstream face of the road embankment is effectively to reduce the width of the opening.'

[86] Britnell, 'Rochester Bridge', 71.   [87] 'Bridges of Bedfordshire', 113.

prevalence of rock for laying foundations, masons created bridges in the north of England, as in southern France, which stand comparison with the masonry bridges of the late eighteenth century. They compare favourably with the arched bridges the Romans built in southern Europe. Indeed, arches could be larger and piers narrower than Roman bridges; as a result, these northern bridges often provided more free waterway. They were utterly different from London Bridge.

Masons in pre-industrial England built bridges which, within their technical competence, met the needs of the site. The crucial test of all these types of bridges is how effectively they performed their function. There are two main measures of this: first, the continued use of the same design, and secondly, the survival of the bridges. Medieval bridges in England pass both tests. Around the twelfth century masons found a way of constructing large bridges in deep, tidal waters which was refined, but not surpassed until the industrial revolution. Typical lowland bridges with narrow arches, first constructed in the eleventh century, were still being built in the nineteenth century. Tall, wide, single-span bridges were being constructed in the highland zone in the 1950s, their profile unchanged from structures of the 1450s.

Many medieval bridges are still standing. More have disappeared, but it is well worth considering why. Some collapsed because of the effects of exceptional floods, inadequate maintenance, or poor construction. On the other hand, many others, which survived into the eighteenth century, were demolished. The peak period for demolition was the century from *c.*1770 to *c.*1870. The main reason was that, like Looe Bridge or the Great Bridge at Burton-on-Trent, which were pulled down in 1853 and 1864 respectively, they were too narrow for increasing volumes of traffic.[88] The bridges, some of which had survived for 500 years, were usually not fundamentally unsound, although engineers and architects with a vested interest in their demolition often claimed they were. They also argued that finally a better type of bridge could be constructed. However, the replacements do not always seem to have been an improvement. An account of the old bridge in the *Burton Weekly News* of 1876 observed: 'Although it may not have attracted special attention the line of the Old Bridge across the valley was one of an almost continuous unbroken water surface here, the channels of the Trent now two in number, being then divided into three, and to this was due the line of curvature of the Bridge, as it was necessary for each buttress to be placed at right angles with the flow of the stream,

---

[88] *Cornish Bridges*, 67–70: 'It is a thousand pities that the builders of Looe Bridge did not make it 9 ft. wide as Wadebridge. If they had done this, the old bridge might have been spared'; Rye, 'Burton-on-Trent Bridge', 17.

and to this fact is due the long life of the Old Bridge.'[89] The author added that the old bridge was not inferior to the modern. The arches of the new bridge, thrown across the west branch of the river, had the advantage in height and span, and the buttresses were also of less bulk. However, because they stood diagonally to the natural flow of the stream, they formed an obstacle to its course of greater area than that of the old bridge, and consequently the freedom of the actual river passage was reduced to less than half the diameter of the arches. Writing over twenty years later, in 1901, H. A. Rye noted that thirty of the thirty-four arches of the old bridge at the time of its demolition were ribbed and therefore likely to be medieval. He concluded: 'This to my mind is very strong evidence that in spite of the storm, flood and age, the old Bridge had stood well, not more than three or four arches had been so destroyed as to necessitate total rebuilding; and had the ancient Bridge been widened throughout its length, as so many of our bridges have been treated, it would have been with us to this day, and I doubt not would, with proper repair, have outlasted the new Bridge.'[90]

[89] Ibid. 18–19.   [90] Ibid. 21.

9

Keeping the Bridge Network in Use

It was one thing for skilled masons and carpenters to build an extensive network of well-designed, mostly stone bridges, another to ensure that they remained in use. The traditional view has been that this proved impossible. Fifty years ago de Maré, following Jusserand and Jackman, concluded that 'the tale of medieval bridges, including even great London Bridge itself, is one of continual catastrophe. The larger ones in particular were always in trouble.'[1] The most recent works continue this long tradition. We are told that: 'Documentary evidence suggests that medieval bridges were so often unsafe and so commonly left in disrepair that a ferry may have been regarded as safer and more reliable.'[2]

These opinions are inherently implausible. We are asked to believe that a fortune would be spent on constructing bridges, but that the effort would be not put into maintaining and repairing them. The evidence supports the contrary view: through the power of the state and the self-interest, generosity, and enterprise of many individuals, vast resources were mobilized for the upkeep of bridges. As a result, the network of bridges was kept open to travellers. Most bridges at most times remained in use.

THE TRADITIONAL VIEW

This is not to deny that the traditional view is superficially attractive and contains some elements of truth. Many bridges collapsed, at least partially, at one time or another. Some fell because of poor workmanship. Exceptionally severe floods swept others away, especially in upland areas. Timber bridges needed constant repair, and stone bridges required regular maintenance. Without it,

---

[1] E. De Maré, *The Bridges of Britain* (London, 1954), 59.   [2] Crook, *Medieval Bridges*, 9.

they could soon fall into serious disrepair, to be followed by the collapse of an arch or arches. River banks, abutments, and piers were an ideal position for vegetation to flourish and this, if unchecked, could cause serious damage to the masonry, with major consequences. As Jervoise pointed out, 'the small decays and weaknesses which a wall may endure unshaken for many years will soon destroy the margin of safety of [a bridge's] piers and arches'.[3] Bridges could also be undermined by small changes to the environment of a river. A log trapped near a pier could scour the foundations (plate 20). Blocked arches could lead to disaster, and the authorities were keen to get obstructions removed. Thus in 1392 an order was made that rafts of timber should not be allowed to obstruct the arches of or damage Ouse Bridge, York.[4]

Nor can it be denied that there is a great deal of evidence about the difficulties facing those who struggled to keep bridges open. The problems of important bridges are well documented. Few were more central to the road system than Huntingdon Bridge on the Old North Road (plate 12). In the fourteenth century, it was described as the 'public passage from north to south'.[5] Unfortunately, it was frequently broken. The records from the late thirteenth to late fourteenth century present a grim picture. In 1276 it was 'so broken that it is almost impassable for passengers on horseback or on foot'.[6] To repair it a pontage was granted in 1279.[7] It was destroyed by a severe flood laden with ice during the winter of 1293–4.[8] Work to rebuild it continued for a number of years: in 1300 the king gave twenty-four oaks for the work on the bridge; a few years later at least 520 marks were spent on it.[9] However, by 1329 it was again 'in a ruinous state, in many places broken through, and at one part threatening to fall'; two years later, to alleviate the problems, permission was given to build a causeway from the bridge to Godmanchester across the king's land.[10] Pontages were granted for its repair in 1344 and 1356.[11] Eight years later we hear that it 'had been long ruinous to the nuisance of all the country and of men passing by'. In 1370 the bridge was either to be repaired or rebuilt, but foundations could not be laid because the water level was too high; orders were given to open all the water gates to mills and ponds by the bridge to reduce the level. Payments of £200 were made for repairing it.[12] In all, this very important

[3] *South*, 4.   [4] *York Memorandum Book*, ed. M. Sellers and J. Percy, 3 vols., Surtees Soc. (1918), i. 33.
[5] *CCR (1364–8)*, 39–40.   [6] *Mid and Eastern*, 100.   [7] *CPR (1272–81)*, 331.
[8] *Rolls etc. of Bishop Sutton*, v. 123.
[9] *CCR (1296–1302)*, 343; PRO E13/27/ Membrane 39 dorse. I am grateful to Dr Paul Brand for this information.
[10] *CPR (1327–30)*, 379; *Calendar of Inquisitions ad quod damnum*, List and Indexes PRO 17, ccxiv, No. 14.
[11] *CPR (1343–5)*, 252; (1354–8), 357.
[12] *CCR (1364–8)*, 39–40; (1369–74), 140; *English Medieval Architects*, 18.

bridge was in a poor state of repair on perhaps seven occasions in little more than a century, and was completely rebuilt at least once.

War was an additional cause of destruction. In 1264, during the Baronial Wars, Henry III ordered his sheriffs to break down all the bridges over the Severn except the bridge at Gloucester which was to be fortified. Fords and ferries were to be obstructed.[13] Eight years later a pontage was granted in favour of Worcester Bridge, which had lately been destroyed by Prince Edward and other 'fideles'.[14] The crossing at Berwick-on-Tweed was particularly difficult to keep in use, both because it formed the boundary between England and Scotland and because of the great width of the river at this point.[15] The bridge was swept away in the floods of 1199, when the town was under the control of the king of Scotland. He wished to rebuild it, but the bishop of Durham, who owned the land on the south bank, initially refused to give his permission.[16] Later the Scots proved to be as troublesome as the river. In 1347 we hear that they had destroyed the bridge when they had held the town, and a pontage was granted for its rebuilding.[17] Whether or not it was reconstructed at this time, there was no bridge at the site fifty years later.[18]

It was not just the most important bridges which were frequently broken. The many pontage grants which were made to provide funds for bridges in need of repair seem to tell a sorry story of the state of many major bridges. In 1332 grants were made which licensed the collection of tolls for between three and five years on traffic crossing a bridge near Nantwich, and on bridges at Atherstone and New Malton. The money was to be applied to the repair of the bridges. In the following year the beneficiaries were the bridges at Wansford, Wigan, Yarm, and Croft. In 1334 grants were issued to repair bridges at Worcester, Maidenhead, Peterborough, Bridgnorth, Holland Bridge, and Hereford.[19]

Lesser bridges seemed to have suffered similar problems. In any year, in any county, a number of bridges and causeways were in need of repair. During the Sussex Eyre of 1279 presentments were made that bridges at Robertsbridge, Stockbridge, and 'Machambrigg' (across the River Medway) were out of repair. If we move on to the next century, the situation is no better. Presentments before the king at Aylesbury in Buckinghamshire in Trinity Term 1351 relate to a bridge between Wolverton and Bradwell and bridges at Long Crendon and Olney which were in a similar state. In 1387 it was claimed that the causey

[13] *CCR* (*1261–4*), 374.   [14] *CPR* (*1266–72*), 639.   [15] *North*, 2–3.
[16] Roger of Howden, *Chronica*, ed. W. Stubbs, 4 vols. (RS, 1868–71), iv. 98.
[17] *CPR* (*1345–8*), 439.   [18] *CPR* (*1399–1401*), 536; (*1413–16*), 386.
[19] *CPR* (*1330–4*), 378, 259, 309, 397, 408–9, 514, 536, 555; (*1334–8*), 12, 14, 53.

from Faringdon to Radcot Bridge, Marcham Causey between Marcham and Abingdon, and *Stokkyngbrugge* near Southcot were in disrepair.[20]

These were bridges which someone was liable to repair. Bridges which no one was bound to repair or which lacked a benefactor were even more likely to have been in a bad state. Reflecting on the problems of Rochester Bridge, which was supported by a well-endowed bridge estate, Jusserand observed:

It may be imagined what fate awaited unendowed country bridges. The alms from the passers-by proved insufficient, so that little by little, nobody repairing them, the arches wore through, the parapets were detached, not a cart passed but fresh stones disappeared in the river, and soon carriages and riders could not venture without danger over the half-demolished building. If moreover a flood should occur, all was over with the bridge and often with the imprudent or hurried travellers.[21]

By 1530 the situation seems to have become so bad, with so many bridges in poor condition and no one responsible for their repair, that Henry VIII's government decided that it had to take action. The Statute of 22 Henry VIII, 'an act concerning the amendment of bridges in highways', reorganized the system of bridge repair. It put JPs in charge of enquiring into defects and awarding process against offenders, and made provision for the county to raise a rate for the repair of those bridges which no one was responsible for.[22]

A NEW INTERPRETATION

Strong though the argument in support of traditional views about the state of bridges might seem, a more considered examination of the evidence leads to a completely different interpretation. From the eighth to the eighteenth century a very considerable effort was put into maintenance and repair and a great deal of money was spent. Most bridges were in an acceptable state of repair for most of the time, but even well-maintained bridges need to be repaired from time to time. The key question is how effectively and quickly repairs could be made. When out of repair, bridges could usually still be used. Temporary repairs with planks could be made if an arch collapsed. If a large part of a bridge fell, a temporary bridge could swiftly be erected while new arches or even a new bridge were constructed. The result was that by the late middle ages, when the evidence is available, at any time the great majority of bridge crossings were useable.

---

[20] PRO, JUST 1/915, m. 23, m. 27d, m. 4d.; Flower, *Works*, i. 22–4; i, 4, 13, 17.
[21] *Wayfaring Life*, 31–2.   [22] *Statutes of the Realm*, iii. 321–3; and see Chap. 11.

At some bridges work was constant. Continuous expenditure on maintenance and repair is recorded in long series of accounts prepared by the bridge
masters and bridge wardens of a number of large, well-endowed bridges. The
most detailed surviving records are the very full week-by-week accounts of
the London bridge masters. Those extant date from 1381, but accounts were
produced before then. The most complete series are the 345 rolls relating to
Exeter Bridge. Annual income and expenditure account rolls of the new bridge
at Rochester were produced soon after the bridge was finished in 1391, although
between then and the mid-sixteenth century quite a few are missing, particularly after 1508.[23]

Accounts relating to a considerable number of other bridges also survive,
albeit the documentation is usually incomplete. Among these are the accounts
for the Henley Church and Bridge Estate which begin in the fourteenth century, and for Kingston-on-Thames Bridge from the sixteenth century.[24] A
considerable number of bailiff's accounts (presumably because they, rather
than bridge wardens, supervised the work on the bridge) survive which record
the work carried out at St Ives Bridge in the fourteenth and fifteenth centuries;
in the following century work on Barford Bridge and Harrold Bridge, further
upstream, is described.[25] These surviving records imply the existence of a much
larger body of evidence. Accounts detailing expenditure on major bridges were
probably very common by the late middle ages.

The fact that accounts were kept at all is a sign of the attention paid to the
upkeep of bridges. In addition, they provide detailed evidence of the endless
activity on routine maintenance and repair, as well as the additional work in
times of trouble. The records demonstrate the many different types of work
which were undertaken. The St Ives accounts show the typical repairs made to
a large timber bridge (it was rebuilt in stone in the next century). In 17–18
Richard II 43s. 6d. was spent *inter alia* on paying for men to saw planks at
Ramsey, carting planks from the wood to the bridge. Two carpenters carried
out repairs at the bridge site; they were paid 4d. per day for twenty-two days.

[23] The London accounts are printed in *London Bridge Accounts, 1381–1538*, ed. V. Harding and L. Wright,
London Rec. Soc., 31 (1995). For the Exeter Bridge rolls, see Dyson et al., 'The Maintenance and Repair of
London Bridge', in *London Bridge*, 119. The Rochester account rolls are fully discussed and summarized in
Appendix B of *Traffic and Politics* see also *York Bridgemesters' Accounts*, trans. P. M. Stell, Historical Sources
for York Archaeology after AD 1100, 2 (2003).

[24] *Henley Borough Records, Assembly Books, i–iv, 1395–1543*, ed. P. M. Briers, Ox. Rec. Soc., 41
(1960–1); *Kingston-upon-Thames Bridgewardens' Accounts, 1526–67*, ed. N. J. Williams, Surrey Rec. Soc., 22
(1955).

[25] The accounts relating to the bridge at St Ives are preserved in the PRO as SC6 883/1–27; for the bridges
at Harrold and Barford, see 'Bridges of Bedfordshire', 28, 55.

This year the river flooded and for eleven days two workmen were also paid 4*d.* per day to shore up and repair the bridge. Work was also regularly done on the approaches to the bridge. Accounts regularly record payments for digging up sand and clay and carrying it to the site to raise the height of the causeway.[26]

Work on stone bridges was equally varied. For instance, the accounts of the wardens of Long Bridge, Barnstaple, for 1458–9 record *inter alia* one day's wages and food for John the helier and his man and £1. 0*s.* 10*d.* on 41 lbs. of lead.[27] The lead was presumably used both to enable iron clamps to be sunk into the stonework, and for pipes and gutters for drainage purposes. A few years later payments were made for breaking up ice around the piers which threatened bridges at Nottingham.[28] Foundations often required attention: sixteenth-century accounts for Barford Bridge refer to workmen who were paid for eight days work digging gravel and earth about the arches and bottom of the bridge. The parapet was mended at the same time; a payment referred to 'creast stones which was taken owt of the water and . . . mending the toppe of the bridge with lyme and stone that was left'.[29]

The weekly expenditure accounts for London Bridge show in great detail the work done at a very large, wealthy bridge, which was in need of constant attention, particularly to the foundations. A permanent workforce was employed, including a core team of masons, carpenters, and 'tidemen', who worked on the bridge starlings. In the later middle ages there were normally a master mason and four to six others, and a larger number of carpenters, often eight or ten, working both on the bridge and its houses, and the properties of the bridge estate. Others worked continuously on the starlings. The accounts from the week ending 19 April 1381 to 4 January 1382 show that about ten hours per week was spent at low tide driving piles, chiefly elm logs tipped with iron pile shoes. By 1480–1 twenty-two labourers were working a huge pile-driver, called a 'gibbet ram', to drive very long piles at the edge of the starlings deep into the river bed. Chalk rubble was purchased by the boatload and used to infill the starlings and the gullies created between the starlings by the current.[30]

Accounts were usually drawn up by bridge wardens or bridge masters, who were appointed specifically to take responsibility for the upkeep of major bridges. They are a further indication of how seriously routine maintenance and repair were taken. There are references to them by the twelfth century, and by the thirteenth century they were relatively common. For instance,

[26] PRO SC6 883/11, PRO SC6 883/20.
[27] *Reprint of Barnstaple Records*, ed. J. R. Chanter and T. Wainwright, 2 vols. (Barnstaple, 1900), ii. 234–5.
[28] *Mid and Eastern*, 10–11.   [29] 'Bridges of Bedfordshire', 28.
[30] Dyson et al., 'Repair of London Bridge', 121–5.

we hear of bridge wardens at York and Henley in the first half of the century, at Wallingford by 1258, and at London by 1284.[31] By the late middle ages it is probable that the affairs of most major bridges were overseen by a bridge warden.

The wardens had two main functions. They looked after the income of the bridge, collecting rents from the endowment, repairing properties owned by the bridge estate, and sometimes encouraging donations. They also checked the state of the bridge, buying materials, authorizing repairs, paying and supervising masons, carpenters, and other craftsmen who did the work which the accounts describe in considerable detail. Occasionally the wardens were masons: the great Henry Yevele was a London bridge master.[32] One of their most important tasks was to inspect the bridge regularly. At Rochester in the later middle ages the wardens routinely checked the depth of the water flowing under the bridge to ensure that its foundations were not being eroded by the force of river.[33] Other tasks included examining foundations, and investigating the underside of arches, looking for cracks. Mr Wallis has provided a good description of what this job involved, when he was the Dorset Bridge Engineer from the 1950s to the 1970s. Such an inspection might have been made at any time after the first stone arched bridges were constructed: 'One day I was in our dinghy probing the foundations of Whitemill Bridge, the Norman style bridge . . . when my ranging rod went right in under the stonework of one of the piers. The more I probed the more cavities I found, and these had obviously been scoured out by the winter's severe flooding.' Some of the timber foundations had rotted and the heavy structure which weighed perhaps a thousand tons was sinking into the river bed (plate 23).[34]

The bridge wardens' importance is shown in a number of ways. First, those responsible for major bridges were often paid a sizeable income, which was at least in part an indication that they were undertaking a vital task. Robert Rowe was bridge warden during the construction of the new bridge at Rochester and for many years after it was completed. He has been described as 'one of the key figures in the management of bridge affairs' during this period. He was of a landholding family but of lower social rank than Sir John Cobham and Sir Robert Knollys, who were the major benefactors of the new bridge. Rowe was paid a stipend for his work as warden of £6. 13s. 8d. in 1398–9. His fellow warden for the period from 1398–9 to 1415–16 was John Wolcy, who seems to have been a junior warden and was paid £2 in 1399–1400.[35]

---

[31] *VCH City of York*, 516; *Henley Borough Records*, 4; *CPR* (1234–58), 651; Watson, *Construction of the Colechurch Bridge*, 84.

[32] Harvey, *Henry Yevele*, 28–9, 44.   [33] Britnell, 'Rochester Bridge', 60.

[34] Wallis, *Dorset Bridges*, 25.   [35] Britnell, 'Rochester Bridge', 58.

Secondly, problems in repairing a bridge were quite often blamed on the lack of a warden or someone similar to supervise its affairs. In 1223 the work on the bridge (*operatio pontis*) at Kingston upon Thames was in desuetude through the absence of assistance and advice (*auxilium et consilium*); accordingly the custody of the bridge and all its appurtenances were committed to Henry of St Albans and Matthew of Kingston.[36] In 1329 a commission found that legacies bequeathed to Huntingdon Bridge had not been applied to its repair, 'for want of a keeper'.[37] When its bridge across the Trent was in trouble in the 1370s, the town of Nottingham, the county, and surrounding counties petitioned parliament for permission to choose two wardens, one from the town and another from the county, 'to buy and receive lands, tenements and rents for them and their successors, without any licence, for the maintenance of the bridge'.[38]

Public officials, in particular the sheriff and his subordinates, brought to bear the power of the state to maintain the bridge network. First, they ensured that those liable for repairs carried them out. By the thirteenth century we can see in detail the routine which had been established to make sure this happened. The sheriff, or a seigneurial official in a private hundred, enquired into the condition of bridges and causeways twice a year at his tourn, and the justices in eyre, at longer intervals, held inquiries into his performance of this duty.[39] Those who failed to maintain their bridge were fined. For instance, in 1395 a Lincolnshire jury found that a bridge between Leadenham and Broughton in the king's road (between Boston and Newark, today the A17) was defective by default of the former township which was amerced 3s. 4d.[40] Aspects of this routine were relatively recent in the thirteenth century, but much of the practice was probably ancient.

There were lengthy disputes about liability, as a number of high-profile cases show, but it should not be assumed that this was the norm. Sometimes those charged with failing to maintain a bridge arrived at court, admitted their liability, and promised to get the work done.[41] The local bridge was often very important for the prosperity of those who had to repair it. At least some of those responsible for the upkeep of a bridge conscientiously applied themselves to the job. Ramsey Abbey maintained the bridge and causeway at St Ives. As the account rolls described above show, its bailiffs seem to have supervised their upkeep diligently. Estate officials performed the same task for Bolton Priory in respect of its bridges at Bolton and Kildwick.[42]

---

[36] *Rot. Lit. Claus.*, i. 558, 579. [37] *CPR (1327–30)*, 379.

[38] *Rot. Parl.*, ii. 350a. Sometimes, others, e.g. hermits, performed some of the functions of a bridge warden; see Chap. 11 below.

[39] H. M. Cam, *The Hundred and the Hundred Rolls* (London, repr. 1963), 104.

[40] Flower, *Works*, i. 262. [41] For an example where liability was acknowledged, see ibid. 24.

[42] Kershaw, *Bolton Priory*, 122.

Very large sums had to be raised to build bridges. It is unlikely to have been the norm to spend so much on construction while repair was totally ignored, although it doubtless happened occasionally. Indeed, we know that often those who built or rebuilt a bridge also had an eye to its future maintenance. Some contracts for constructing a bridge also include a payment to the mason to maintain and repair it. Nicholas Blackburn made provision in his will for his executors to make good any faults in the four large Yorkshire bridges he built in the 1420s and 1430s. New bridges were endowed, as at Abingdon, and a number of major bridges built up large endowments. Inevitably those repairing bridges thought they had insufficient funds and some bridges suffered from a shortage of funds, but it is by no means certain that this was a general failing.[43]

Although the construction of new bridges at new sites was uncommon between 1550 and 1750, maintenance, repair, and reconstruction continued. The records of the quarter sessions show the same constant activity as earlier records. For instance, in the 1580s and 1590s the justices at North Riding quarter sessions authorized the expenditure of £200 on Greta Bridge; the 'pillars' were undermined, and unless the work were done immediately the whole bridge would go. Two hundred marks were spent on repairing Ulshaw Bridge.[44] C. Chalkin has examined expenditure by counties on bridges between 1650 and 1830. The biggest spender was the West Riding of Yorkshire, which was spending *c.*£530 per year on repairs and rebuilding in the early eighteenth century.[45]

There is some evidence that the funds raised and the very considerable effort put into bridge maintenance were not wasted: bridges in the late middle ages and beyond were in a far better state of repair than has usually been assumed. A few very big bridges like Berwick Bridge or Rochester Bridge were constantly in trouble, but they were probably the exception.[46] While there is evidence that many other bridges were at one time or other broken, it is important to put this into perspective. There were a very large number of bridges in medieval England: at any time some were out of repair, fewer out of use, and an even smaller number had completely collapsed. It is, however, not surprising that this should have been the case, or that there should have been disputes about who should repair them, or that those undertaking their repair or rebuilding should seek money or other assistance. Bridges are always in need of repair, and collapses have continued to happen, even in recent times. It is likely that any

---

[43] The cost of construction and major repair, and the extent of endowments are described in more detail in Chaps. 10 and 11.

[44] *North Riding Quarter Sessions, 1605–1791*, iii. 17, 21, 31.   [45] Chalkin, *Public Building*, 104.

[46] See Chap. 8. Britnell observed that shortage of funds was not the main problem at Rochester; rather it was the inadequacy of the technology available: Britnell, 'Rochester Bridge', 75.

bridge which survived for 500 years would be broken at some time or other. The evidence of the sheriff's tourns and the eyres in the late middle ages and of the quarter sessions in the seventeenth century provide a very similar picture of the condition of England's bridges. They do not suggest an endemic crisis. Rather, it seems that a relatively small percentage of bridges were out of repair at any time, let alone unuseable.

Even what seems like the best evidence that the bridge network was in crisis by the late middle ages—the Bridge Statute of Henry VIII, and the countless entries in the Patent Rolls year after year of pontage grants—are not as convincing as they might at first appear. The Statute seems very important in retrospect, because the system it established had such an important future and led eventually to the county taking responsibility for most of the bridges within its boundaries. It is, however, not certain that it was needed to deal with a national failure of the bridge network. Its first purpose was to pass the responsibility for hearing cases about bridge repair and enforcing liabilities to JPs.[47] It was part of a general expansion of their work. At the same time it was decided to make the county directly responsible for repairing bridges which no one was bound to repair. There were a significant number of such bridges, but not all lacked the resources necessary to repair them. Many a bridge was funded by benefactors. It would not be surprising if the origins of this section of the Act lay in a few high-profile cases.

The Crown's grant of pontages, that is, the right to take tolls on vehicles passing under or over the bridge for its repair, is also undeniably evidence that most major bridges were in disrepair from time to time. However, in almost every case the grant makes clear that, although it might be in a poor, even dangerous state, although it might pose a great risk to life, the bridge was still in use because tolls were to be taken on travellers, vehicles, and goods passing over it.[48] Occasionally tolls were only taken on river traffic, because the bridge was impassable, and we know of at least one bridge which collapsed before the grant had expired or repairs could be undertaken.[49] These seem, however, to have been the exception. Usually tolls were collected on goods crossing over the bridge and repairs were undertaken.[50]

---

[47] *Statutes of the Realm*, iii. 321.

[48] Sometimes the grants permitted the collection of tolls on goods passing under the bridge (but many bridges were not across the navigable sections of rivers).

[49] By 1280 London Bridge was in a poor state because its huge endowment had been granted after the Baronial Wars to Queen Eleanor, who neglected it. In January 1281 it was granted a pontage, but it was too late, and in February the bridge fell (Dyson and Watson, 'London Bridge is Broken Down', in *London Bridge*, 128–9).

[50] See Chap. 11.

The *Life of St Anselm* contains the following story which describes the crossing of a broken timber bridge between 1109 and 1114 by a monk called Robert, who was in the service of Ralph, bishop of Rochester. It vividly demonstrates that a bridge in considerable disrepair could still be used :

At about this time he was going over London Bridge when he was visited by a sudden misfortune through an accident to his horse which carried his baggage. The bridge was broken in places, and as the horse was being led without proper care by a servant, it fell into the river, at a point where the force of the current and the depth of the water were at the greatest. The brother was unmindful of everything else in his great anxiety for the book of Father Anselm of blessed memory which was packed in his bag, among his other things. He went across the bridge as best he could, praying the Lord for the safe-keeping and recovery of the book, by the memory of him who had written it.

As we might expect, the horse swam to the shore, and the book was found safe and dry.[51]

Through neglect, the overwhelming power of nature, a combination of the two, or some other misfortune, sometimes an arch or arches or even an entire bridge collapsed. This eventuality which, at least temporarily, made the bridge unuseable, was a regular occurrence in the north, although less common in lowland England. Even London Bridge, for all its faults, remained in use for all but a few years. De Maré, as we have seen, thought the history of London Bridge was one of continual catastrophe, but he noted of the bridge, which stood for 600 years: 'Its only major structural calamity in the stone fabric itself was the collapse of five arches in 1282 due partly to the severity of the winter and the pressure of the ice, partly to the serious state of neglect the bridge had suffered through lack of those funds Queen Eleanor had misappropriated.'[52]

A fallen stone arch could often be patched up with planks for a modest sum. The manorial bailiff's accounts for 1532 list repairs to the bridge at Harrold (Great Ouse) (plate 4). A carpenter was paid 12*d.* for felling timber, sawyers 2*s.* 8½*d.* for sawing it into planks. The cost of carriage was 6*d.* Finally, the carpenter and his man were paid 11*d.* per day for two-and-a-half days for laying the planks. The total cost was 6*s.* 6*d.*[53] Repairs could also quickly be made to timber bridges. In 1088 there was a serious rebellion in favour of Robert Curthose. The rebels devastated lands as far as Worcester, the see of the aged St Wulfstan. To prevent them from approaching the city the defenders damaged the bridge

[51] Eadmer, *The Life of St. Anselm, Archbishop of Canterbury,* ed. and trans. R. W. Southern (Oxford, 1962), 148.
[52] De Maré, *Bridges of Britain,* 77; as we show below, a number of arches also fell in the 15th cent.
[53] 'Bridges of Bedfordshire', 55–6.

over the Severn. Subsequently it was decided to mount an attack from the city, and emergency repairs seem rapidly to have been made to the bridge.[54]

Where a significant part of a major bridge collapsed a temporary bridge was usually erected. This could be done relatively swiftly. In the first week of January 1437 damage was done to London Bridge by the build-up of ice around the piers. Then, between 5 and 12 January, the Stonegate and its two adjoining arches collapsed. Immediately a gang of seventeen carpenters were paid to work day and night on the bridge. Their task was probably to shore up the remains of the tower and of the bridge to prevent further collapse. Elm logs, normally used as starling piles, which were stored in the Bridge House Yard, seem to have been employed to stabilize the masonry. Work began in the next week on the construction of a pontoon bridge, and payments were made in the week ending 2 February for the carriage of two great posts and for 'two cart loads of braces and rails' for this bridge. By 9 March thirty carpenters were at work, and by the end of March it may have been possible to cross the bridge on foot.[55]

At York too the city authorities reacted rapidly after the two central arches of Ouse Bridge fell in January 1565. A ferry was in place by February. A temporary wooden bridge supported by boats was erected by April. It was not possible to rebuild the bridge that year because by September the river levels made it impossible to work on the foundations, but work began the following year. The winter break seems to have allowed time for reconsidering the design. In April 1566 it was decided to build a single bow (plate 3). The new arch, described by Camden as the largest in England, was built with great speed and had been completed by October.[56]

Finally, there seem to be two key pieces of evidence which suggest that the basic system of repair was, for all its faults, essentially effective. The first is that so few bridges disappeared. Had the situation been as bad as some have suggested this would not have happened: lack of resources, combined with incompetent organization, would have meant that once a bridge collapsed it would have been lost for ever. However, we only know of a handful of sites where this happened, and these losses were outweighed by the construction of new bridges.[57] With very few exceptions, if a bridge or part of a bridge fell, it was eventually rebuilt.

Secondly and most importantly, travellers did not commonly complain about the condition of bridges. They complained about highwaymen.[58] They

---

[54] *John of Worcester*, 25.　　　[55] Dyson and Watson, 'London Bridge is Broken Down', 129–130.
[56] Camden's comments are quoted in Palliser, *Tudor York*, 266–7; Horsley shows a plan of the temporary bridge at Newcastle following the collapse of arches of Tyne Bridge in 1771 (Horsley, *Eighteenth Century Newcastle*, 14).　　　[57] See Chap. 4.　　　[58] Fiennes, 225.

complained about the state of the roads, particularly across the midland clays and the fens.[59] On her way from Ely to Huntingdon through the fens, Celia Fiennes approached a bridge, but 'the road was so full of holes and quick sands I durst not venture, the water covering them over'.[60] Bridges are occasionally referred to: at Ripon she mentions that 'there are two good Bridges to the town, one was a rebuilding pretty large with several arches called Hewet (Hewick) Bridge, its often out of repair by reason of the force of the water that swells after great raines'.[61] This, however, was the exception. For the most part Fiennes, Defoe, and other travellers were impressed by the fine bridges they saw.[62]

Over 150 years before Celia Fiennes the situation was similar. Leland set off on his journeys in the same decade that the Henrician Bridge Statute was enacted. Poor bridges were not an obstacle to him. His *Itineraries* provide an excellent snapshot of the state of bridges. He crossed a huge number of them over a wide area of England and Wales, but rarely came across a bridge which was out of use. Very exceptionally, he noted that a bridge could not be used or had disappeared: 'Finkley Bridge . . . was throwne down 2 or 3 yeres ago for lake of reparations in tyme. It stode a mile above Dovesme [Durham].' He had to cross the Ure at West Tanfield by ferry, probably because the bridge had fallen.[63] However, for the most part he recorded not disasters of this kind, but lists the fine bridges he saw or heard about. Leland was not alone. A sixteenth-century German traveller, Von Wedel, observed that 'in England there are fine stone bridges everywhere even over small streams'.[64]

Leland and later Fiennes and Defoe were able to enjoy the benefits of a highly effective bridge network for a number of reasons. For the most part, by the end of the middle ages bridges were well built, substantial structures. Routine maintenance and repair was common. When bridges were out of repair they often remained useable, and when part of them collapsed they could be patched up. If the damage was very serious, temporary bridges could be erected until rebuilding had taken place. This achievement required huge resources and impressive organization. We turn to these subjects in Part III.

---

[59] Defoe, *Tour*, ii. 120–7. [60] Fiennes, 159. [61] Ibid. 83.
[62] e.g. Defoe, Tour, ii. 113. [63] Leland, v. 128–9; i. 83.
[64] Quoted in D. M. Palliser, *The Age of Elizabeth, 1547–1603* (Harlow, 1983), 272.

PART III

Economics and Society

10

Costs

The building, rebuilding, repair, and maintenance of the network of bridges was a huge task. Large labour forces were employed. Enormous quantities of stone, timber, lime, chalk, iron, and lead were used in construction, and very large sums of money spent. Ten thousand piles were found in the river bed at Rochester when the medieval bridge was demolished in the mid-nineteenth century.[1] The largest bridges were among the most expensive projects of their age. In the early nineteenth century £1 million was spent on Waterloo Bridge, making it the greatest public work of its age. In comparison the major new churches funded by the Church Building Acts of 1818 and 1824 were a fraction of the cost, between £10,000 and £20,000, a major hospital in the next decade £40,000, King's College, London University, £140,000.[2] Once a bridge was built spending did not end. Expenditure on their maintenance was probably greater than on any other type of building. Timber bridges required constant attention. Even stone bridges had to be regularly repaired and maintained. A few required very heavy, continuous expenditure: in the fifteenth century over £500 was spent, year in year out, on London Bridge; more when major repairs had to be carried out.[3] This was the same as the annual income of some members of the lay peerage.[4]

CONSTRUCTION COSTS

Over the centuries there is ever more evidence about investment. By the eleventh century we can see the size of the labour force mobilized for the repair of large bridges. By the later middle ages there is evidence about expenditure on

[1] Britnell, 'Rochester Bridge', 49.   [2] Chalkin, *Public Building*, 17–22.
[3] Dyson and Watson, 'London Bridge is Broken Down', 130.
[4] H. L. Gray, 'Incomes From Land in 1436', *EHR* 49 (1934), 607–39.

bridges of different construction and sizes in different parts of the country. It comes from many of the sources discussed in earlier chapters: accounts and contracts, wills, licences to alienate land, and legal and administrative records. Of course these documents have their shortcomings: in particular, until the sixteenth century none gives us the full cost of construction, nor even the estimated total cost. The surviving medieval contracts take the form of an agreement with a mason or carpenter, recording how much he was paid, but not the sums the clients spent on materials, carriage, foundations, and other works. All the extant bridge wardens' accounts post-date the construction of the bridges they relate to. Nevertheless, for all their limitations these sources are a good, if rough, guide to the often very large amounts spent.

From the early seventeenth century there is much fuller evidence: there are detailed estimates, which both show the total cost of construction and the relative costs of different aspects of the work, including piling, erecting arches, shaping stones, and the carriage of materials to the site. It is apparent that construction costs could vary considerably, even for bridges of similar overall span, depending on the site, foundations, and materials. Occasionally the differences were staggering: an eleven-arched brick bridge across the Thames at Sonning was built in 1773 for as little as £1,150; the contemporary bridge of seven stone arches at Maidenhead, less than 20 miles downstream, cost £15,424, an amount which was not unusual for a large stone bridge in this period.[5] Both bridges are still standing. Variations of such magnitude were, however, relatively uncommon. The type of foundations made a difference, but even the use of extensive piling instead of shallow foundations would usually not have added more than about 25–30 per cent to the cost. A bridge, founded on 'starlings', was built at Hexham from 1777 to 1780 for £5,700; its successor, constructed to an identical design from 1790 to 1795, but supported by a 'forest of piles', cost £8,000.[6]

Bridges in Yorkshire

We are particularly well informed about bridges in the West Riding in the seventeenth century, because the Riding had taken responsibility for many of them within a century of the passage of the Statute of Bridges, and details of expenditure on them is to be found in the quarter sessions records. These records are supplemented by other documents, in particular a number relating to building bridges over the Aire and Calder, which were published early in the last century. Together they show that the cost of stone bridges *c.*30 to *c.*50 metres long in this part of Yorkshire in the first half of the seventeenth century

---

[5] Ruddock, *Arch Bridges*, 240–2.   [6] Ibid. 98–101, 238.

was in the range of *c.*£200 to *c.*£450. The most expensive was a bridge of one giant arch over the River Aire at Kirkstall. Its span would probably have been on a par with the spans of Framwellgate Bridge (plate 5); that is, it would have rivalled the largest spans yet built in England, since by 1752 it had been replaced by a bridge of three arches, each of a 45 foot span. A paper endorsed 'A note taken of Cristall Bridge this 29th April, 1616' breaks down the cost of construction.[7] The total estimate for the bridge was £419. Among the major components was £50 for 140 piles to support the abutments. This included taking the timber to the site, preparing it, and driving the piles into the river bed. Building the abutments was estimated at £80. The charges for the erection of the arch were as follows: £20 for the timber for the centring of the arch, and £25 for erecting the centring in the river; £44 for the voussoirs for two arch rings, and £15 for putting them in place. Finally £90 was to be spent on the parapets, infill, and paving.

W. E. Preston, who published the Kirkstall Bridge agreement, also found a contract of 1601 for the construction of a bridge a few miles upstream at Apperley. Thomas Wallimsley, a mason, was to build in a year a two-arched bridge with spans of 44 feet for a mere £99. This was not the total cost, since it excluded materials, and carriage, which in the construction of Kirkstall Bridge had amounted to almost £100; the clients were also to provide workmen to help Wallimsley empty the coffer dams of water.[8] Nevertheless, even allowing for these additional costs, Apperley Bridge was significantly cheaper than Kirkstall Bridge. Possibly shallow foundations were used; possibly it was built of rubble.[9] Other near-contemporary Yorkshire bridges of similar total length cost a little more than Apperley Bridge and a little less than Kirkstall. Estimates made between 1638 and 1640 for rebuilding Cooper's Bridge over the Calder, Gargrave Bridge over the River Aire, and Hampsthwaite Bridge over the Nidd, all of *c.*40 metre total span, were all in excess of £350.[10]

Larger bridges in Yorkshire of over 50 metre total span usually cost rather more than £400 in the seventeenth century. In 1673–4 £1,000 was spent on reconstructing Ulshaw Bridge over the River Ure with four segmental arches. The most expensive bridge in the north of England of the late seventeenth century was constructed at Corbridge in 1674, at a probable cost of £3,000.[11] By way of comparison, expenditure on rebuilding major provincial churches in

---

[7] It is printed in Preston, *Aire and Calder Bridges*, 146–8.   [8] Ibid. 142–5.
[9] Several such relatively cheap, rubble stone bridges were constructed in Scotland after 1715 (Ruddock, *Arch Bridges*, 20–1).
[10] *West Riding Session Records*, ed. J. Lister, Yorks. Arch. Soc. Rec. Ser., 54 (1915), 67, 70, 200.
[11] Chalkin, *Public Building*, 111.

the first half of the eighteenth century varied from £2,000 to £5,000: for instance, a new church at Penrith cost £2,252 in 1720–2.[12]

The figures we have for the amounts spent on major medieval bridges in Yorkshire, although not precise, suggest that they cost similar amounts to the seventeenth-century bridges, taking account of the inflation in building costs. Although far from ideal, the best measure of these building costs currently available is probably that of building craftsmen's wage rates. These doubled between 1300 and 1400 and had doubled again by 1600; by the 1640s they were at three times their 1400 levels.[13] Ninety pounds, probably the equivalent of about £350 three hundred years later, was spent between 1304 and 1308 by Bolton Priory on rebuilding the still extant Kildwick Bridge over the Aire; it has four arches spanning in total *c*.40 metres.[14] Works on Scarborough Castle in 1336–7, the principal of which was building the great Stone Bridge, cost £74.[15] In 1435 the large sum of £100 was left for completing Kexby Bridge, today a seventeenth-century structure of *c*.45 metres total span.[16] A contract of 1485 provided 100 marks, excluding the amount spent on materials and their transport to the site and so on, for rebuilding Lady Bridge, Sheffield, with five relatively small 21 foot spans. This figure is rather lower than the others, but the full cost of Lady Bridge, which survived until the twentieth century, is likely to have considerably higher, probably well over £100.[17] Haulage alone would have been a significant expense, and could account for up to a third of the total construction cost of a small bridge.[18]

Catterick Bridge was considerably larger than these bridges with a total span of *c*.90 metres. As we have seen, under the contract of 1421 masons agreed to erect the stonework of the bridge of three very large arches for 260 marks (£173. 6*s*. 8*d*.).[19] This sum, once again, excluded other costs, including the materials (mainly stone and timber), haulage to the site, the coffer dam, and the work of carpenters on making the centring and scaffolding. Judging by what we know about these excluded items from the detailed breakdown of figures in the

---

[12] Chalkin, *Public Building*, 7.

[13] The following index is an approximate measure of building craftsmen wage rates in southern England, derived from Table 1 of H. Phelps Brown and S. Hopkins, *A Perspective of Wages and Prices* (1981): 1300—100; 1400—200; 1600—400; 1650—600. It does not take into account the cost of materials and transport. The 'index' is probably a reasonable if very rough guide to changing building costs.

[14] Kershaw, *Bolton Priory*, 122.   [15] *King's Works*, ii. 830.

[16] *Test. Ebor.*, 50. Some years earlier, in 1427 and 1429, recognizances had been enrolled on the Close Rolls for 500 marks in respect of building this bridge and Thornton Bridge over the lower Swale (*CCR (1422–9)*, 473).

[17] Hunter, *Sheffield*, 337.

[18] In 1710 £60 was spent on a small bridge between Rainford and Billinge in Lancashire, of which £20 was for carrying stone, sand, and other materials to the site (Chalkin, *Public Building*, 106).

[19] The contract is discussed at length in Chap. 7.

Kirkstall Bridge contract, the total estimate for the bridge would have been significantly more than 260 marks, probably well in excess of £250, and considerably more if the foundations were piled. The cost of constructing the great span of the central arch of Ouse Bridge, York, in the mid-sixteenth century was about £400, similar to the cost of Kirkstall Bridge. It presumably included reinforcing the foundations of the piers on which it rested.[20]

Bridges in the Midlands and South

Although the large inland bridges of the midlands and the south lacked the enormous spans of northern bridges, they were still very expensive. Several examples show the scale of expenditure. The first is Huntingdon Bridge, still a medieval structure of six arches with an overall span of more than 80 metres (plate 12). Part of the bridge may date from about 1300, when over 500 marks were contracted to be spent on it. Later, in 1370–5, £200 was spent on repairs or rebuilding.[21] The second is Redbridge, the lowest crossing of the Test in the tideway. In the seventeenth century it consisted of a main bridge, a number of smaller bridges, and a causeway. It was constantly damaged by tides. Works had to be carried out *c*.1320, when it was estimated that the repair of the bridge would cost 200 marks and its maintenance £2 per year.[22] By the time we have better documentation of the work undertaken it is clear that such expensive repairs were common. In 1682 a Fordingbridge mason had finished repairs to the bridge for £1,000. In 1696 £1,400 was needed. In 1725, when 'great rains and flouds' destroyed two stone arches and damaged the rest of the bridge, works cost over £1,100.[23]

The third example relates to the bridges at and near Abingdon and the long causeway between them. The 'Abingdon Bridge' poem tells us that Geoffrey Barbour, a Bristol merchant who retired to Abingdon, gave 1,000 marks for their construction. This very large sum may have been spent between 1416 when work began and 1417 when Barbour died; it covered the wages of the 300 men at work on the bridge in the summer of 1416. However, it by no means covered the full cost the undertaking. We know of other very generous benefactors. One, Sir Peter Bessils, provided the stone for the bridges from his quarries.[24] This was a generous donation: at this date the wardens of Rochester Bridge were paying 5*d.* per ton for ragstone, 10*d.* per ton for large ragstone, and

---

[20] £400 was ordered to be raised for the bridge by a local tax: *York Civic Records*, 6, ed. A. Raine, York Arch. Soc. Rec. Ser., 112 (1946), 100–23; and see Palliser, *Tudor York*, 267.

[21] *RCHM Hunts.*, 151; PR. E13/27/ Membrane 39 dorse; *English Medieval Architects*, 18.

[22] *Cal. Inq. Misc. (1307–49)*, 454.   [23] Chalkin, *Public Building*, 111–2.

[24] Leland, v. 77–8, 113–18.

4*d.* per foot for ashlar.[25] The three bridges near Abingdon would have required thousands of tons of stone (plate 15). Considerable amounts were also spent on middling-sized lowland bridges. The surprisingly large sum of 500 marks was left in 1426 for building Eastford Bridge over the Blackwater in Essex,[26] and over £200 was spent on repairing Chelmsford Great Bridge in the mid-sixteenth century.[27]

Smaller Medieval Bridges

Smaller, high-quality bridges were not cheap: in 1372 the eminent architect Henry Yevele contracted with the abbot of Westminster to rebuild Moulsham Bridge (*c.*15 metres span) over the River Can in Chelmsford for £23. 6*s.* 8*d.*[28] Simple stone bridges cost less. Two centuries later a contract survives for the construction of a small single-arched bridge at Polwheverell. It was to be 7 feet wide and had a 7 foot span. On 24 May 1572 Roger Hallard, a local mason,

hath bargained to make of new-hewed stone of moore stone . . . before the day of St James the Apostle [25 July] next ensueing under the manner and form following:

First the same Bridge is to be made with an Arch of hewn stone, the water course between the two side walls to be 7 foot broad with 2 squinches on the upper side and the walls of every end of the side walls to be of length 112 foot, and to make two crests of every side of the passage and ye Bridge, to be hewn stone above the Bridge rising 2 foot; and between the same two crests to be clear 7 foot way for wain-carriage and the bridge and the Arch to rise in altitude 7 foot and the parish to pay him for his labour £3 6s 8d and to find cleavers and all lime and sand.

Roger was bound to the sum of £6. 13*s.* 4*d.* to do the work, and he also agreed to maintain and repair the bridge during his lifetime.[29]

Timber and Brick Bridges

Timber bridges and brick bridges were considerably cheaper to build than stone bridges. In 1827 a bridge at Brigg in Lincolnshire was rebuilt in stone for the sum of £2,100, which was £650 more than a brick bridge.[30] In 1753 an estimate of £194 was made for a timber bridge at Lamberhurst on the borders of Kent and Sussex; this was 40 per cent cheaper than the stone bridge which was built.[31] The cost of a timber bridge over the Nene at Fotheringay of about

---

[25] Britnell, 'Rochester Bridge', 68.

[26] *The 50 Earliest Wills in the Court of Probate, London, 1387–1437,* ed. F. J. Furnivall (1882), 70.

[27] PRO SC6 Edward VI/91 Receiver of Duchy of Cornwall's Acct. for 3–4 Ed VI.

[28] Harvey, *Henry Yevele,* 31; the span of the present bridge is 14 m.

[29] *Cornish Bridges,* 24–5. Moor stone is the name for the granite stones found lying in the fields of Devon and Cornwall.

[30] Chalkin, *Public Building,* 117.   [31] Ibid. 104.

30 metres span was put at £60 in 1551. This was one-third the cost (£180) of a bridge, built twenty years later, of 'three stone piers in the river and two "jammes" with a timber superstructure for which ten trees were felled and quartered'.[32]

Although substantial timber bridges cost less than stone bridges of similar span, they were, nevertheless, a significant expenditure. The contract for building a predominantly timber bridge at Newark in 1485 provided £40 for a carpenter to build a wooden bridge of twelve spans of oak between stone abutments.[33] In the early sixteenth century John Gye, a carpenter, agreed to take down and rebuild the Great Bridge over the Cam at Cambridge for £40.[34] The same sum was left in 1545 to complete the building of a timber bridge, over 100 metres in total length, at Chepstow across the Wye near its junction with the Severn.[35]

The Great Bridges

Finally, there was a small number of very large bridges. The work undertaken at, and expenditure on, these structures was on a quite different scale from expenditure on other bridges. It is evident that in the eleventh century very large work forces were assembled for their repair, as, we can reasonably assume, they had been for centuries. The Domesday Book entry for Chester—that the reeve could summons a man from each hide of the county for the repair of the wall and bridge—give some idea of the potential scale of the work at what would have been a very busy construction site.[36]

Dee Bridge was a timber deck bridge. From the late twelfth century the great estuarine bridges began to be rebuilt with stone arches, at immense cost. We do not know the total expenditure on any of them, but we can get a glimpse of its scale from the substantial repairs carried out in later centuries. The first of these bridges was Old London Bridge, where work began in 1176. Records of the cost of repair and maintenance begin in the fourteenth century. Major work was very expensive: in the year when the Stonegate and two adjoining arches collapsed, £825 was spent, and expenditure on reconstruction continued for many years.[37]

Two other large bridges had been built within fifty years of the completion of London Bridge. The first was Exe Bridge, Exeter, which was constructed *c*.1200 (plate 2). The *Description of the Citie of Excestre*, written *c*.1600, claimed that Nicholas Gervys and Walter, his son, built the bridge:

[32] *King's Works*, iii. 249–51.   [33] Salzman, *Building*, 546–7.
[34] *English Medieval Architects*, 127.   [35] *Wales and Western*, 124.   [36] See Chap. 11.
[37] Dyson and Watson, 'London Bridge is Broken Down', 130–1.

In their tyme was no bridge of stone over Ryver of Exe but onely certaine Clappers of Tymbre . . . in the wynter the passage was very daungerose and many people thereby perrished and wer carryed awaye with the floudde and Drowned. Theise twoo good men . . . thought . . . to devise howe abridge their might be buylded. . . . [They decided] to make a generall Collection throughout the whole Realme . . . And . . . the founde such favor and love emonge all men both highe and lowe that in fewe yeres they had Collected . . . of all good men . . . Contribushions to the valewe of £10,000 which mony they so husbandryed that they Dyd not onely buylde a very fayre bridge of stone but also purchased certaine Lande which they gave to the same for a perpetual meanetenance therof.[38]

This account was made 400 years after the deeds it records, but even if the figures were invented, they had presumably to be plausible to a sixteenth-century audience. The second bridge was Tyne Bridge, Newcastle, traditionally dated to the mid-thirteenth century. In 1369 the cost of repairs to the foundations and other parts of it were estimated to be in excess of £1,500.[39]

Great stone bridges continued to be constructed in the fourteenth and fifteenth centuries. Dee Bridge, Chester, with its seven red sandstone arches and total span of *c.*130 metres (plate 13), is thought to have been rebuilt to the design of the Black Prince's mason, Henry de Snelleston, in the fourteenth century. Unfortunately we can only get a glimpse of the cost: in 1347–8 Sir Thomas de Ferrers, the justiciar of Chester, undertook for £150 to complete the arches and their parapets and to construct a tower at the Flintshire end of the bridge; in 1349–50 the sum of £83. 6s. 8d. was paid to Sir Thomas.[40] Rochester Bridge, constructed in the deep, tidal River Medway in the late fourteenth century, was an even greater undertaking. Sir John Cobham and Sir Robert Knolles, its major benefactors, together with others were purchasing stone for the bridge for the huge sum of £360 in 1387, and in the account of 1392 receipts of £250 were received from Sir Robert's private clerk. This can only have been a fraction of the total cost. Heavy expenditure was recorded subsequently in the bridge wardens' accounts when the bridge had to be repaired. In the late fifteenth and early sixteenth centuries the bridge was in a very bad state, and it seems likely that parts of it fell. There are only two accounts for the period between 1480 and 1520: that for 1500 records expenditure of £394, and for 1507–8, £160.[41]

After the ancient bridge over the Tweed at Berwick was swept away in 1294, its reconstruction was attempted on a number of occasions over the next hundred

---

[38] John Vowell alias Hoker, *The Description of the Citie of Excestre*, Devon and Cornwall Rec. Soc. (1919), 602.

[39] *Cal. Inq. Misc. (1348–77)*, no. 718.

[40] *King's Works*, ii. 612; *Wales and Western*, 27–8. Major work was also undertaken in the 1380s (36th Report of the Deputy Keeper of the Public Records, Appendix II, 94)

[41] Britnell, 'Rochester Bridge', 90, and see 311–35.

years. About 1400 Hotspur was provided with £1,000 from the customs at a number of ports for this purpose, but this attempt seems to have been unsuccessful like the others. There was, however, by Henry VIII's reign a wooden structure.[42] By the 1540s this bridge had broken and was later rebuilt, also in timber. Then in 1607–8 ice coming down river carried away ten of its piers. It seems to have taken some time to start on a new bridge. Inigo Jones was consulted. Estimates were made both for a stone bridge and for a bridge with seven stone arches over the deepest part of the river and the rest of timber. The former was chosen. Presumably, a substantial bridge was required following the union of the crowns. Huge, iron-shod oak piles up to 23 feet long and 18 inches square were driven into the river bed. In all 873 oak trees were used. Unfortunately, in 1621 the unfinished structure was severely damaged by an exceptional flood. Despite this, the bridge, which is still standing, was probably largely complete by 1624, although over the next decade some further work was done. Total expenditure for the period from 1611 to 1634 was £14,960.[43]

The next large structure was the timber bridge begun in 1729 over the Thames at Fulham at a cost of £23,000.[44] About a decade later work began on Westminster Bridge, a few miles downstream. Thomas Ripley, the comptroller of the King's Works (1726–58), estimated £26,000 for a timber bridge at New Palace Yard, but far more for a stone bridge: he thought the cost of the foundations alone of a such a structure would be £100,000. He also proposed an alternative, which seems to have involved founding the stone piers on wooden piles projecting from the river bed in the medieval tradition at an estimated cost of £80,000.[45] Labelye's design for a stone bridge was chosen instead. He claimed that the its eventual outturn cost was £218,000, but others put it at £389,500, that is, fifteen times Ripley's original estimate for a timber bridge.[46] Within twenty years there was another major bridge in London, Blackfriars, built for the considerably lesser sum of £160,000. The next, however, Waterloo Bridge (1811–17), cost over £1 million.[47] Even allowing for an increase in building costs over the fifty years which separated the bridges, Waterloo Bridge was considerably more expensive in real terms.

Indeed, Waterloo Bridge dwarfed all other building expenditure in the early nineteenth century. The £1 million spent on it was the equivalent of the annual expenditure on all public buildings in England at the time. It was over twice the amount spent on Somerset House between 1775 and 1801.[48] We do not have precise figures for the cost of constructing the largest medieval bridges at

[42] *CPR (1399–1401)*, 536; *North*, 2–3.   [43] *King's Works*, iv. 769.
[44] Walker, *Old Westminster Bridge*, 51.   [45] Ibid. 77.   [46] Ibid. 225–6.
[47] Chalkin, *Public Building*, 22.   [48] Ibid. 15.

Newcastle, Rochester, or London, and they were built to a cheaper design than Waterloo Bridge, but there is every reason to believe that they were also massive investments.

Expenditure on other bridges was not in this league, but was still sizeable compared with the cost of other contemporary buildings. A church at Catterick, built at about the same time as the bridge there and under similar conditions, was to cost 160 marks (*c*.£106), that is, 100 marks less than the value of the bridge contract.[49] The £90 spent between 1304 and 1308 on rebuilding Kildwick Bridge, a relatively modest structure, exceeded by a considerable margin the other investments made by the Priory, including the building of barns and mills in those years.[50]

UPKEEP

The cost of keeping bridge crossings of similar size in use, like the cost of construction, varied greatly, depending on the type of structure and its location. Wooden bridges were particularly costly to keep in repair. The commissioners appointed under 'An Act for Building a Bridge across the Thames from the new Palace Yard in the city of Westminster to the opposite shore in the county of Surrey' questioned Thomas Ripley about the cost of repairing a timber bridge. He replied that, provided it were well made, the cost over fifty years would be equal to its being rebuilt twice over.[51]

Dealing with flood damage was especially costly. Bridges in every part of England might be swept away in an exceptional disaster, even lowland bridges. In 1696 'great water floods' destroyed Bungay Bridge on the border of Norfolk and Suffolk and damaged at least two other bridges.[52] However, events of this kind were less common in the lowlands than the uplands. In Warwickshire only one county bridge was rebuilt between 1650 and 1750.[53] Highland-zone bridges, by contrast, were far more prone to destruction by flood. While a significant number of great medieval northern bridges have survived to the present day, at a number of locations a succession of bridges were swept away and had to be rebuilt. The giant single-arched Kirkstall Bridge, which had been built in 1616, had collapsed within 130 years.[54] The superb three-arched Hewick Bridge, near Ripon, which Leland had crossed and which must have had individual spans of 20–30 metres, had been replaced by a timber bridge by 1675.[55]

[49] Salzman, *Building*, 487–90, 497–9.   [50] Kershaw, *Bolton Priory*, 121–2.
[51] Walker, *Old Westminster Bridge*, 63, 77.   [52] Chalkin, *Public Building*, 108–9.   [53] Ibid. 222.
[54] *YWR Bridge Book*.   [55] Leland, v. 139; Ogilby, plate 95; Fiennes, 83.

Hexham Bridge suffered worse than most from floods in the late eighteenth century. There had been a bridge over the Tyne in the thirteenth century, but at some time in the late middle ages it collapsed. In 1767 work began on a new bridge. It was finished in 1770, but was destroyed by the great flood of the following year. Smeaton designed a new bridge which was built from 1777 to 1780. This, in turn, survived only two years. In March 1782 it was destroyed by another flood which occurred after heavy snow, followed by rain and a quick thaw. Work began on the third bridge in less than thirty years in 1790.[56]

Stone bridges required constant maintenance, even if it was relatively minor such as rebuilding parapets, which were prone to being damaged by vehicles, or repairs to paving or causeways. The sums were normally modest, but major repairs were also often necessary. Before the late eighteenth century the total reconstruction of a stone bridge was a last resort. Unless a bridge completely collapsed, it was usual for it to be repaired. This could involve substantial work and hence there are many references to sizeable donations, like the bequest of £40 given by Richard, Lord Scrope of Bolton, in 1400 for the repair of Wensley Bridge.[57] Such large sums must have been spent on major works to foundations or on rebuilding an arch or arches. Later we can see in more detail what was involved. A typical example is Sowerby Bridge in the West Riding. A four-arched stone bridge was constructed here in the sixteenth century in place of an earlier structure; in 1674 its two central arches were rebuilt at a cost of c.£200.[58] Since repairing major bridges and causeways was a heavy responsibility, it is not surprising to find that in the early fourteenth century the abbess of Barking paid £200 to be rid of any liability for maintaining the bridges and causeway at Stratford atte Bow.[59]

Considerable though this was, expenditure on the repair and maintenance of the great bridges was in a different league. By the mid-fifteenth century Exe Bridge, Exeter, was much patched; arches which were weak or had fallen had been replaced by spans of timber. John Shillingford, the mayor, stated that the 'grete part of the seid brigge by dyvers tymes hath fallen adown and made up agen with tymber'. He estimated the cost of repair at £2,000.[60] In 1409–10 £156 was spent on Rochester Bridge when large cracks in the stonework appeared, in 1425–6 £252, following the collapse of two arches, and £471 in the two years 1444–6, when the bridge was so badly damaged that it was useable for over seven months. Spending was high even when the bridges were in a sound condition, mainly because new piles had constantly to be driven round the starlings. In the 1450s, a decade when there were no calamities, spending on

---

[56] Ruddock, *Arch Bridges*, 98–100, 238.   [57] *North*, 76.   [58] Ibid. 101.
[59] *CCR (1313–18)*, 337.   [60] *Devon Bridges*, 63.

Rochester Bridge varied from £49 to £86, most of it spent on reinforcing the foundations.[61] Expenditure on Old London Bridge was even higher. According to Dyson and Watson an annual average of £521 was spent between 1404 and 1445.[62] This would imply expenditure on the bridge over the whole century of in excess of £50,000. Incidently, this is the same sum that Edward III spent on Windsor Castle, admittedly over a shorter period—from 1350 to 1377—which was the highest cost recorded for any single building operation in the history of the king's works in the middle ages.[63]

TOTAL EXPENDITURE

The replacement cost of English bridges in 1500 would have been huge. There were over eighty bridges across the five largest rivers in the country and more than fifty across the major Yorkshire rivers.[64] This was but a fraction of the total number of bridges in England. Many of the largest structures have already been described in the earlier parts of the book, such as the long causeways across the Trent valley, including the mile-long *pons cordis* at Swarkestone.[65] Over the Thames too, as well as the large timber bridges of the middle reaches, there were the great causeway bridges of the upper river: Newbridge, Grandpont, Abingdon, and Wallingford.

Some idea of what the replacement cost might have been can be seen by examining the bridges of the West Riding. In 1752 there were 115 county bridges in the Riding, all but a few on the site of a bridge standing in 1500. Over a quarter, more than thirty bridges, had total spans of over 40 metres, and probably each cost in excess of £100 to build in the late middle ages. Some—for example, North Bridge, Ripon, Tadcaster Bridge, Ferrybridge, Castleford Bridge, Wakefield Bridge, and Wetherby Bridge—were much larger (plate 8). It is likely that all would have cost more than several hundred pounds to replace in the fifteenth century, and a few much more.

Chalkin has calculated that annual expenditure on county bridges in the West Riding alone in the 1750s ranged from £491 in 1750 to £1,007 in 1758, and this was before the increase in expenditure associated with widespread rebuilding in the late eighteenth century.[66] He estimates total spending on county bridges from 1640 to 1760 at between £250,000 and £350,000.[67] This is likely

[61] Britnell, 'Rochester Bridge', 47, 49, 315.
[62] Dyson and Watson, 'London Bridge is Broken Down', 130.   [63] *King's Works*, ii. 881.
[64] See Tables 2.1 and 2.2.   [65] See Chap. 8.   [66] Chalkin, *Public Building*, 215.
[67] Ibid. 112.

to be less than half the total expended on bridges, probably considerably less, since it excludes expenditure on the many bridges which were not a county responsibility, including the very large bridges which had their own endowment. There is every reason to think that expenditure in the late middle ages was comparable. The cumulative spending on building and maintaining bridges was prodigious. The more we examine investment in the pre-industrial transport infrastructure, the more apparent it is that it was one of the most impressive and least recognized achievements of pre-industrial England.

II

Funding Mechanisms

The bulk of the information we have about bridges in the thousand years from the mid-eighth to the mid-eighteenth century relates to the efforts made to maintain and repair them. By the later middle ages, when we can see what was happening in some detail, the repair of bridges was financed and organized in a multiplicity of ways. Some look decidedly eccentric. Here the king gave oaks, there a lord provided timber and his men the labour. The men of a village were responsible for the pier of one bridge, a bishop granted an indulgence to those contributing to another. For the fabric of other bridges, tolls were collected; a widow bequeathed a few bushels of corn in her will; a hermit sought alms from passers-by.

At first sight there seems to be neither rhyme nor reason to this miscellany, but behind the apparent mishmash it is possible to see three main methods of funding bridge construction and maintenance. The first, wide category consists of methods involving state compulsion. In the middle ages certain landholders were made liable for specific bridges. Later the funding came from a county rate and later still from general taxation. The second method was the imposition of a toll on those crossing the bridge. Finally, the task could be left to private contributions. The government exhorted and encouraged such contributions, but whether or not funds were raised depended on the charity, civic responsibility, and self-interest of those who gave donations. All general works on medieval bridges give examples of these methods of funding, but there has been no comprehensive consideration. Nor has there has been any attempt to assess the relative contribution each made to keeping the large network of bridges in repair, and how and why it changed over time.

Perhaps the best place to start any consideration of this process is not with a work on bridges, but with a pioneering study of the funding of another public work, town fortifications, which had much in common with bridges.[1] H. L.

---

[1] H. L. Turner, *Town Defences in England and Wales: An Architectural and Documentary Study A.D. 900–1500* (London, 1971).

Turner has shown that in the Anglo-Saxon period the walls of *burhs* were built and maintained by *burh-bot*, an obligation she describes as 'vested in the land in the vicinity of the defences'.[2] After the Norman Conquest the *burh-bot* system collapsed; by the twelfth century it was unlikely that the 'King was able to enforce the performance of labour services in land'.[3] In its place the Crown introduced a new system of funding known as the murage. This was a grant to townsmen of the right to collect tolls to fund the construction and repair of walls from those entering the town. Subsequently the murage ceased to raise adequate sums, and new sources of revenue were developed, including the acquisition of property to provide an income.[4]

The history of bridge building and maintenance has many similarities with that of town walls, but also significant differences. The key to both the construction and maintenance of a large bridge network and a system of *burhs* was the Anglo-Saxon state's ability to compel landholders to provide a work-force for the task. Whereas *burh*-work disappeared after the Norman Conquest, with certain important exceptions many bridge-work liabilities survived. It was, however, difficult to impose new burdens, that is, difficult to compel anyone to build a new bridge at a new site. By the twelfth century it is evident that major new bridges were funded by charitable donations. Gifts to bridges remained one of the most important good works throughout the middle ages. In the early thirteenth century we find another parallel between bridges and town fortifications: soon after the Crown devised the murage grant to fund the construction of walls, an equivalent for funding bridges was instituted. This, the pontage grant, made a useful contribution to the repair of major bridges, but it probably never raised funds on the scale of the bridge-work liabilities or donations.

In 1530 the first act of parliament concerned solely with bridges, the Statute of Bridges, was enacted. One of its provisions reinforced the principle of placing the burden of repair on local property-owners; the county was now to raise a rate for the reconstruction and repair of bridges for which no one was liable. Although the medieval system of financing provided the bulk of the funding for the next two centuries, gradually, at very different rates in different counties, most major bridges became the responsibility of the county. After 1760 new arrangements were found for funding the new bridges which began to be built in significant numbers. Some were funded by the county rate, others by tolls and loans, but as in the middle ages, private funds paid for many major new structures.

---

[2] Ibid. 28.   [3] Ibid. 30.   [4] Ibid. 39–44.

ANGLO-SAXON ENGLAND: THE BRIDGE WORK LIABILITY

The capacity of the old English state to mobilize men and materials for major civil engineering projects is well known. The state which built Offa's Dyke and the system of *burhs* also undertook the creation and maintenance of the extensive late-Saxon bridge network. Charitable donations may have played a more prominent part than the scant references to them suggest, but there seems little doubt that the state took the lead role.

We know a great deal about the liabilities to mend bridges from late medieval sources. The plentiful records of proceedings held at the view of frankpledge commonly contain bridge repair cases.[5] One of the few surviving records of the proceedings of a county court, the rolls of the pleas of Bedfordshire and Buckinghamshire for 1332–4, contains an instruction to distrain the townships of Elstow and Kempston because of the failure to repair a bridge on the *regia strata* from Bedford to Ampthill, presumably on the site of the current bridge over Elstow Brook on the A418 between the two towns.[6]

Flower implied that such obligations were created ad hoc, determined by whoever benefited most from the bridge. He observed that they were usually undertaken *ratione tenurae*, adding: 'It is reasonable to assume that the township was called on to maintain works adjacent or beneficial to its common fields and that the lord of the manor was liable when the work benefited him or was situated near the demesne land.'[7] However, his evidence suggests that the liabilities did not arise in the utilitarian way he proposed. The emphasis of the court cases is on repairs which were done *de jure* by the person responsible and his predecessors.[8] The expression *ratione tenurae* used in the court records, which Flower drew attention to, was a reference not to whose land most benefited from the bridge, but to the fact that long-standing liabilities rested on land.[9] It is worth noting that something very similar survives to this day: the charge which falls on a small number of properties to pay for the repair of a church chancel. The clinching argument is that there were many bridges which no one was liable to repair, although they must have been of utility to someone. Not untypical was Till Bridge near Saxilby to the west of Lincoln (probably on

---

[5] e.g., *Court Rolls of the Manor of Ingoldmells*, ed. W. O. Massingberd (London, 1902), 140, 155, 211, 280–1.

[6] *Rolls from the Office of the Sheriff of Beds. and Bucks., 1332–4*, ed. G. H. Fowler, Beds. Hist. Rec. Soc., quarto memoirs, 3 (1929).

[7] Flower, *Works*, ii. p. xli.   [8] Ibid. i. 88–90; ii. 140.

[9] Of course, specific liabilities could arise in a variety of ways. Some groups or individuals were responsible because they accepted an endowment to undertake the repair (see below). Liabilities could be imposed by a mistaken or corrupt jury, and likewise they could be avoided in this way. Occasionally jurors did make a decision based on utility (e.g. Flower, *Works*, ii. 72–4), but such decisions were surely only made because there was already a widespread sense that someone must be responsible for the repair of a bridge.

the site of the bridge which today takes the A57 over the River Till), the cause of a series of disputes in the fourteenth century. Eventually it was found that neither the local townships which had been charged with repair nor any holder of land there ever made or ought to repair the bridge.[10]

In Western Europe landholders' duty to repair bridges dates back over a millennium before the dispute about Till Bridge. N. P. Brooks has described its development in the late imperial period, when it became increasingly difficult to fund bridges from taxation. Instead, the empire turned to landowners to provide men for their maintenance.[11] In the 370s and 380s imperial decrees emphasized bridge-building as a public service: an instruction issued in AD 370 to the vicar of Italy and preserved in the Theodosian Code stated that the bridge of Livenza should be restored by the landholders of the municipality.[12] At this date the great and the good were exempt. Chapter 11.16.8 of the code dating from AD 390 exempted them and 'the land of churches and of rhetoricians and grammarians of both branches of learning from the obligation to construct bridges and highways'.[13] However, by the next century these exemptions could no longer be sustained. In 423 it was decreed that 'no class of men by merit of any high rank or veneration should be exempt from the repair of roads and bridges'.[14]

As we have seen, it is not impossible that similar liabilities existed in Roman Britain and, where Roman bridges remained in use, survived the end of imperial rule. They may have survived into the eighth century, when they provided a model for new developments.[15] To this date belong the Mercian charters, which contain the earliest English references to the obligation to build bridges and which exempt land from all services except work on bridges and fortresses.[16] Behind these exemption clauses lay the state's capacity to compel a work-force to build and repair bridges. By the late-Saxon period work on bridges, *brycgweorc* as it was described in one source, was important throughout England.[17] The obligation continues to be included in later charters: for instance, Cnut frees the lands of the church of Exeter from all burdens except military service, bridge repair, and assiduous prayers.[18]

Although there are many Anglo-Saxon charters which reserve bridge work, they provide no indication of what was involved in the liability. Fortunately

---

[10] Flower, *Works*, i. 229–31.   [11] Brooks, 'Medieval Bridges', 15.
[12] *The Theodosian Code*, ed. and trans. C. Pharr (Princeton, 1952), cap. 11.10.2.
[13] Dating from AD 390 (ibid.).   [14] Ibid., cap. 15.3.6.   [15] Brooks, 'Rochester Bridge', 12–15.
[16] See Chap. 3.
[17] The term 'brycgeweorc' is used in the *Rectitudines Singularum Personarum* of *c*.1000 (Liebermann, *Gesetze*, i. 446).
[18] F. W. Maitland, *Domesday Book and Beyond* (Fontana edn., London, 1960), 346.

two eleventh-century sources help to fill that gap. One is the statement in Domesday Book of the customs of the city of Chester under King Edward: that the reeve could summons a man from each hide to rebuild the bridge and the town walls. If he did not obey, his lord would be fined 40s.[19] The other is the vivid description of the liabilities to repair Rochester Bridge, which is contained in a (probably) eleventh-century document. This records the estates in a part of Kent which were responsible for the upkeep of the piers and provided timber for the beams and planks of the road way. It begins:

This is the labour-service for the bridge at Rochester.

Here are named the estates from which the labour is due.

First the bishop [of Rochester] undertakes to construct the land pier on the [eastern] arm, and to plank three rods, and to set in place 3 beams [to support the road way]: that is from Borstal, Cuxton, Frindsbury and Stoke (these were episcopal manors).

The list goes on to name in a similar manner those who were responsible for the remainder of the nine piers and the wooden spans between.[20]

The Chester example also demonstrates another principal element of bridge work. The liability commonly rested on the major administrative units of late Saxon England: counties, hundreds, and vills, the basic units of royal authority.[21] The responsibility of the men of Cambridgeshire, Huntingdonshire, and Nottinghamshire, as well as of Cheshire, for their county bridge is well attested.[22] Hundreds were also liable: for instance, the hundred of Blackheath repaired Deptford Bridge on the London–Dover Road in the fourteenth century.[23] The vills of Bisley Hundred in Gloucestershire acknowledged their duty to repair the middle third part of 'Dodebrugge by Stonehouse' (Dudbridge over the River Frome).[24]

As the vills of the whole hundred were liable for a part of Dudbridge, so smaller groups of vills or others might be responsible for bridges of local importance. In 1389 it was claimed that Totisbrigge (River Great Ouse) was broken and that the master of St John the Baptist's Hospital, Oxford, should repair the

---

[19] 'Ad murum civitati et pontem reaedificandum, de unaquamque hida comitatus unum hominem venire prepositus educebat. Cuius homo non veniebat dominus eius xl solidos emendabat regi et comiti. Haec forisfactura extra firmam erat' (*DB*, i. 262).

[20] The list is published in Yates and Gibson, *Traffic and Politics*, App. C. The document is first recorded in the 12th-cent. cartulary of Rochester Cathedral, the *Textus Roffensis*, in both a Latin and an old English version. They are both undated, but are considered to have been based on an 11th-cent. Old English original.

[21] The role and importance of these units are discussed in Campbell, *Anglo-Saxon State*, 16.

[22] *Rot. Hun.*, ii. 407; *CCR (1364–8)*, 39–40; and see N. Neilsen, 'Customary Rents', in *Oxford Studies in Social and Legal History*, 4 (Oxford, 1910), 137–40.

[23] Flower, *Works*, i. p. xxxvi; and see i. 197–203.

[24] Ibid. i. 117. The river is not large here, but Dudbridge may have been a relatively substantial causeway.

abutment (*pedem pontis*) and one arch on the side of Thornborough in Buckinghamshire, and the men of Leckhamstead and Foxcott the abutment and two arches on the side of their townships.[25] Of the approximately 100 court cases about bridge repair recorded in Flower's collection, in a third a vill or vills were liable for repair, while in about a quarter named individuals, sometimes the lords of the manor, were responsible. Sometimes the burden was shared: for instance, the lords of Bungay provided the timber, and the men of the township used it to repair the bridge.[26]

The burden of repairing major bridges rested on the Old English taxation unit, the hide (or its equivalent). This was the situation not only in respect of Dee Bridge, Chester, but also of Great Bridge, Cambridge. Here 6*d.* a hide was levied on those lands which paid the charge in the thirteenth century.[27] By this date there is evidence that the liabilities had become attached to specific tenements. An inquisition of 1277–80 provides not only details of the estates assigned to the repair of Rochester Bridge, but also information about which tenements from the estates were responsible, indicating the liability of holders of smallholdings of land. The men of Hollingbourne were responsible for the sixth pier; among them were the 'heirs of Thomas de la Dane's five acres'.[28] We seem to find similar arrangements for other bridges: thus Robert Bacon, Knight, was obliged to repair *Wolvesdonebrigge* by reason of four acres of meadow called Wolvesdonemede belonging to his manor of Bacons in Essex.[29]

By the late middle ages the duty to work on the major bridges had often been commuted into a money payment.[30] Those liable to repair bridges commonly paid craftsmen to undertake the work, as bridge wardens' accounts show. Originally, however, the obligation seems to have been a labour service. This must be the interpretation of the Chester Domesday entry.

The role of lords in Cheshire in 1066 was to ensure, subject to a stiff penalty if they did not, that their men turned up and repaired the bridge. This illuminates the earliest references to bridge repair which appear in early eleventh-century law codes and tracts. Canute's code lays down the very heavy penalty of 120*s.* for failure to perform *brigbot*. A contemporary tract, the *Rectitudines singularum personarum*, includes a section on the thegn's law which describes the thegn's principal public duties: he is to contribute to the three common burdens in respect of his land, including the repair of bridges as well as *fyrd*

---

[25] Ibid. i. 28–30.   [26] Ibid. ii. 142–6.   [27] *Rot. Hun.*, ii. 407.
[28] Brooks, 'Rochester Bridge', 38–9.   [29] Flower, *Works*, i. 75.
[30] This was the situation in Cambridgeshire (*Rot. Hun.*, ii. 407) and Cheshire (Stewart-Brown, *Dee Bridge*, 66).

service and *burh* work. Archbishop Wulfstan and his circle, who compiled these works, seem to have had a clear idea of the importance of bridges, and the role of landholders in ensuring that their men maintained them.[31]

Thus the creation and maintenance of a large bridge network may have been one of the priorities of the Old English state. It is an achievement which must be seen alongside the other, better-known attributes of that state: the establishment of a coinage, of a system of taxation, and, closely associated with bridge construction, the building of a system of *burhs*. It is another and outstanding testimony to the power of the Old English state which a generation of Anglo-Saxon scholars has impressed upon us.

THE ELEVENTH TO THE SIXTEENTH CENTURIES: LIABILITIES, CHARITY, AND TOLLS

The Bridge Work Liability

Survival and Change

After the twelfth century the public duty to repair bridges remained extremely important. The condition of bridges and causeways was systematically examined, not only in the county court and at the twice-yearly sheriff's tourn, but also, at longer intervals, by the justices in eyre. Other sources too show that there was a general expectation of liability: the *Modus tenendi curias* of the early fourteenth century states that broken bridges were repaired by the vills nearest the bridge.[32]

However, bridge work ceased to have the prominence it had enjoyed in late Anglo-Saxon England. Exemptions from bridge work were widely granted. While most liabilities probably survived, obligations to repair very large bridges fell into disuse. We can see the difficulties in the post-conquest history of Dee Bridge, Chester, which R. Stewart-Brown unravelled in the 1930s. In the thirteenth century the ancient obligation of the men of the county to repair the bridge came near to disappearing. It survived because of the reference in Domesday Book. In 1251 the justiciar of Cheshire was ordered to see if the

---

[31] Liebermann, *Gesetze*, i. 353, 444. The background to the laws and *Rectitudines* and the role of Wulfstan and his circle are discussed in P. Wormald, *The Making of English Law*, 2 vols. (Oxford, 1999). The references to bridge repair are considered in i. 344, 355, 387–9.

[32] Cam, *The Hundred and the Hundred Rolls*, 105; id., 'Studies in the Hundred Rolls', in *Oxford Studies in Social and Legal History*, 6 (1921), 94–5; *The Court Baron*, ed. F. W. Maitland and W. P. Baildon, Seldon Soc., 4 (1891), 88.

bridge's repair pertained to the king. He must have paid for it, since five years later his successor was instructed to distrain the people of Cheshire to return more than £20. The reason for the instruction was that the king had heard from the barons of the Exchequer that, according to Domesday Book, the communities of Cheshire were bound to repair the bridge. As M. T. Clanchy has shown us, this was a time when Henry III's officials were beginning to search the volumes, now almost two centuries old, to check up on royal rights. Possibly an official familiar with Domesday Book remembered that he had seen a reference to the bridge's repair.[33]

From this time on, what seem like a continuous series of disputes about liability are recorded. Most involved those who had been granted an exemption: the abbey of Chester argued that the sheriff had wrongly taken ten of its oxen to the value of £10 from its grange at Sutton-in-Wirral as its share of the cost of repair; the sheriff's action was unlawful, since under its foundation charter of 1093 the abbey was freed from all such works or payments. The court found in the abbey's favour, as it did in further disputes. Others claimed exemption too.[34]

These, however, were irritants, further reducing the willingness to repair the bridge, but those who were not exempt continued to shoulder the burden. The big change seem to have come in the fourteenth century, when the present impressive and expensive bridge with seven stone arches was built in place of the ancient structure which had a timber roadway with stone abutments and possibly stone piers (plate 13).[35] Those liable must have been alarmed. The abbey was again charged to contribute and again objected. The prince of Wales, as earl of Cheshire, in consideration of these great costs, granted that all those of the county 'who were anciently and by custom so liable and their heirs, as well as the abbot of Chester, should forever be discharged therefrom and of all forced contributions thereto', provided that the parties responsible should complete the bridge on this one occasion only.[36]

Many of the problems encountered in repairing Chester Bridge recurred at other major bridges. Exemptions from liability for bridge work as for other public services seem to have been casually issued to favoured institutions and courtiers, without apparently much thought for the resentment and difficulties

---

[33] Stewart-Brown, *Dee Bridge, CCR* (*1251–3*), 17; (*1254–6*), 264–5, *CLibR*, iv. 282; M. T. Clanchy, *From Memory to Written Record* (London, 1979), 19.

[34] Stewart-Brown, *Dee Bridge*, 70–1.   [35] See Chap. 10.

[36] Stewart-Brown, *Dee Bridge*, 73–5; *Register of Edward the Black Prince, etc.*, 4 vols. (London, 1930–3), iii. 8, 15, 19.

they must have caused. The many exemption clauses in charters imply a host of angry people left to shoulder a bigger share of the burden.[37]

No doubt the traditional liabilities to repair major bridges disappeared for a variety of reasons, including poor record-keeping and/or the effects of granting exemptions. It is, however, notable that as seem to have happened at Chester, so at almost every one of the other large crossings we have evidence for, the decision to build an arched, stone bridge was the key factor. Those responsible continued to repair London Bridge after the Norman Conquest. In 1096 we hear that 'many shires, whose work pertained to London were badly afflicted through the wall which they constructed around the Tower, and through the bridge which was well-nigh washed away . . .'[38] The bridge was probably still being repaired by outlying liable estates in Henry I's reign, when the tenants of Battle Abbey were freed from the obligation.[39] However, after Peter of Colechurch's bridge was constructed we hear no more of such obligations, and by the thirteenth century the maintenance of the bridge was financed by a bridge estate. Liabilities for Rochester Bridge too effectively ended with the construction of the new bridge in the 1380s.[40] The large estuarine structures were national assets, and their reconstruction in stone was beyond the means of local communities. It is of interest that one of the few county bridges which continued to be maintained and repaired by the traditional contributions long after the middle ages was Great Bridge, Cambridge, where the bridge remained timber until the eighteenth century. The contributions ceased after it was reconstructed in stone in 1754.[41]

As ever, the history of these large estuarine bridges was quite different from that of typical lowland bridges. The cost of reconstructing the latter in stone, though heavy, was modest in comparison. Those liable for them often lived locally or had local interests and could see direct personal advantages in paying for their bridge.

The Fossilization of Liabilities
It is likely that work-forces from the mid-eighth and to the mid-tenth centuries had been compelled to construct bridges in place of fords and ferries. Later,

---

[37] A 14th-cent. dispute illustrates the problems caused by exemptions. The tenants of the honour of Huntingdon claimed to be exempt from work on bridges, but the other inhabitants of Huntingdon, not surprisingly, objected. The royal justices were concerned that: 'for default of the men and tenants of the said honour the bridge should remain for even in ruins unrepaired, to the peril and hurt as well of the king as of his whole people since the public passage north and south is by the same' (*CCR (1364–8)*, 39).

[38] *ASC*, 234.

[39] *Sir Christopher Hatton's Book of Seals*, ed. L. C. Lloyd and D. M. Stenton, Northants Rec. Soc., 15 (1950), 61.

[40] Britnell, 'Rochester Bridge', 43–6, 51–2.   [41] *VCH Cambs.*, iii. 114.

however, obligations fossilized: those traditionally liable repaired bridges, but the state seems to have ceased trying to get people to build new bridges at new sites. Charters of the eighth, ninth and early tenth centuries refer to the construction of bridges.[42] In the second half of the tenth century they speak of repair; for example, *CS* 1067 of AD 961 states 'ex rata videlicet exped. pontis arcisive restauratione'.[43] Canute's law of the eleventh century is concerned with the repair or rebuilding of bridges. The Latin version of II Canute 65 translates *brig bot* as *emendationem* or *refectionem pontis*: 'Si quis burhbotam vel brigbotam (id est burgis vel pontis emendationem [refectionem])'.[44] This change in terminology may reflect a change in practice. It is even possible that the law codes begin to mention bridge work around 1000 because there were serious problems in getting bridges repaired.

Magna Carta provides further evidence of the resistance to attempts to impose new burdens. Chapter 23 states: 'No vill or man shall be forced to build bridges at river banks, except those who ought to do so by custom and law.' This clause had a very specific application to the repair of bridges when the king was hawking, a device which the Angevins were probably using to raise money.[45] Its provisions, however, were symptomatic of the general difficulty in imposing new obligations.

By the later thirteenth century it is clear that the system had become completely fossilized. Some bridges were repaired by liable communities; others were repaired by alms, and nobody could be made responsible for them. An inquisition was held in 1280 on a complaint by Peter of Berghfield that he was wrongly charged with the repair of a bridge. The question it had to answer was: 'whether he or his ancestors were accustomed to repair the said bridge wholly out of charity or because he was bound to do so'; if the former, he was not obliged to repair the bridge.'[46]

Charitable Donations

Because it was impossible for the state to create new liabilities, after the eleventh century, new bridges had to be financed in a different way. In every

---

[42] The charters are discussed in Brooks, 'Military Obligations', 72. *CS* 178 (AD 749) refers to *instructionibus pontium*, *CS* 274 (AD 793–6), to *structionem*, *CS* 848 (AD 792) to *constructionem*, *CS* 370 (AD 822) to *constructione*. Such formulae are noted in Wessex as well as Mercian and Kent charters (e.g. *CS* 451, AD 846). See also *CS* 753, 758, 763, 764, 770, 775, 777, 787, 795.

[43] See also *CS* 1066, also produced at Abingdon, and *CS* 1080 produced at Winchester.

[44] Liebermann, *Gesetze*, i. 353.

[45] W. S. McKechnie, *Magna Carta* (Glasgow, 1905), 352–8, and see *CCR* (*1234–7*), 9, 33, 158, 196–8, 378; (*1237–42*), 147–8. The key phrase is 'at river banks' (*ad riparias*), which also appears in later instructions to royal officials recorded on the Close Rolls. The clause refers to the obligation to repair bridges when the king went hawking by rivers.

[46] *CPR* (*1272–81*), 408.

known case, from Robert d'Oilly's building of Grandpont to the construction of the new bridges at Abingdon by a consortium of local merchants and aristocrats three centuries later, they were privately funded. The state was not the prime mover in these works. There were two strands to the provision of private funds. First, there were the many well-documented charitable donations to bridges. Secondly, bridge building may in some places have been a straightforward estate investment, or an essential investment in the infrastructure of a town by its lord and have been seen as such.

A few—but only a few—seigneurial accounts record such expenditure. Consider the bailiff's account of Thorncroft by Leatherhead for 1347–8, which refers to expenditure of 6s. 8d., 'ad facturam pontis de Ledred precepto seneschalli', or the Bolton Priory accounts which detail the money spent on rebuilding Kildwick Bridge.[47] These were public bridges on public roads, not estate bridges on private roads. There is no mention of charity. Some of the accounts could be recording repairs undertaken as a bridge work liability, but possibly not all.

In contrast to the sparse references to estate investment in bridges, there are numerous examples of charitable gifts. They were being made by the late-Saxon period at the latest. We only know this because of a lone early reference recommending as penance facilitating 'people's journeys, by bridges over deep water and foul ways'.[48] This single clause may offer us a glimpse of a world where charitable gifts to bridges were frequent, as they most definitely were in Scandinavia. Here in the period of the conversion to Christianity many rune stones record the erection of bridges. The following inscription from Sweden is typical: 'Sigrid, mother of Alrik, daughter of Orm, made this bridge for the soul of Holmgeir, her husband, father of Sigurd.'[49]

By about 1100 we are on firmer ground in England. We begin to hear of aristocrats, senior ecclesiastics, and royalty who paid for very substantial bridges, including, in addition to Robert d'Oilly and Ranulf Flambard, Queen Mathilda, the wife of Henry I, who paid for the construction of Bow Bridge over the Lea valley at Stratford, near London. The project is particularly well documented thanks to a long series of subsequent disputes about its repair in the thirteenth and fourteenth centuries. The road from London to Essex had formerly crossed the Lea at Old Ford, but because of the dangers of the crossing the queen decided to build a causeway and a series of bridges, including

[47] Merton College Records 5728 (for 1347/8); Kershaw, *Bolton Priory*, 122.
[48] *Ancient Laws and Institutes of England*, ed. B. Thorpe, 2 vols. (London, 1840) ii. 283.
[49] Quoted in Brooks, 'Medieval Bridges', 20.

Bow Bridge, over the marsh. It is probable that an approach road was constructed from Bow to London at the same time. K. G. T. McDonnell, who examined the intricacies of the project, considered that 'the whole operation was one of the most considerable of all medieval public works in England'.[50]

These large donations have to be seen in the context of similar gifts to other medieval institutions which were also funded by private benefactors.[51] At about the same time that Bow Bridge was built, a few miles to the west Mathilda founded the hospital of St Giles, Cripplegate, and Rahere was founding St Bartholomew's Hospital and Priory.[52] Hospitals, university colleges, schools, and bridges received very large sums throughout the middle ages.

The supporters of these good causes competed for funds in the past, as they do now. On the death of Cardinal Beaufort in 1447, his executors received numerous begging-letters and petitions. Over £300 was given to Oxford University. The city of Exeter asked for money to rebuild its bridge. The wardens of Rochester Bridge went to great lengths to secure funds: at least two visits were made by representatives of the bridge, and eventually a gift of £30 was made.[53]

Like hospitals and educational foundations, many bridges were largely or wholly dependent on the generosity of benefactors. A fourteenth-century inquisition found that 'the bridge of Wollebrigge is and always has been maintained by alms and no one is bound to repair it'.[54] It was typical of many others.[55] Donations were also given to bridges which someone was liable to repair. The men of the county were responsible for Huntingdon Bridge, but that did not stop people from making 'divers legacies' for its upkeep.[56] Biddenham Bridge, further upstream on the Great Ouse, was repaired by four neighbouring vills in 1383, but it also benefited from gifts: between 1501 and 1509 four separate donations to the bridge are recorded, comprising 8*d.* and 20*d.* and three and two measures of barley.[57]

[50] K. G. T. McDonnell, *Medieval London Suburbs* (Chichester, 1978), 68–71.

[51] The funding of schools and hospitals is discussed in N. Orme, *English Schools in the Middle Ages* (London, 1973) and id. and M. Webster, *The English Hospital, 1070–1570* (London, 1995).

[52] Pevsner, *London*, i. 148; William Dugdale, *Monasticon anglicanum*, ed. J. Caley et al., 6 vols. in 8 (London, 1846) 6/ii. 635–6.

[53] G. L. Harriss, *Cardinal Beaufort: A Study of Lancastrian Ascendancy and Decline* (Oxford, 1988), 379–82.

[54] *Cal. Inq. Misc. (1307–49)*, 1848.

[55] e.g. *CPR (1345–48)*, 87; *Cal. Inq. Misc. (1307–49)*, 228, 229, 348,1940, 2024; *(1348–77)*, 871; *(1377–88)*, 34.

[56] *CPR (1327–30)*, 379.

[57] Flower, *Works*, i. 1; *Bedfordshire Wills, 1490–1519*, ed. P. Bell, Bed. Hist. Rec. Soc., 45 (1966), 47, 108, 177, 180.

The Donors

Small contributions of this type were numerous. P. Goodfellow has discovered many such bequests to Northamptonshire bridges. In 1243 William de Pavelli left 5s. to Cademan Bridge. The bridge of Great Bowden benefited in 1523 from William Southerey's legacy of 6s. 8d. In his will of 1540 T. Werwyke bequeathed 'to the bridge of Kislingbury a heyffor of five years with a white baby', and in 1500 Richard Clerke left to 'the bridge called Stabulbrigge XXd. and to the bridge called Brekebridge XXd.'.[58] A small but significant proportion of the late medieval population made such donations. Some statistical information is available from collections of wills: a quick examination of a sample of late medieval Bedfordshire wills shows that from 5 to 10 per cent contain a bequest to a bridge.[59] A large survey found that between 1480 and 1540 1.48 per cent of the lower gentry's, 7 per cent of yeomen's, and 16 per cent of tradesmen's charitable benefactions were spent on 'municipal betterments', which included bridges and other public works.[60]

The large sums of money necessary for major construction were given by a few of the very wealthy, whose munificence has been described throughout this look. Some were members of the aristocracy. In 1316 Eleanor de Percy, 'late wife of Henry de Percy, executrix of the will of Richard de Arundel ... [was] beginning to build and repair Wetherby Bridge for his soul'.[61] Rich merchants were also major benefactors. Clopton Bridge at Statford-upon-Avon was built by, and is still named after, one of the town's most successful sons. On the third pier from the eastern end was formerly a stone pillar which carried the inscription: 'Sr. Hugh Clopton, Knight, Lord Mayor of London, built this bridge, at his own expence, in the reign of King Henry ye Seventh' (plate 21).[62]

Such extravagant generosity was unusual, and is often to be explained by special circumstances. Leland observed that one of the most generous of donors, Nicholas Blackburn, 'had very onthrifty children; wherefore he made at Yorke 4 cantuaries . . .'[63] He also tells us the background of the founder of Burford Bridge, Abingdon: 'Sum say that one Joanne de St. Helena aboute that tyme [c. 1416] had 2 daughters, and for lakke of issue of them it shoulde go to mayntaynaunce of the hospitalls and the bridgs. The land devolv'd to that use.'[64]

---

[58] Goodfellow, 'Northants Bridges', 151–7.
[59] *Bedfordshire Wills, 1490–1519; English Wills, 1498–1526*, ed. A. F. Cricket, Beds. Hist. Rec. Soc., 37 (1957).
[60] W. K. Jordan, *Philanthropy in England, 1480–1660* (London, 1959), 385–7.
[61] *Cal. Inq. Misc.* (*1307–49*), 228; *CPR* (*1313–18*), 449. Wetherby Bridge carries the Old North Road across the River Wharfe.
[62] *Wales and Western*, 163; Leland, ii. 49–50.   [63] Leland, v. 144.   [64] Ibid. 78.

Motives were mixed and are hard to disentangle. Presumably many charitable bequests were motivated by piety, mixed with civic pride and the desire to be well-thought-of by contemporaries. Doubtless self-interest was often a significant factor, but explicit statements to this effect are rare. An exception was the finding in the 1320s that Godfrey Woderowe of Uppecham, 'of his alms assigned a sum of money in aid of making a causeway and Brand bridges in Kent and because men with carts carrying timber from Sussex and the Weald to the port of Newehethe perceived that the causeway and bridge would be for their convenience they gave aid for making them'.[65]

Some good works, we are told, were an act of repentance. This, according to the monks of Abingdon, accounted for the benevolence of Robert d'Oilly. He had a dream in which he saw the Virgin Mary:

Robert fell victim to a severe illness, in which he suffered for many days without repentance, until one night it seemed to him that he was standing in the palace of some great king. On one side and the other a multitude of important men were standing by; in the midst of them a certain glorious figure was sitting on a throne, in female clothing and extremely beautiful. Before her were standing two brethren from the number of the aforesaid community [of Abingdon], whose names he knew. And when these two had seen him entering the palace, they genuflected before that Lady, saying, with a deep sigh, 'Behold, Lady, that is he who is usurping for himself the possessions of your church and has recently taken from your monastery the meadow, which is the reason for our outcry.' She, incensed against Robert, ordered him to be thrown out of doors, taken to the meadow which he had stolen from the monastery, and there tortured . . . And immediately most rascally boys gathered there, carrying hay from that very meadow on their shoulders, laughing and saying to each other, 'Look! There's our dearest friend. Let's play with him.' Then they took the bundles off their shoulders, urinated on them, and thrusting a firebrand beneath, thus fumigated him . . . others set fire to his beard. Robert indeed, finding himself in such straits, began to cry out, though still fast asleep, 'Holy Mary, take pity on me! Any moment I shall die' . . .

A few days afterwards, at the instigation of his wife, he had himself rowed to Abingdon and there, before the altar, in the presence of Abbot Rainald and with all the congregation of the brethren and his friends standing around him, he fully restored the revenue . . . For, just as before that vision he was a plunderer of churches and of the poor, so, afterwards, he became a repairer of churches and a restorer of the poor and an accomplisher of many good works.[66]

One of the most impressive of these works was the construction of Grandpont.

---

[65] *Cal. Inq. Misc.* (*1307–49*), 841.

[66] *Abingdon Chron.*, ii. 13–15. The translation, which is taken from Blair, *Anglo-Saxon Oxfordshire*, 173–4, is by Mrs M. Lockwood.

The Religious Background

Private individuals had paid for bridges a thousand years before Robert
d'Oilly. Under the Roman empire the state had the primary role in the provision and upkeep of bridges, but its work was supplemented by the generosity
of benefactors.[67] For centuries this meant that most benefactors were pagans. A
bridge over the River Bibey in the north-west of Spain has two original
inscribed columns remounted at its eastern end, one of which refers to the
reconstruction of the bridge. Trajan, adopted son of Nerva, 'reconstructed this
bridge at his expense'.[68]

Later, donations to bridges became part of the Christian life: helping travellers was an act of charity.[69] Throughout the middle ages, in the words of
Bishop Veysey in 1536, 'devout christian people . . . for the love of God and
their neighbours [built] highways and [made] bridges'.[70] Contributions were
particularly fitting as a good work because broken bridges could lead to death,
and, worse, sudden death before the last rites could be dispensed. In the
register of Thomas de Cobham, bishop of Worcester (1317-27), there is a model
letter commending the construction and repair of bridges as a work of mercy
pleasing to God, which notes that 'the ruin and damage of bridges is frequently of peril to souls and bodies'.[71] The state also lent its support: for example, letters patent were issued which provided special protection for those seeking
alms for bridges.[72]

For the medieval church, gifts to bridges, like other good works, were associated with a reduction of the time spent in Purgatory. The church issued
indulgences, which guaranteed penitents remittance from penance for sin for a
certain number of days if they contributed with their labour or money to the
repair or building of a bridge. Indulgences are recorded in some of earliest surviving episcopal registers; for instance, in 1233 Archbishop Gray of York granted an indulgence for ten days to last until the following Easter to all those who
contributed to the construction of the bridge at Wetherby.[73] In the following
centuries they were frequently sought and frequently issued on behalf of
bridges. In 1366 the men of Towcester had indulgences from seven bishops of
four different bishoprics.[74] The indulgences seem to have brought in small but
useful sums. In 1504-5 the bridge wardens of Barnstaple Bridge received 8s. 2d.
'for Indulgences'.[75]

---

[67] Brooks, 'Medieval Bridges', 14; B. Ward-Perkins, *From Classical Antiquity to the Middle Ages: Urban Public Building in Northern and Central Italy, AD 300–850* (Oxford, 1984), 186–91.
[68] O'Connor, *Roman Bridges*, 39.   [69] Brooks, 'Medieval Bridges', 16.   [70] *Cornish Bridges*, 18.
[71] *Register of Thomas de Cobham, Bishop of Worcester, 1317–21*, ed. E. H. Pearce, Worc. Hist. Soc. (1930), 164.
[72] *Rot. Lit. Pat.*, 87b.   [73] *Register of Archbishop Gray of York*, ed. J. Raine, Surtees Soc., 56 (1870), 60.
[74] J. Wake, 'Communitas Villae', *EHR* 37 (1922), 413.   [75] *Barnstaple Records*, 239.

Gifts were encouraged by churchmen with varying beliefs: Lollards and those who sympathized with them may have been particularly keen to promote the repair of bridges as a practical demonstration of devotion. Wyclif criticized priests because they enjoined men to have masses said as penances rather than to give alms to poor men and 'maken broken bridges and causeis where men and bestes and catel perischen ofte'.[76] It may not be a coincidence that Sir John Cobham, one of the principal donors to Rochester Bridge, had Lollard sympathies. So possibly did Sir Gerard Braybrooke, builder of Barford Bridge, whose brother was one of the husbands of Joan Cobham, later wife of Sir John Oldcastle. This does not mean that orthodox clergy did not see the construction or repair of bridges as an important act of charity. We have already seen that Bishop Skirlaw of Durham, who is known to have prosecuted Lollards, built bridges at both Yarm and Shincliffe.[77]

Bridge Chapels

Perhaps the clearest sign of the connection between religion and bridges was the bridge chapel, built either on or near the bridge, where priests said masses for the souls of the bridge's benefactors. Such chapels were being built in the east by the time of Justinian.[78] The earliest English references are not until the twelfth century, but of course they may have been built earlier.

By the sixteenth century there were many bridge chapels. We know of about a hundred, but there were probably more: a detailed examination in Devon found at least ten.[79] They were common at major bridges in towns. Leland saw and recorded a number on the eve of their dissolution. Two of the finest were 'owr Lady Chappel on Avon Bridge', Bristol, and 'a chapelle or chirch [St William] on Ouse bridg', York.[80] Several, such as St William's Chapel and the 'chaple of St. Sythe' which stood on Bridgnorth Bridge survived long enough to be illustrated in the late eighteenth century (plate 3). This chapel was demolished a few years later when the bridge was remodelled, but the wider pier on which it rested can still be identified.[81] A few chapels remain. The most impressive are those at Rotherham, St Ives, and Wakefield, which are built on top of the bridge piers; the last two are relatively large buildings and the piers project far into the river (plate 17).[82] Among others is the much-restored 'chapel at the est end of the bridge entering the toune of Rofecestre from London'.[83]

---

[76] *Select English Works of John Wycliff,* ed. T. Arnold, 3 vols. (Oxford, 1869–71), iii. 283.

[77] *DNB,* xviii. 357–8.   [78] Brooks, 'Medieval Bridges', 16.

[79] At Barnstaple, Bideford, Taddiport, Clyst St Mary, Colyton, Exeter, Ottery St Mary, Tiverton, Plym Bridge, and Totnes (*Devon Bridges,* 5).

[80] Leland, v. 90; i. 55.

[81] Wilson and Mee, *Ouse Bridge*; Blackwall, *Historic Bridges of Shropshire,* 7–9. Sandby's illustration is reproduced in Morriss, *The Shropshire Severn,* 65.

[82] *North,* 106, 108; *RCHM Hunts.,* 216.   [83] Leland, iv. 44; Britnell, 'Rochester Bridge', 49.

Where there was no bridge chapel there might be a substitute. At Birmingham there was a chantry chapel in the local church associated with the beneficiaries of the bridge. On many bridges a cross was erected, such as the one planned for Newark Bridge in 1485. They are less well documented than bridge chapels, but were probably very common.[84]

Chapels served a variety of functions. Some were very practical; it was claimed that the chapel by Biddenham Bridge, over the Great Ouse to the west of Bedford, acted as a refuge for anyone escaping from the thieves who plagued the neighbourhood. Their main purpose was as a place where masses were said for the souls of benefactors to reduce their time in Purgatory. The chaplains of London Bridge were recorded in 1478-9 as 'synging placebo dirges and masses of Requiem for ale the benefactors of the Bridge iiij tymes this yere'.[85] The masses also ensured that posterity remembered them. Benefactions could be listed in the bridge chapel, sometimes in a book. Leland found 'owte of a table in the chapel' at Rochester an impressive list of major benefactors, including Knolles and Cobham, who was described as the 'principale benefactor to the making' of the bridge. Among the other donors were four archbishops, four bishops, and several knights and London merchants, including Richard Whittington, who left £40 to the bridge in 1423-4.[86] The memorial in St Helen's Hospital, Abingdon, probably contained the longest account of the founding of a bridge, but it was unlikely to have been the only tablet which recorded the deeds of benefactors.[87] There may well have been boards, like those of a later date which still survive in some churches, listing charitable bequests. Benefactors were also recalled in other ways: at Warkworth Bridge in the eighteenth century there was 'an upright stone pillar on the middle, with the Percy arms sculptured'.[88]

The cost of maintaining chapels and chaplains was high. In 1395, soon after he had overseen the rebuilding of Rochester Bridge, Sir John Cobham obtained a royal licence to found a chantry which was eventually served by three chaplains supported from the bridge endowment. Expenditure was about £16 a year from 1398-9 to 1478-9; this was about 25 per cent of the cost of maintaining the bridge.[89] At the beginning of the fourteenth century John le Palmer and Alice, his wife, had been looking for funds to rebuild the long bridge over the Trent at Nottingham. It seems to have been quite an effort.

[84] Salzman, *Building*, 546-7.
[85] R. Lloyd, 'Music at the Chapel of St Thomas, London Bridge, in the Later Middle Ages', in *London Bridge*, 114.
[86] Leland, iv. 44-5.   [87] Ibid. v. 115-18.
[88] J. Wallis, *Natural History and Antiquity of Northumberland*, 2 vols. (London, 1769), ii. 355.
[89] Britnell, 'Rochester Bridge', 49-50, 70.

Nevertheless, their first step had been to endow a chapel of the bridge: in 1303 a licence had been obtained for the alienation in mortmain of £6. 13s. 4d. rent to support two chaplains to celebrate divine service ('for their souls and all who assign their goods for maintenance of the bridge') daily in the chapel of St Mary Hethebrigge.

As these strenuous efforts to find funds suggest, there was perhaps more to the bridge chapel than its obvious function as a place were masses were said and benefactors remembered. Chapels were seen as an essential feature of major bridges, just as they were of hospitals, almshouses, or schools and other important charitable institutions. It may also have been thought that a chapel would help guard against bridge collapse. This perhaps is what the following recognisance of 1427 was getting at: 500 marks was 'payable at All Hallows next . . . on condition that, before St Peter's Chains next, they shall cause a stone bridge at Kexby and another at Thornton which are begin to be new built to be completed in a workmanlike manner in the fashion of Catterick Bridge with chapels and other things which affect the security thereof'.[90]

Hermits

Another characteristic presence at bridges in late medieval England were the hermits who assisted with their repair. Most were from the lower echelons of society, and, in the words of V. G. Davis, 'quietly laboured away, performing useful social tasks'.[91] Hard though it is for us to appreciate it in the twenty-first century, their devotion commonly took the form of building and repairing bridges and roads. Their work on these projects is not just a literary convention. We know of several by name. In 1399 John Jaye 'heremite' was collecting tolls for the repair of 'small bridges' between Cambridge and Barton; by 1406 his place had been taken by Thomas Kendall. Hermits, identified by name, were also responsible for the collection of tolls for the aid of bridges at Oxford, Attlebridge, Cambridge, and Stony Stratford.[92] Indulgences were issued to others who were seeking funds for bridges at Farnham and Wandsworth.[93] Others took the lead in constructing bridges. It was claimed that at a date before 1352 Cloud Bridge, near Coventry, an important crossing of the River Avon, was first built by a hermit from the alms given to him in charity.[94]

Despite the good work that many of them undertook, hermits had their critics. Langland accused them of abusing their position. There was particular

---

[90] *CPR* (*1422–9*), 410.
[91] V. G. Davis, 'The Rule of St. Paul, the First Hermit, in Late Medieval England', in W. J. Sheils (ed.), *Monks, Hermits and the Ascetic Tradition*, Studies in Church History, 22 (Oxford, 1985).
[92] *CPR* (*1399–1401*), 90; (*1374–7*), 280; (*1403–8*), 84; (*1399–1401*), 273; *VCH Cambs*, iii. 114.
[93] Davis, 'Rule of St. Paul', 212–3.   [94] Flower, *Works*, ii. 217.

criticism of those who did not belong to an order, followed no rule, dressed up in clerical gowns, and paraded as hermits for the sake of an easy life. Such comments may have played a part in encouraging some to seek a formal role, which provided a degree of respectability. The Rule of St Paul, by which many claimed to be governed, commanded: 'Also to avoyde idelness ye be bounde to laboure youre prayers . . . and to repair wayes and brigges to youre power.'[95] Installation could take the form of a very formal ceremony. On 29 October 1423 the mayor of Maidenhead and many prominent men from the town and district stood by the rebuilt hermitage, and received a solemn profession from the new hermit, Richard Ludlow. He promised to be continent and chaste and 'to eschew all open spectacles, commone scotales, tavernys'. He agreed to attend mass, to pray, and to fast. Whatever gifts he received he would spend on repairing the bridge, 'and ye common weyes longing to ye . . . town', taking only sufficient for his sustenance. The warden then blessed the hermit's habit, admitted him to the hermitage, and he passed into the chapel *iuxta pontem.*[96]

Endowments

While the upkeep of bridges was often a key part of the hermit's life, it was not in the same way essential to the monastic vocation. Monasteries and priories did not see the upkeep of bridges as one of their principal functions. Giving was essentially a matter for individuals. In *Piers Plowman* the repair of roads and bridges is recommended as a work of charity, especially for merchants.[97] Many ecclesiastics, like the many archbishops and bishops who gave money to Rochester Bridge, did make charitable donations to bridges, but they were rarely acting on behalf of their institution.

Of course some monastic houses did maintain bridges. However, this was usually not because as institutions they made charitable donations to them, but for one of three reasons: where they were lords of towns or estates they might maintain a bridge for sound economic reasons, or they might hold lands which were anciently liable, or they might have been given an endowment in return for maintaining a bridge. Even where such an endowment had been received, it was rare for the repair of the bridge to be a major function of a monastery or priory.

There was a small group of exceptions, but they were the exceptions which prove the rule. One was the small Gilbertine house of St Saviours at Bridge End, which was established and endowed by Godwin the Rich of Lincoln. Its chief function, according to B. Golding, the historian of the Gilbertine order,

[95] Davis, 'Rule of St. Paul', 212.   [96] The hermit's profession is printed in *VCH Berks.*, ii. 20.
[97] William Langland, *The Vision of Piers the Plowman, Text B*, ed. W. W. Skeat, EETS 38 (1869), 112.

was to maintain a section of Holland Bridge, the large causeway which carried the main road from Grantham to the important port of Boston.[98] The prior held land worth £20 a year for its upkeep. There were also a number of hospitals associated with bridges. For instance, St Nicholas Hospital, which stands at the north end of Harnham Bridge, Salisbury, shared common endowments with it. The warden of the hospital was responsible for spending the revenues of the estate on the priests of the chapel on the bridge, the poor of the hospital, and the bridge. Thirteenth-century remains of hospital, chapel, and bridge survive.[99]

While it was rarely their main purpose, the endowment of ecclesiastical institutions to secure the repair of bridges seems to have been relatively common in the twelfth and thirteenth centuries. For example, St John's Hospital, Nottingham, St Batholomew's Hospital, Gloucester, and St Catherine's Hospital by the Tower of London were each responsible for the major bridge in their towns—if, in the latter case, only for a short period (plate 1).[100] They were given charge of the endowments for a number of reasons. One was very practical, as a chance comment in the long series of legal proceedings about the repair of Bow Bridge at Stratford shows. As well as paying for the construction of the bridge, Queen Mathilda endowed Barking Abbey with land, the rent from which maintained the bridge. The reason for endowing the abbey is clearly stated: 'because a layman's heirs might fail.'[101]

How to ensure that bequests, especially gifts of property, were applied to the fabric of the bridge in perpetuity was a difficult task. Could a bridge own property? Who would ensure that rents from the property were collected and spent on the bridge? It is not uncommon to find that 'divers legacies bequeathed in the past for the support of the bridge . . . have not yet been used for that purpose'.[102] The difficulties led some donors in the twelfth century to trust bridge endowments and repair to monastic houses and hospitals.

By the fourteenth century the situation had changed. Although some religious institutions continued to repair bridges up to the Reformation, others ceased to do so: by the fourteenth century London Bridge, Harnham Bridge, Salisbury, and Trent Bridge were no longer maintained by the wardens of nearby hospitals. Monasteries and hospitals had received the endowments, but, it

---

[98] B. Golding, *Gilbert of Sempringham and the Gilbertine Orders, c.1130–c.1300* (Oxford, 1995).

[99] *H Wilts.*, iii. 344; Pevsner, *Wilts.*, 458–9; *South*, 72–3.

[100] *Rot. Lit. Pat.*, 87b; *CPR (1216–25)*, 320; M. H. Ellis, 'The Bridges of Gloucester and the Hospital Between the Bridges', *Trans. Bristol and Glos. Archl. Soc.*, 51 (1929), 169–210; Watson, *Construction of the Colechurch Bridge*, 84. The Master of St Catherine's Hospital seems not to have been endowed with the bridge's properties, but to have been given temporary custodianship of them.

[101] *VCH Essex*, vi. 59.   [102] *CPR (1329)*, 379.

was often claimed, had failed to undertake the upkeep of the bridges. Jurors in the fourteenth century claimed that many years earlier the wealthy abbey of St Mary's, York, had been provided with 140 acres of land and pasture with appurtenances in Ellenthorpe by Stephen, a former earl of Richmond, for the upkeep of the bridge at Myton-on-Swale. However, the bridge had collapsed and it had not been rebuilt; the only crossing was by the abbot's boat on payment of money.[103] There were many similar disputes.[104] Donors probably came to believe that the repair of a bridge would be a low priority for a monastery or hospital.

Other ways of managing a bridge endowment which did not involve religious houses became more popular. Some were in place by an early date; for instance, in 1179–80 five London bridge gilds are mentioned; presumably they were raising funds for the new bridge.[105] Elsewhere town officials, usually bailiffs, oversaw the repair of bridges; grants of tolls were frequently issued to them for this purpose, and it is likely that they also collected rents from property given to the bridge and managed that property. Bridge wardens, specifically chosen to undertake this task by townsmen, were common. We have shown that there were wardens by the thirteenth century at several Thameside towns, including London, Wallingford, and Henley, where the 'bridge and church' estate is recorded by the fourteenth century.[106] By the late middle ages arrangements like this were common. When a town was incorporated it might be granted permission to acquire an endowment to support its bridges.[107]

This option was relatively effective, judging by the provisions of the statute of 1391 which extended the terms of the original mortmain legislation to cover gilds and fraternities, cities, boroughs, and market towns. In future they were to seek licences from the Crown to acquire any land for themselves, 'because mayors, bailiffs and commons and cities, boroughs and other towns which have a perpetual commonalty, and others which have Offices perpetual, be as perpetual as people of Religion'.[108] Evidently, for some time it had been unnecessary to entrust a bridge endowment to a monastery.

In some places religious gilds held endowments to supervise the upkeep of bridges. The commissioners of Edward VI found that the gild of the Holy Cross, Birmingham, which had been established in the reign of Richard II, 'mainteigned . . . and kept in good reparacions two greate stone bridges, and divers foule and dangerous high ways'. Gilds also undertook the repair of bridges at Stratford-upon-Avon, Abingdon, Ludlow (where the wealthy

---

[103] Flower, *Works*, ii. 270–3.   [104] *CPR* (*1340–3*), 298–9.
[105] Watson, *Construction of the Colechurch Bridge*, 84.   [106] See Chap. 9; *Henley Borough Records*, 4.
[107] *CPR* (*1405–8*), 366.   [108] *Statutes of the Realm*, ii. 80.

Palmers Gild supervised three stone bridges), and Maidenhead.[109] In the latter there was 'the gild of the chantry, originally founded by a legacy of £100 bequeathed by John Hosbonde, citizen and *bladere* of London'.[110]

The wardens of wealthy bridge estates had two main requirements: that they should be able to hold land in perpetuity, and should be able to plead in law suits. For instance, in 1391 Cobham and Knolles, with reference to Rochester Bridge, 'petitioned the crown that the wardens could sue and be sued as such rather than as individuals'. A yet more satisfactory solution was found in 1399, when Richard II allowed the property of the bridge to be vested in the 'Wardens and commonality' which consisted of those formerly liable to contribute to its repair. In practice, as Britnell has described, this meant that the Rochester wardens were, for the most part, left to run the estate. The constitution was confirmed by parliament in 1421, and the commonalty established the right to have a common seal for all the business of the bridge. The surviving bronze seal is in now in the British Museum. It bears the inscription 'sigillum gardianorum communitatis pontis roffensis'.[111]

By the fifteenth century gilds or bridge estates administered by wardens, who were usually appointed by townsmen, were clearly seen as more appropriate to supervise endowments and undertake the upkeep of bridges than monasteries or hospitals. They were also more fitting for what were evidently important communal enterprises. In *Westward Ho!* Charles Kingsley describes a lavish dinner given by bridge trustees, which gives a vivid impression of the position of the trust at the centre of Bideford society in the late sixteenth century: 'The bridge is a veritable esquire, bearing arms of its own (a ship and bridge proper on a plain field), and owning lands and tenements in many parishes, with which the miraculous bridge has, from time to time, founded charities, built schools, waged suits at law, and finally . . . given yearly dinners, and kept for that purpose (luxorious and liquorish bridge that it was) the best stocked cellar of wines in all Devon' (plate 19).[112]

The whole population of Abingdon took a great interest in the construction of the town's bridges:

> Wyves went oute to wite how they wrought:
> V. score in a flok it was a fayre syght.

---

[109] *English Gilds, the Original Ordinances from MSS. of the Fourteenth and Fifteenth Centuries*, ed. L. Toulmin Smith, EETS (1870), 249; R. Bearman, *The History of an English Borough, Stratford-on-Avon, 1196–1996* (Stroud, 1997), 53; *CPR (1441–6)*, 36; J. J. Scarisbrick, *The Reformation and the English People* (Oxford, 1994), 121. Scarisbrick also provides a brief account of the role of gilds (pp. 19–31).

[110] *CPR (1446–52)*, 576.   [111] Britnell, 'Rochester Bridge', 53–9.
[112] C. Kingsley, *Westward Ho!* (London, 1885), 234.

In bord clothes bright white brede they brought,
Chees and chekens clerelych A dyght.[113]

While Geoffrey Barbour and John of St Helens took the lead in providing the
funding, many other prominent men and some women in the neighbourhood
were involved. In 1441, twenty-five years after work had begun, a licence was
granted which permitted a perpetual gild to be founded '. . . for 13 poor, weak
and unfortunate men and women' and 'for the repair of the road from
Abingdon to Dorchester over the water of the Thames through Burford and
Culhamford between the said towns'.[114] Its founders included William, bishop
of Salisbury, William, earl of Suffolk, Thomas Bekynton, clerk, and John
Golafre. The latter may have improved other crossings in the Abingdon area.
In the seventeenth century it was said that he had built Newbridge on the
upper Thames near his manor of Fyfield. This may be right: the bridge, which
still exists with it ribbed arches, is of very similar construction to the bridges in
Abingdon. The gild was allowed to acquire 'lands, rents and possessions held in
burgage, socage or other service to value of £40; and of impleading and being
impleaded in any court and that they have a common seal and hold meetings
as often as need be'.[115]

A number of bridge estates were as rich. Richard II's charter of 1393 authorized the city of York to purchase lands to the value of £100 a year to provide for
the upkeep of its bridges. By 1443–4 the wardens and commonalty of Rochester
Bridge had an income from property very close to the 200 marks which
Richard II had authorized them to acquire.[116] The London Bridge estate had
the largest income: in 1537 it was £796. 14*s*. 4$\frac{1}{2}$*d*. Smaller estates were, of course,
more typical. The Maidenhead gild was allowed to acquire rents to the value of
10 marks per year for the repair and maintenance of the timber bridge over the
Thames, which may have been just adequate, with the tolls it received, for the
task.[117]

Of course, many bridges were not supported by a formal bridge trust or
gild. Property was often invested in trustees or feofees, as at Wadebridge in
Cornwall.[118] Many bridges must have received small propertied endowments,
such as the inn, called the Cock, which Thomas Pygot devised 'to feofees for
evermore to the sustentation and maintenance of the brigg of Stony Stratford'.[119] Most bridges relied heavily on small gifts of cash or kind. Donations of

---

[113] Leland, v. 117.　　　[114] *CPR* (*1441–6*), 36.　　　[115] Ibid.
[116] *London Bridge Accounts, 1381–1538*, ed. V. Harding and L. Wright, London Rec. Soc., 31 (1995),
pp. xvii–xviii; Britnell, 'Rochester Bridge', 77.
[117] *CPR* (*1446–52*), 576.　　　[118] *Cornish Bridges*, 24.　　　[119] *Mid and Eastern*, 84.

very varying values, which usually took the form of cash or kind rather than property, were made to all the bridges over the Great Ouse in Bedfordshire: the construction of Barford Bridge was not only funded by a large donation, but it also received several small bequests for its upkeep over the next century: in 1534 Richard Wylshire left a quarter of malt to the 'reparacyions'. Thomas Knight left 13s. 4d. for Bedford Bridge in 1522; gifts of a similar size were provided for the bridges at Biddenham, Harrold, St Neots, Stafford, and Turvey.[120] In addition to small bequests, collections might be made in local churches. In 1471–2 the Long Bridge at Barnstaple had an income from its small endowment, but also received £2. 4s. 5d. from collections in churches.[121] Thus, by the late middle ages the donations of private individuals were vital to the upkeep of bridges of all kind. Such gifts, together with ancient liabilities, were the principal means by which bridges were kept in use.

Tolls

Tolls had probably been collected at bridges in Anglo-Saxon England, but the first references to their collection at specific bridges occur in the twelfth century. Charters of this date grant *inter alia* exemptions from *pontagium*, which could mean the commutation of bridge work for a financial payment, but also the collection of tolls at a bridge.[122] The latter meaning is surely implied by a writ of Henry II (1155) which states that 'the men, horses and belongings (res) of the abbot of Fountains should be quit of *thelonium, passagium and pontagium* and all other customs, especially at Boroughbridge'.[123] This was the bridge on the Old North Road in Yorkshire, where it crossed the River Ure. A number of references in the Hundred Rolls in the next century appear to record royal rights which may well have originated centuries earlier. A complaint was made that 'Lord R. took tolls at the bridge of Billing (near Northampton) which the King and his bailiffs were wont to take there'.[124] There is no information about what happened to the money raised: it could have been used to repair the bridge or the road; on the other hand, Billing Bridge and Boroughbridge might simply have been convenient places to collect a tax.

It is likely that in Anglo-Saxon England it was unlawful to take tolls at a public bridge on a public road without appropriate authorization. By the thirteenth century there is explicit evidence to this effect. Particularly pertinent are cases involving the prosecution of those charged with collecting tolls illegally. At a date between 1236 and 1269 it was claimed that William de Beauchamp had

---

[120] *Beds. Latin Wills 1480–1519*, 47, 66; *Beds. English Wills, 1498–1526*, 37d, 192, 23.
[121] *Barnstaple Records*, 236.   [122] Neilsen, *Customary Rents*, 137–9.   [123] *EYC*, i. 75.
[124] *Rot. Hun.*, ii. 2, 15.

unjustly levied a toll on carts on the high road from Droitwich to Worcester. In his defence he claimed that the toll was taken only from carts which used a private bridge on his land when the pubic high road was unusable.[125] The outcome of the court case is unknown, but his defence implies that he agreed that the tolls would have been unlawful if the bridge had been on a public road.

There were two main ways that tolls could be authorized. The first was by ancient custom, which seems to have been the reason why the king collected tolls at Billing Bridge. Ancient custom may also explain why tolls were taken at London Bridge and a number of other major bridges throughout the fifteenth century. The other form of authorization was by a royal grant. Around 1200 the Crown seems to have adopted a policy of granting the right to take tolls as a way of raising funds for the upkeep of bridges. Such grants, sometimes called a *pontagium* (pontage grant), are commonly recorded in the patent rolls, one of the categories of new royal administrative documents which survive from the years around 1200.[126]

Because relevant documents do not survive from earlier it is impossible to be certain, but it looks as if pontages were new at this time. An early example of a grant is recorded in the patent roll for 1228 which permitted a charge to be levied on goods crossing the very important bridge of Ferrybridge in Yorkshire, where the Old North Road met the Aire. The grant is addressed to the 'custos pontis (the bridge warden) de Ferie', and concedes, 'in auxilium pontis de Ferie reparandi et emendandi', that for a year from Easter the 'custos' may take sums of money from a variety of items passing over the bridge. Finally, we are told how the public is to be informed about the tolls: the sheriff is ordered to proclaim the grant through the county.[127] It seems to have been a new type of instrument, or at least one only rarely used before: the Ferrybridge document appears tentative, suggesting an initiative which was novel and which the government thought might arouse resentment. It was probably right to think so, since the new charge could not have been popular with those who had to pay it or with others whose income was threatened.[128] Hence the grant was only for a year, and hence the emphasis on its temporariness: 'cadat illa consuetudo et peritus aboleatur.'

The pontage was the companion of the murage grant, the licence to levy a toll on goods coming for sale in the town, which was spent on town defences.

---

[125] *The Cartulary of Worcester Cathedral Priory*, ed. R. R. Darlington, Pipe Roll Soc., 76 (1968).

[126] The first grant to be recorded (for the benefit of Brentford Bridge) was, however, enrolled on the Close Rolls (*Rot. Lit. Claus.*, i. 590).

[127] *CPR* (1225–32), 173.

[128] A pontage obtained in aid of Chippenham Bridge was rescinded because it damaged the interests of the Lady of the town: *CPR* (1374–7), 170, 185.

Both started *c*.1200, but murage grants became popular more quickly, either because they were more eagerly sought or more freely granted. Pontage grants were infrequent until Edward I's reign and made for short periods. Their heyday was the fourteenth century, that of murage grants a little earlier.[129] Grants recorded on the patent rolls in the thirteenth and fourteenth centuries were similar in form to the Ferrybridge pontage. They are long, largely because they list the items which might pass over (and sometimes under) the bridge on which tolls could be taken, and the rates to be charged. They provide an extraordinary insight into the great variety of goods being traded or which it was thought might be traded. The following from a grant issued in aid of St John's Bridge, Lechlade, in 1387 is typical of the lists of commodities: 'for every cartload of grass for sale, one halfpenny; for every horse, mare, ox, and cow for sale, one farthing; for every hide of a horse and mare for sale, one farthing; for every hundred-weight of skins of goats, stags, hinds, bucks, and does, for sale, one halfpenny . . . for every horse-load of cloth for sale, one halfpenny . . .' The list continues at great length.[130]

The grant on behalf of Ferrybridge shows the chief characteristics of all pontages. They always state that the sums raised are to be spent on repairing, or occasionally rebuilding, the bridge. There is no indication that they were ever intended to be a general tax on travellers. For this reason there are prosecutions for misappropriation: following another grant in favour of Ferrybridge in 1359, John de Cotyngton of Pontefract was charged with not spending the money raised from tolls on the repair of the bridge.[131] Such cases show that abuses could occur, as they always can, but also serve to reinforce the point that the sums raised were to be applied to the bridge fabric.

Which Bridges Received Pontage Grants?

Between 1200 and 1500 several hundred pontage grants were enrolled on the patent rolls. This may have been a relatively high proportion of those issued; where other documents refer to a pontage, the initial grant can, as at Ferrybridge, often be found on the patent rolls. The most striking feature of the grants is that they were usually issued for the benefit of important bridges. There were good reasons for this. Obtaining a grant was relatively expensive and troublesome. The men of Wakefield paid £2 in 1345 as a fine to obtain a grant for three years, and other expenses would also have been involved.[132] It

---

[129] Dr Turner concluded 'it seems that by the middle of the fourteenth century the murage grant of the early fourteenth century had outlived its usefulness and was in need of replacement' (Turner, *Town Defences*, 40).

[130] The translation is taken from 'Account of Lechlade Bridge', i. 18–34.

[131] *CPR* (*1358–61*), 296; Flower, *Works*, ii. 317–19.   [132] *CPR* (*1343–5*), 549.

would not have been worth spending this money to secure a pontage either for bridges which did not generate the volume of traffic that would raise sizeable sums of money, or for smaller bridges on major highways which were relatively cheap to repair.

That said, pontages were granted to a few relatively minor bridges through the influence of a powerful patron. A good example is Burford Bridge in Oxfordshire, for which Hugh Despenser, Edward II's favourite, who was the lord of the town, secured a grant in 1323.[133] Without a suitable patron it could be difficult to obtain a grant. The men of Leicester spent 3s. on expenses to 'carry bills to Parliament for obtaining pontage' in 1323–4 in aid of the town bridge, but their request was rejected. In contrast, the earl of Leicester received one for the bridge a few years later in 1330.[134]

Yet although patronage was important, what really mattered was a good case, and high levels of traffic. In this situation it looks as if those who were determined enough could usually find a powerful figure to put their case. The patent rolls record pontages in favour of about sixty bridges. Most were either large bridges spanning big rivers or were on the most important national routes. In Shropshire it was the great bridges over the Severn, at Shrewsbury (plate 10), Montford, Bridgnorth, Atcham, and Buildwas (plate 11), which received grants. Three-quarters of the sixty bridges were across a few major rivers: the Thames, Severn, Trent, Great Ouse, and Nene. Most of the other bridges which received grants were, like Ferrybridge, on national highways. Pontages were issued on behalf of all but a few of the major crossings on the Old North Road.

Whereas most bridges received grants infrequently and for fairly short periods of from two to five years, pontages were issued to a few bridges for longer periods. Some continued to receive grants well into the fifteenth century, when they had become rare. Staines Bridge was the beneficiary of pontages throughout the thirteenth, fourteenth, and fifteenth centuries. The first grant to the bridge warden was recorded in 1228. Others were subsequently issued to the good men and bailiffs of the town: in 1286 for five years, in 1325 for two, and in 1360 for a further year. From the next decade the bridge was in almost permanent receipt of pontages. They were given regularly and for longer periods than before. As late as 1549 a grant was made for ten years.

A small number of other bridges also received grants for very long periods: a pontage was issued for fifty-one years on behalf of Kingston upon Thames Bridge in 1451, the same year that Maidenhead Bridge received a grant in per-

[133] *CPR (1321–4)*, 307.

[134] *Records of Borough of Leicester, 1103–1603*, ed. M. Bateson, 3 vols. (Cambridge, 1899–1905), 345; *CPR (1330–4)*, 28.

petuity.[135] Holland Bridge and the bridges at Newcastle upon Tyne, Redbridge, and Windsor (plate 7) received grants which in total lasted for more than fifty years. The bridges at Nottingham and Lancaster (where the main west coast road crossed the River Lune) received grants for more than twenty-five years.

These bridges do not, at first sight, have much in common, but in fact they were all structures which required heavier and more regular expenditure on maintenance than typical stone bridges. The Thames bridges were timber. Holland Bridge was a causeway of great length, incorporating many small bridges crossing lowlying fen. Redbridge consisted of bridges and a causeway across the River Test, near its junction with the tidal Southampton Water. Trent Bridge, Nottingham, and Tyne Bridge, Newcastle, were stone bridges in deep water founded on starlings, which required continuous reinforcement. They also lacked the huge endowments of Old London Bridge or Rochester Bridge. For these bridges pontages provided the money to fund regular maintenance.

In contrast, the majority of pontages were issued to bridges at moments of crisis when major repairs had to be undertaken, as some entries on the patent rolls emphasize. In 1344 a grant was made on behalf of Wallingford Bridge, 'which threatened to become a ruin'.[136] At times of emergency, grants were sought even by the bridge wardens of the best-endowed bridges. One had been obtained on behalf of London Bridge shortly before it collapsed in 1282.[137] The Rochester Bridge wardens sought and obtained grants during two of the major crises they faced in the first half of the fifteenth century: when cracks were found in the stonework in 1409–10, and when the abutments were in danger in 1431.[138]

In issuing pontages, the government took into account a number of other factors as well as the condition of the bridge. It was usually keen to ensure that by granting a pontage it did not thereby relieve anyone of his liabilities. Grants were issued more readily in aid of those bridges which relied on charity alone. Eleanor de Percy petitioned for a pontage for Wetherby Bridge; she was allowed one if it were found by inquisition that no one was bound to repair it. A grant was subsequently issued for three years in 1316.[139] Others were issued to assist those who were liable to repair a bridge, but in such cases the Crown was keen to stress that their liability continued. A pontage issued for the benefit of Holland Causey pointed out that the obligation of certain people to repair the bridge was not removed by issuing the grant.[140]

---

[135] *CPR (1446–52)*, 231, 576; *(1452–61)*, 273.   [136] *CPR (1343–5)*.   [137] *CPR (1281–92)*, 30.
[138] Britnell, 'Rochester Bridge', 70–1.
[139] Flower, *Works*, i. p. xxxiv; *Rot. Parl.*, i. 340a; and see *Cal. Inq. Misc. (1348–77)*, 297.
[140] *CPR (1292–1301)*, 576.

Strangely, for all the attention the government gave to how and why a pontage might be granted, and for all the effort which went into obtaining them, the money raised from the grants was surprisingly small relative to other sources of funds. The evidence is limited, but all points in the same direction. Two pontage grants were issued on behalf of Pershore Bridge in Edward III's reign. Each raised £10.[141] In 1362 two presentments were made about the funds levied at Ferrybridge from a pontage granted in 1359: it was claimed that Philip Otere had raised £20 (over an unknown period) at the bridge by adopting a forceful approach and presumably ignoring the claims of those with exemptions. He put bars on the bridge and let none pass without payment. John de Cotyngton had collected £6 in forty-six weeks for which he had to account.[142] By the sixteenth century even less was being raised: in the period 1537–65 the tolls at Kingston upon Thames Bridge were farmed out for 33s. 8d. a year. This represented 15 to 20 percent of the annual net receipts of the bridge of around £9.[143] It was a useful contribution to bridge finances, but nevertheless a modest sum.[144]

The money levied at the largest bridges represented an even smaller percentage of their income. The Rochester Bridge accounts record collections from pontage tolls of a minimum of 1s. and a maximum of £6; in comparison, the annual income from land was usually about £100. More was raised from tolls at London Bridge, but the sums were still modest compared with the total income. In 1381–2 £24. 8s. 5d. was collected from the toll on carts, in 1420–1 £7. 6s. 11d., in 1461–2, £43. 15s. 7d. By the end of the fifteenth century the toll was farmed for £23 per year, which was less than 5 percent of the estate's income. At 2d. per cart, which was probably the rate charged, this is the annual sum which would be produced from fewer then ten carts per day paying the toll at the bridge.[145] By this date, as H. L. Turner argued, the many exemptions may have meant that few paid. Nevertheless, it is surprising to discover that so little was collected.

It is something of a paradox that the pontage grants should have raised relatively little money, but are the most comprehensively documented method of funding bridge repair, with grants regularly and meticulously recorded on the

---

[141] Flower, *Works*, ii. 361–2; *CPR* (*1334–8*), 414.   [142] Flower, *Works*, ii. 317–19; *CPR* (*1358–61*), 296.

[143] *Kingston Bridgewardens' Accounts*, pp. x–xi, 231.

[144] It is possible that the surviving sources give a distorted picture since we know that murages could raise very large sums: a grant at Newcastle provided £120 in 1280; the largest amount collected was the £200 taken at Southampton in 1377–8 (Turner, *Town Defences*, 233–5). However, the sums raised by pontages are likely to have been less: all traffic had to enter a town past one of several collection points; and tolls on bridges could be avoided by using a ford, ferry, or alternative bridge crossing.

[145] *Traffic and Politics*, 312–4; *London Bridge Accounts*, pp. xx–xxi.

patent rolls. In contrast to the pontages, the other main sources of finance are documented in a haphazard way. Just a fraction of the many donations made to bridges are recorded. The ancient liabilities owed by many landholders are largely known from court cases which dwell on the minority of cases which involved difficulties of enforcement. Yet, despite the relatively scanty documentation, it is evident that the funds raised from those anciently liable and from the numerous private donations dwarfed the sums raised from tolls.

POST-1530

1530–1760

Historians have long claimed that two important developments in the 1530s and 1540s had a significant impact on the system of bridge repair. First, as result of the Statute of Bridges in 1530, those bridges which no one was bound to repair became the responsibility of the county. Secondly, it is argued that the English Reformation had practical consequences for bridge repair and construction. In place of the piety and good works characteristic of the monastic vocation and late medieval Christianity, we are told that there was a new attitude to charitable donations which was less favourable to bridges. The Chantries Act of 1547 suppressed the religious gilds: henceforth there were no more bridge chapels and endowments of these gilds were confiscated. As a result of the dissolution of the monasteries their vast lands were transferred to new owners, who failed to carry out the ancient liabilities which fell on them.

The 'Acte conc'nyng the amendement of Bridges in Highe Wayes' had two principal provisions. First, Justices of the Peace were now to ensure that those responsible repaired damaged bridges, 'as the Kynges Justices of his Benche use comonly to doo'. Secondly, it tackled the problem of bridges which no one was liable to repair: 'And where in many partes of this realme it can not be knowen or proved, what Hundrede, Riddynge, Wapentake, Citie, Borough, Towne, or Parisshe, nor what [person] or body politic ought of right to make suche bridges . . . by reasone wherof suche decayed bridges for lacke of knowledge of suche as owen to make them for the moste parte lyen longe withoute any amendement, to the greate anoyaunce of the Kynges Subjectes . . .' To remedy this the JPs were given the power to charge the inhabitants of the relevant town, city, or county for repairs, and appoint both collectors of rates and surveyors to inspect and carry out repairs to the bridges.[146] In the long run the statute was

---

[146] *Statutes of the Realm*, iii. 321–3.

to be of great importance, but the short-term effects varied from county to county.

We can begin to trace its consequences by the late sixteenth century. The earliest records of expenditure by a county at the quarter sessions come from the North Riding of Yorkshire and Norfolk in the 1560s and 1570s. By the early seventeenth century Devon, Staffordshire, and the West Riding were also repairing bridges.[147] As the act intended, some bridges formerly repaired by alms became the responsibility of the county.[148] In addition, it is possible that here and there counties took some responsibility for bridges formerly repaired by liable individuals and communities, but the extent of this practice cannot be known.[149]

Fortunately we have good quantitative evidence of the effects of the Bridge Statute because of C. Chalkin's detailed analysis. He shows that its impact varied enormously from county to county. In the period 1650 to 1760 nine counties were responsible for between twenty and fifty bridges, and eleven others handled between fifty and 200 bridges. Devon had the most county bridges, with over 200 by in the seventeenth century. In contrast, about half of English counties took responsibility for a mere handful of bridges.[150] These figures are not just a reflection of the number of major bridges in the county; for instance, there were many important bridges across the Thames, but few were the responsibility of the quarter sessions.[151] Evidently as late as the mid-eighteenth century ancient methods of repairing bridges remained very important.

The notion that the Reformation led to a reduction in charitable donations to bridges has been advanced intermittently in studies of bridges, and continues to be. It is an appealing theory because, if right, it might explain why so few new bridges were built at new sites in the period 1550–1750.[152] It is, however, wrong. Although doctrines which had encouraged good works, in particular the doctrine of Purgatory, were rejected at the Reformation, charity did not stop, and gifts continued to be made to bridges. Protestants, like the Lollards before them, stressed practical acts of charity. Under Elizabeth's injunctions of July 1559 for 'the suppression of superstition', 'clergy were to discourage dying parishoners from making any religious obit provisions other than bequests to the poor and to highways'.[153]

There is ample evidence that gifts to bridges continued: for instance, in 1583 donations to the wardens for Rochester Bridge totalled £50, in 1584, £45.[154] It

---

[147] Chalkin, *Public Building*, 97.   [148] 'Bridges of Bedfordshire', 27–9.
[149] Chalkin, *Public Building*, 98–9.   [150] Ibid. 93–7.   [151] Ibid. 97–8.
[152] *Cornish Bridges*, 22; Crook, *Medieval Bridges*, 15, 47.
[153] E. Duffy, *The Stripping of the Altars: Traditional Religion in England, 1400–1580* (London, 1992), 568.
[154] J. M. Gibson, 'Rochester Bridge, 1530–1660', in *Traffic and Politics*, 150.

was not only large bridges which benefited. In 1615 Sir John Howley of Howley Hall in the West Riding of Yorkshire appealed to the inhabitants of Leathley to contribute to the reconstruction of Newlay Bridge, noting that: "one James Cootes of Headingley hath owte of his charitable minde and disposition to do some good worke which might tende to a general good of the Country, given four score pounds to the building of a bridge over the water of Aire at Newlath . . . where sometime an olde bridge hath bene.'[155] Jordan's classic examination of philanthropy shows broadly similar levels of charitable benefactions to 'public works, roads etc.' throughout the sixteenth century. He undertook a survey of charitable benefactions made in a sample of counties from 1480 to 1660. In the sixteenth century spending ranged from £1,500 to £3,000 per decade, except for the 1540s, when it was £4,631, and the 1520s, £1,166.[156] It tended to be higher in the second half of the century, so allowing for inflation it probably remained relatively stable in real terms. Gifts continued to be given for the upkeep of bridges in the early eighteenth century.[157]

It is therefore evident that changing attitudes to charity are unlikely to explain the decline in new bridge construction after 1550. In that case, what was the explanation? The existence of so many bridges was a major factor, as it had been for three centuries. That is there was not much demand for new bridges at new sites. However, it is also likely that the decline was in part an unintended consequence of the Statute of Bridges: a generous bequest to fund a new bridge could end up creating a long-term burden on the county ratepayer.

What of other steps taken at the Reformation? Some bridge endowments were affected by the suppression of the chantries because the assets of religious gilds, which had been used to maintain bridges, were confiscated. Most were at least partially restored, if only after a protracted effort on the part of townsmen, and sometimes after they had had to buy back their own assets. Maidenhead was particularly unlucky: after the gild was suppressed support for the bridge was not provided until 1582, when the town was incorporated.[158] After much effort, and at some cost, the men of Ludlow also regained property with which *inter alia* they maintained their three bridges.[159] The men of Stratford-upon-Avon were more fortunate: the town was incorporated in 1553. It had an income of £80 per year to support school, almshouses, and the bridge.[160] Similarly in Abingdon: the fraternity of the Holy Cross was suppressed, but was restored as Christ's Hospital five years later. Its new endowment was over £65 per year, which was probably sufficient to enable it to repair its bridges and roads.[161]

---

[155] Preston, *Aire and Calder Bridges*, 139–40.   [156] Jordan, *Philanthropy*, 372.
[157] 'Bridges of Bedfordshire', 74.   [158] Phillips, *Thames Crossings*, 111;
[159] Scarisbrick, *Reformation*, 121.   [160] *Stratford-on-Avon*, 83.
[161] Scarisbrick, *Reformation*, 115, 118; *VCH Berks.*, ii. 93.

It was the bridges attached to religious gilds which suffered. Fortunately most bridge estates were not associated with such gilds. Instead, they were in the hands of a secular organization: some, for instance, were in the possession of city corporations, as at York. Inevitably some of these estates lost that part of their endowment which funded the priests of the bridge chapel, but not all: the Rochester Bridge wardens were able to prevent the £18 annual stipend for the priests from falling into the hands of the Crown.[162]

We are also told that the dissolution of the monasteries was bad for bridges: monastic houses were involved in bridge repair, 'both as an expression of piety, and because good communications helped the efficient administration of large monastic estates'.[163] There is, however, little if any evidence to support this opinion. In some places the reverse was the case: it is notable that the abbot of Abingdon seemed to be one of the few prominent local figures who did not make a significant contribution to the construction of bridges near the town. Reformers said they wanted to use the assets of the monasteries for practical good works. In practice this was not the norm, but occasionally it happened. A commission of Northamptonshire gentlemen used the proceeds of demolishing part of the collegiate church at Fotheringay, together with a £100 from Sir Walter Mildmay, to rebuild the bridge over the Nene there.[164]

More plausibly it has been argued that the dissolution of the monasteries had another effect: the 'new owners of monastic land did not inherit ancient obligations along with the rest of the property.'[165] This was sometimes the case: an inquiry of 1588 found that St Neots Priory had been largely responsible for the bridge of the town, 'but since [its] suppression the inhabitants of the parish and various well-disposed people in neighbouring counties had maintained it'.[166] Elsewhere, however, liabilities were inherited. For instance, the monks of Beaulieu Abbey, as lords of the manor of Faringdon, were partially liable for the repair of Radcot Bridge on the upper Thames; their successors remained liable into the twentieth century.[167] This must have reflected the legal position. Of course, in the dislocation caused by the massive change of ownership, some landowners probably were able to avoid the liabilities which were vested in the land they acquired, but it is far from clear that this was common. It should also be remembered that, even though so much land changed hands, most of the land in the country was unaffected by the Reformation and remained in the same ownership.

---

[162] Gibson, *Rochester Bridge, 1530–1660*, 111–13.   [163] 'Bridges of Bedfordshire', 10–11.
[164] *King's Works*, iii. 251.   [165] Ibid.   [166] Ibid.
[167] Phillips, *Thames Crossings*, 24–7; and for another example see Chalkin, *Public Building*, 97.

It is, therefore, not surprising that many liabilities remained. We have seen that the survey of Willey Hundred in Bedfordshire in 1630 found that the bridges across the Great Ouse at Bromham, Harrold, Stafford, and Turvey were still being repaired by individuals or parishes anciently liable.[168] Towns which had repaired their bridges in the middle ages continued to be responsible for them: many Thames bridges were still being repaired by the town or city authorities in the nineteenth century.[169] At York the corporation repaired its bridges up to the nineteenth century, using the endowment it had acquired in the late middle ages.[170]

In the early eighteenth century the system of bridge repair may have remained essentially medieval. Ancient liabilities and charitable donations and endowments probably still provided the bulk of the funding, albeit they were supplemented, to a greater or lesser extent, by tolls and, depending on the county, by the new provisions established by the Bridge Statute 200 years earlier

1760 to the Present Day

During the eighteenth century there was a gradual and almost imperceptible shift to a new system of funding bridges. After 1760 there was a large increase in expenditure on county bridges. Total expenditure was c.£250,000–£350,000 in the 120 years from 1640 to 1760. It was almost double this sum in real terms in the forty years from 1760 to 1800, and had doubled again in the period from 1800 to 1830.[171] The rise in expenditure was in part because the number of county bridges increased. Bridges, previously repaired by their owners, became county bridges: for instance, three Surrey bridges at Cobham, Leatherhead, and Godalming were adopted by the county in 1782.[172]

The main reason, however, for the increase in expenditure was the very extensive reconstruction of existing bridges in the late eighteenth and early nineteenth centuries. Some counties spent large sums on major bridges: Atcham Bridge in Shropshire was rebuilt by the county in 1768 to the designs of John Gwynn at a cost of £8,647.[173] Elsewhere it was the number of bridges which is striking: in the North Riding in the 1770s and 1780s about twenty bridges were widened or rebuilt, at costs varying from £120 to £1,715.

The cost of reconstruction was often too great for those traditionally liable, and in many places led to the end of ancient funding arrangements. In 1810 the

---

[168] 'Bridges of Bedfordshire', 11.
[169] e.g. at London, Kingston, Windsor, Maidenhead, Henley, Wallingford, and Oxford (Phillips, *Thames Crossings*).
[170] *VCH City of York*, 516–19.   [171] Chalkin, *Public Building*, 129.   [172] Ibid. 119.
[173] Ibid. 118–20.

city corporation began work on rebuilding Ouse Bridge, York. Progress, however, was slow because funds were inadequate. Work was suspended in June 1814, and an act of parliament was obtained in the following year. Authority for the work was removed from the corporation and vested in the justices of the three Ridings and the city. The total cost of the new bridge was estimated to be £80,000.[174]

The arrangements for funding the boom in the construction and reconstruction of major bridges after 1760 contained a number of common elements. An act of parliament often authorized a group of trustees to undertake the work. The funds were usually provided either by subscription or by a loan. The act also commonly provided that the loan, and sometimes the subscribers, would be reimbursed from the proceeds of a toll which was typically granted for a limited period. It is worth noting that, although some of the institutional arrangements had changed, many of the elements of the organization and funding of major projects would have been instantly recognized by those involved in constructing Abingdon Bridge three centuries earlier.

Consider, for example, another Shropshire bridge. In 1766 an act was passed 'for Repairing and Widening the Stone bridge in the Town of Shrewsbury', which gave responsibility for the works to a group of trustees. The project was supported by subscribers, including Lord Clive, the MP for the town and the wealthiest man in the neighbourhood, who gave £1,000 in July 1767. In September of that year it was decided not to widen the existing bridge, but to build a new bridge to the design of John Gwynn. In May 1769, after eighteenth months spent putting the funds in place for the project, a contract was signed. The foundation stone was laid, 'amidst the Acclamations of a great Number of Spectators', on 29 June in that year. However, it relatively soon became clear that funds were insufficient. More money was raised, not only from the subscribers, but now also from the local turnpike trusts. The bridge eventually cost almost £16,000, of which the subscribers paid around £11,500.[175]

Bridge acts commonly gave the trustees the right to take tolls to cover the initial costs. This did not happen at Shrewsbury, possibly because the corporation already had the right to take tolls and was unwilling to assign them to the trustees. Tolls, however, financed Gwynn's third bridge across the Severn, at Worcester.[176] Similarly, at Bedford an act 'for the Improvement of the Town of Bedford, and for rebuilding the Bridge over the River Ouze, in the said Town' of 1803 permitted the collection of tolls to repay monies raised through public

---

[174] *VCH City of York*, 517.
[175] The construction of the bridge is described in detail in Ward, *Bridges of Shrewsbury*, 41–77.
[176] Ruddock, *Arch Bridges*, 111–13, 243.

subscription. A further act in 1810 allowed additional funds to be raised. Among the chief contributors were the duke of Bedford and Samuel Whitbread. The new bridge opened on 1 November 1813. Tolls were charged until 1835.[177]

Smaller bridges were financed in a variety of ways. The funds for some came from local worthies.[178] Navigation commissioners made contributions, especially when bridges had to be rebuilt to improve navigation. Thus when Monk Bridge in York was rebuilt in the 1790s, a grant of £100 was made by the Foss Navigation Company. Turnpike trusts too built and rebuilt bridges, especially minor bridges, as Defoe observed.[179] They also constructed a number of more important bridges. It was the Biggleswade to Alconbury Hill Turnpike Trust which paid for the first cheap timber bridge at Tempsford on the Great Ouse in 1736.[180]

Throughout the nineteenth century the county's role in the upkeep of bridges continued to increase. Sometimes an agreement with bridge owners was reached; sometimes the county gave up the legal struggle to make those liable pay for repairs. The Gloucestershire justices continued to attempt to get the landowners, whom they believed had inherited the liabilities, to repair Lechlade Bridge, but they were unsuccessful: when the bridge needed repairing in the 1830s and 1880s the county paid for the work. A number of the ancient bridges over the Great Ouse in Bedfordshire became the responsibility of the county: Blunham Bridge was adopted as a county bridge in 1839, Turvey Bridge in 1881. In this county the turnpike trusts were wound up between 1868 and 1877, and liability for their bridges was transferred to the county. Finally, in 1888 the responsibilities of counties, supervised by JPs at the quarter sessions, were transferred to the new county councils which have continued to maintain most of the country's bridges.[181]

Nevertheless, at the beginning of the motor-car age bridges were still being repaired by landowners who had inherited a liability almost a thousand years old, or from funds from bridge estates which had been established almost as long. Over the next fifty years the remains of these funding arrangements disappeared. In 1926 it was decided that Abingdon Bridge needed to be reconstructed; the cost was beyond the means of Christ's Hospital and the two counties of Berkshire and Oxfordshire agreed to assume responsibility for it. At Wallingford the bridge estate properties had been sold in the nineteenth century and the proceeds invested in consuls. In 1934, when the bridge needed

---

[177] Chalkin, *Public Building*, 34–5.   [178] For an example see 'Bridges of Bedfordshire', 52.
[179] Defoe, *Tour*, ii. 127.   [180] 'Bridges of Bedfordshire', 73.
[181] Phillips, *Thames Crossings*, 22–3 'Bridges of Bedfordshire', 11–12, 69.

extensive reinforcement, the fund proved inadequate and the county councils took on the work. A few of the bridge estates lasted even longer. It was not until March 1968, following the collapse of an arch, that the Ministry of Works took over the responsibility for and maintenance of the fabric of Bideford Bridge, subject to the trust contributing £1,000 a year in perpetuity. The trust has maintained its substantial property holdings and investments, which it uses for charitable purposes.[182]

[182] Phillips, *Thames Crossings*, 61, 75–6; Whiting, *Long Bridge of Bideford*, 18–19.

12

Conclusions: Bridges, Transport, and Pre-industrial Society

This book has attempted to trace the history of bridges and other river crossings in England over the last 2,000 years. It begins with the impressive programme of construction undertaken by the Romans. The remnants of a few of their finest structures can still be seen. By the seventh century, however, most Roman bridges had collapsed and, although there were major exceptions, few new bridges had been built. Bede describes a society where bridges seem to have been scarce. However, within twenty years of his death renewed emphasis was being given to the building of bridges. Over the following centuries a new road and bridge network was established which owed surprisingly little to its Roman predecessor. By the late Anglo-Saxon period major crossings had been built in timber, or stone and timber, at key crossings, including Nottingham and London, Bristol, Worcester, and Huntingdon, and many lesser sites. By the thirteenth century, and possibly earlier, the network of bridges which was to last until the eighteenth century was largely complete: at most places where there was a bridge in 1750 there had been a bridge 500 years earlier, and at many sites long before that. The national road system which these bridges supported suddenly comes into full view in the fourteenth century when it is described on the Gough Map, but it is likely that it is older. It survived with few changes into the twentieth century. Although their number and location did not change, the bridges themselves were rebuilt in stone from c.1100 onwards. This process was largely complete by 1500; only around the Thames did many major timber bridges survive until the late eighteenth century. From this period much began to change: new bridges were built in place of ferries, older bridges reconstructed, and many others widened.

The history of bridges has very important implications for our understanding of transport and, more generally, of society in pre-industrial England. It provides insights into many subjects: the road system, the amount of traffic using it, the extent of internal trade, the development of the economy, and even the nature of the state. It also highlights the problems caused by historians' specialization in relatively narrow periods. Because bridges are easily identified, because they can be counted, and because a surprising amount can be found out about them from an early date, we can take a very long view of the development of this important part of the transport infrastructure. We can put post-medieval changes in the context of the medieval transport system, and we can get a clearer perception of the significance of the medieval road network by comparing it directly with later periods. Thus it is possible to overcome the drawback that most works on road transport and internal trade in pre-industrial England have tended to examine different periods in isolation.

BRIDGES AND ROADS

Those who have studied the medieval road system have emphasized that investment in it was concentrated on bridges. Sir Frank Stenton argued that 'it was not by the making of new roads, but by the building of bridges that [medieval] Englishmen set about improving their communications'. More recently B. P. Hindle has claimed that 'bridges and causeways . . . attracted more attention in medieval times', A. R. H. Baker that 'improvement of roads was highly localised and concentrated especially on bridges'.[1]

There is no doubt, as this book has stressed, that very large sums were spent on bridges. There were several reasons why this should have happened. The most obvious and important was the need to establish and maintain safe, dry crossings. But a dense network of bridges was also a requirement of an age when transport, dependent on horse traction, was slow by the later standards of railways and motor vehicles. A modern car driver loses only a few minutes if he has to go out of his way because there is no bridge; a medieval carter could lose hours from a similar diversion. That bridges over major rivers were often only 5 miles apart shows the sort of detour which it was thought necessary to avoid.

However, to stress the scale of spending on bridges is not to say that roads were ignored. Too much emphasis has been given to the supposed dichotomy between an impressive network of bridges, on which large sums of money were spent, and roads, which were neglected. Bridges were built as part of the road system. The quality of roads and investment in them have not been thoroughly studied, and it is beyond the scope of this book to look at them in any

---

[1] Stenton, 'Road System', 238–9; Hindle, *Medieval Roads*, 11; A. R. H. Baker, 'Changes in the Later Middle Ages', in H. C. Darby, *A New Historical Geography of England Before 1600* (Cambridge, 1973), 237.

detail. Nevertheless, even though our knowledge of the subject is very limited, the notion that medieval roads were little more than rights of way and that the medieval road system consisted of splendid bridges joined together by oceans of mud seems inherently implausible. There is some evidence that such views are excessively pessimistic. There were many long causeways, for example, at the approaches of bridges and across the fens. There are also many examples of the maintenance of roads by such methods as the application of gravel and other stones and by the scouring of ditches.[2] Bequests were frequently made for the upkeep of roads, which presumably included work of this type: in 1427 Sir Gerard Braybroke left £100 'to foule wayes in Bedfordshyr and Buckyng-hamshir and also in Essex', in addition to his bequest to Barford Bridge; in 1434 Joan, Lady Abergavenny, bequeathed £100 for 'the makyng and emendyng of feble brugges' and another £100 for 'foule wayes'.[3] It is possible that as much if not more was spent on the repair of roads as on bridges. Roads continued to prove troublesome, not least where they crossed the heavy clays of the midlands and the Weald or where gradients were very steep, but that should not detract from the considerable efforts made to maintain and improve them. Moreover, such failings continued long after the middle ages. Major improvements in the productivity of road transport did not begin to occur until the middle of the eighteenth century.[4] Heavy clays still created difficulties long after.[5]

BRIDGES AND ROAD TRANSPORT

Demand and Supply

The information about bridges not only gives an insight into the quality of the road network, but also provides an important indicator of the extent of road transport and internal trade. It is likely that the number of bridges is related to transport demand. Of course the situation is complex. The paucity of statistics on road transport makes it difficult to prove any link between the volume of road traffic and the number of bridges, and there is unlikely to be a universal rule governing the relationship.

There were several important supply-side factors which affected the construction and reconstruction of the network. Important political and military, as well as economic, considerations lay behind the bridge-building undertaken

---

[2] e.g. see Flower, *Works*, ii. pp. xvi, 91, 241.
[3] *Register of Henry Chichele*, ii. 412, 536; many similar examples could be given.   [4] See Chap. 6.
[5] Pawson, *Transport and Economy*, 275–9.

by Saxon kings. Charitable impulses encouraged construction: a wealthy merchant with no heirs might make a large bequest which determined whether a bridge was constructed. Growth in per-capita wealth, which is such a notable feature of the fifteenth century, not only stimulated traffic growth but also, because more people had money to spare for such projects, encouraged construction. There were also special circumstances at some locations which caused a bridge to be built; for instance, a ford may have became unuseable.[6]

Yet underpinning all these supply-side factors which might influence individual decisions was the demand to travel. Many of the major Saxon bridges, such as those constructed at London and Nottingham, may have been built for reasons of state, but they also met a latent demand. They rapidly became indispensable to all kinds of traveller and all types of transport. In general, the supply-side factors had only a relatively small effect on the number of bridges. Consider one of most important: donations to bridges. Such gifts were a pious and charitable act, and both large and small sums of money were bequeathed for their building, rebuilding, and repair. Yet these gifts were made to meet transport needs: they were given to existing bridges because those bridges were important to travellers, and to new bridges because there was a strong potential demand. Proof of this is that there is no evidence of an over-supply of bridges which bore little relation to the needs of society. Indeed, it is hard to find the medieval equivalent of the Humber Bridge, planned in the 1960s for essentially non-transport reasons and underused. Medieval bridges were not white elephants.

Clopton Bridge, Stratford-upon-Avon, still stands as a lasting memorial to its builder, Hugh Clopton (plate 21). This does not mean that it was simply a testimony to his piety, or vanity, built without regard to how much it would be used. On the contrary, he was praised because his new bridge and causeway made the journey across the Avon much safer and more convenient, and increased the number of people going to Stratford. Leland recounts that:

Clopton aforesayde made also the great and sumptuouse bridge apon Avon at the este end of the towne. This bridge [hath] 14 great archis of stone, and a long cawsey made of stone and now waullyd on eche syde, at the west end of the bridge.

Afore the tyme of Hughe Clopton there was a but a poore bridge of tymber, and no causey to come to it; whereby many poore folkys [and] othar refusyd cum to Stratford, when Avon was up, or cominge thithar stoode in jeoperdy of lyfe.[7]

Bridge building was considered a charitable act largely because it was useful.

---

[6] e.g. the building of mills and weirs could sometimes deepen the water at fords, possibly making them unuseable for much of the year (Flower, *Works*, i. 195; ii. 199).

[7] Leland, ii. 49–50.

There are several other reasons for thinking that bridges funded by charitable offerings were built in response to demand. First, the location of bridges over major rivers suggests that they were built at rational and cost-effective locations, where the demands of the traffic were greatest, often in or between towns. If bridge building had been determined by pious motives without thought for utility, grand bridges would have been built in unexpected places. They were not. Secondly, if the bridges had been built with little regard to need, one might have expected that little interest would have been taken in their maintenance or repair, and that in the course of time they would have collapsed and disappeared. With a few exceptions, this did not happen. Finally, there is evidence that new bridges attracted considerable amounts of traffic; for example, following the generous bequests which led to the construction of bridges in and near Abingdon a new major road from London to Gloucester and Wales was formed.[8]

It is also unlikely that supply-side factors provide the main explanation for the relatively low rate of new construction during the late middle ages, and in particular in the sixteenth and seventeenth centuries. There is no evidence that charitable donations declined significantly. Gifts continued to be given to bridges throughout this period and into the late eighteenth century. Some were very generous. The opposition of vested interested may have discouraged bridge construction, but only to a limited extent. A powerful corporation, like the City of London, might for some time be able to prevent the construction of a bridge which was seen to threaten its interests. Another factor was that, as a consequence of the Statute of Bridges, there was a reluctance to build new bridges because their maintenance would be a charge on the county rate.[9] However, these factors had a relatively marginal importance. They might explain why fewer new bridges were built in the 150 years after 1530 than in the previous 150 years. They do not explain the remarkable stability of the network in the 500 years after 1250. This is because in the long run the size and nature of the network reflected the requirements of road users.

The best indication of this is the change that came about as a result of the economic growth and increasing volumes of traffic in the second half of the eighteenth century. Most of the remaining unbridged river crossings on secondary roads were bridged. New bridges were built in cities, most notably in London. A small number of new routes were opened up and bridges built on them.[10] The change in the late eighteenth century may, of course, have been

---

[8] See Chap. 4.
[9] See Chap. 11. The opposition of the City of London to the construction of Westminster Bridge is described in Walker, *Old Westminster Bridge*, 45–6.
[10] See Chap. 4.

a delayed response to a demand which had been building up for some time, but it is surely no coincidence that new construction occurred when the economy and population were beginning to grow rapidly. The contrast between the events of the mid-sixteenth to the mid-eighteenth centuries with those from the late eighteenth century on is very striking.

Secondary Sources

The existence of a large network of bridges in the middle ages which supported a busy inland trade fits in well with the researches undertaken by medieval historians over many years. Even in the 1920s and 1930s, when most historians believed that eighteenth-century land communications were poor and had been worse earlier, a few medievalists had presented a more positive view, arguing that medieval roads were adequate for the requirements of a relatively vibrant economy.[11] Stenton long ago concluded that the road network was ancient and extensive.[12] J. Willard noted that carts carried a wide range of commodities along these roads, from wool, grain, and building-stone to government records and corpses, over both short and long distances.[13] He considered that carts were the most important method of conveying goods: 'there was a division of labour between [carts, pack-horses, and barges] but the greater share of the burden was borne in the fourteenth century by the cart'. He also argued that the quality of roads was better than has often been thought, and the cost of carriage was less than has sometimes been supposed: 'it was by no means prohibitive.' Along the roads, 'the most vivid impression is that of the large amount of movement'.[14] The evidence was impressionistic, based on the manner, cost, and speed of a few recorded journeys, but sufficient to show the scale and variety of road transport. O. Coleman's more quantitative work on the Southampton Brokage books provided a similar account, showing the large number of carts leaving Southampton for all parts of the country in the late middle ages; some went as far north as Kendal.[15]

Recent work has supported these earlier views. J. Langdon's very thorough study of haulage and transport, based on a large national sample of manorial documents, traces among other trends the shift from ox to horse traction and the associated efficiency gains. He also shows that on the great majority of manors peasants had acquired carts.[16] J. Masschaele, in a study of the costs of road transport using purveyance records, argued that fourteenth-century

[11] Jackman, *Transportation*, i. 8–9, 43, 45.   [12] Stenton, 'Road System', 252; see Chap. 6.
[13] Willard, *Inland Transportation*, 364–8.   [14] Ibid. 374; Willard, *The Use of Carts*, 250.
[15] *The Brokage Book of Southampton, 1443–4*, ed. O. Coleman, Southampton Rec. Soc., 4 (1960).
[16] Langdon, *Horses and Oxen*, 22, 86–118, 176–229; Langdon, *Horse Hauling*, 37–66.

transport costs were similar to, if not lower than, those of the eighteenth century. Given that the cost of fodder was, as D. Gerhold has demonstrated, such an important factor, it is unlikely that transport costs were lower, but nevertheless it is of considerable interest that the costs may have been very broadly similar.[17]

Others studies have shown that trade was extensive. C. Dyer has found traces of a 'hidden trading network . . . well established by the eleventh century'. His researches have demonstrated that in the later middle ages a wide range of consumers made frequent use of the market, often over long distances. He notes that: 'London's tentacles in the 15th century spread over the whole kingdom', and 'even the bishop of Carlisle and the cellarer of Durham Priory bought spices from merchants in the capital'.[18]

The increasing sophistication of the medieval economy has been linked to improvements in road transport. B. M. S. Campbell has shown that the proposition that urbanization was linked to the development of regional specialization and integration can be applied to the thirteenth as well as to the sixteenth and seventeenth centuries. He considers that: 'The large size of towns (especially London, now thought to have had a population of at least 90,000 in 1300) . . . symptomatic of rising agricultural productivity and an evolution towards a specialized and integrated pattern of food production and supply . . . is certainly a development to which more widespread use of the horse may have made an indirect contribution . . . Horse haulage increased the speed and range of market transactions.'[19]

It should, moreover, come as no surprise that many bridges had been constructed by an early date. Increasingly, historians see the late Saxon period as formative in the development of English wealth. There has been increasing acceptance of the view that by the time of Domesday Book England was very rich. Professor James Campbell concluded: 'Some of the most important changes which took place in late Anglo-Saxon England were economic. It could be that these were more significant than any which took place in the sixteenth century or even later; for example in the development of towns and of large scale manufacture; in the extensive (and strongly capitalized) exploitation

---

[17] J. Masschaele, 'Transport Costs in Medieval England', *EcHR*, 2nd ser. 46 (1993), 266–79; on the importance of the cost of fodder in determining transport costs, see D. Gerhold, *Road Transport in England Before the Railways: Russell's London Flying Waggons* (Cambridge, 1993). If the cost of fodder was not lower, roads (or another factor, e.g. the quality of horses) would have had to be significantly better.

[18] Dyer, *Hidden Trade of the Middle Ages*, 284–303; C. Dyer, 'The Consumer and the Market in the Later Middle Ages', in id. *Everyday Life in Medieval England*, 257–81.

[19] B. M. S. Campbell, 'Towards an Agricultural Geography of Medieval England', *Agric. Hist. Rev.*, 36 (1989), 98, 87.

of the countryside) . . .'[20] Professor Dyer has recently come to a similar view: 'some of the crucial ingredients in transforming the medieval economy must be the creation of an enduring framework for production and exchange in the two centuries after 850.'[21]

The scale of bridge construction in the middle ages accords with recent research about medieval road transport and trade. In contrast, the evidence that the number and quality of bridges remained much the same between c.1540 and the third quarter of the eighteenth century, and the suggestion that this roughly mirrors the levels of road transport and the requirements of road users, is contrary to much, though not all, of the work undertaken since the 1970s. Studies have stressed the expansion in internal trade during the early modern period, the growth in the volume of road transport as the main instrument of that trade, and the importance of improvements in both the road transport industry and the roads themselves.

The dismal view taken by the Webbs about these issues has been revised.[22] Albert, who published his research on turnpike trusts in 1972, showed that contrary to the Webb's conclusions, turnpikes formed a system of improved roads much earlier than had traditionally been supposed. He argued that 'far reaching economic changes underlay the political and social changes taking place from 1641. The growing demand of industry and the steady rise in the volume of trade, especially from 1688, created new pressures on many traditional institutions. The transport system was one of those.'[23] Pawson's work was published soon afterwards, in 1977. It demonstrated that turnpikes had important effects on road transport and on the economy.[24]

Subsequently, other historians claimed that significant changes had begun to happen in the sixteenth century. They have argued that the volume of road traffic increased considerably between the sixteenth and eighteenth centuries, and that these centuries saw much growth, development, and improvement. For example, Chartres refers to 'the magnitude of the growth in the effective capacity of the road transport industry between 1500 and 1700—it may have grown by at least three or four-fold'.[25]

Undoubtedly there was some growth in internal trade and road transport in the sixteenth and seventeenth centuries, but these claims almost certainly exaggerate it. The evidence does not support them. Quantifiable data are scarce, so

---

[20] Campbell, *Anglo-Saxon State*, 17

[21] C. Dyer, *Making a Living in the Middle Ages: The People of Britain 850–1520* (London, 2002), 365.

[22] Webb and Webb, *King's Highway*, and see also Jackman, *Transportation*. An excellent summary of the work done since 1970 is contained in Barker and Gerhold, *Rise of Road Transport*, 14–15.

[23] Albert, *Turnpike System*, 6.   [24] Pawson, *Transport and Economy*.

[25] Chartres, *Internal Trade, 1500–1700*, 40–1.

there are 'practically no series of figures for national agricultural or industrial production'.[26] Equally, there are few statistics relating to road transport, and Chartres provides little evidence for his suggested growth in the road transport industry, especially in the sixteenth century. One of the few sets of statistics on road transport relates to regular road carrying services from London, and it is far from clear that these can provide an accurate index of the levels of road traffic throughout the country.

Albert, Chartres, and Pawson rightly argued that the inland trade was important, but also, wrongly, sought to belittle earlier achievements, thereby giving greater emphasis to the degree of change at a later date and overstating improvements. Albert and Pawson give the misleading impression that the road system before the turnpikes was primitive. While criticizing the Webbs' views of the turnpike age, Albert relies heavily on their study of the King's Highway for his view of the condition of pre-turnpike roads. Pawson's comment that, without improved road surfaces brought about by the turnpike, waggons would not have been able to 'supplant' pack-horses is an excellent example of how he failed to get the right context for his own researches; he was clearly unaware that the cart as much as the packhorse had been characteristic of pre-turnpike travel.[27] Other works commonly ignore medieval developments, possibly because the evidence is less easy to assemble, leaving the impression that little of note happened. In contrast, the achievements of the turnpike age have been stressed.[28]

In the late 1980s Gerhold began to reassess the work undertaken in the previous decade, and has now modified our views of the period. He presents a view which is far more compatible with the bridge evidence. He has demonstrated that claims about the increase in the volume of road transport in the sixteenth and seventeenth centuries have been exaggerated. Chartres used the evidence about road carrying services from London to produce estimates of a twenty-twofold increase in the number of services and a seventy-sixfold rise in ton-miles between 1637 and 1840. Gerhold, however, has shown that these estimates are grossly exaggerated. He suggests a 'trebling of London carrying services between 1681 and 1838'.[29] He has also demonstrated that in many areas

---

[26] K. Sharpe, *Early Modern England* (London, 1987), 127.

[27] Pawson, *Transport and Economy*, 281–2.

[28] e.g. Hey's *History of Yorkshire from 1000 AD* (Harlow, 1986) is typical in describing improvements from the 18th cent. (pp. 212–21), but makes no reference to medieval improvements.

[29] J. A. Chartres, 'Road Carrying in England in the Seventeenth Century: Myth and Reality', *EcHR*, 2nd. ser. 30 (1977), 73–94; id. and G. L. Turnbull, 'Road Transport', in D. H. Aldcroft and M. J. Freeman (eds.), *Transport in the Industrial Revolution* (Manchester, 1983), 64–99, 80–8; D. Gerhold, 'The Growth of the London Carrying Trade, 1681–1838', *EcHR*, 2nd ser. 41 (1988), 392–410.

major improvements in productivity in the long-distance carrying trade began in the mid-eighteenth century. There were similar productivity gains in coach travel which partly explain the very large reductions in the time taken for journeys. In 1757 a coach from Exeter to London took three days in summer, four in winter; by 1776 it took twenty-four hours.[30]

TRANSPORT AND SOCIETY BEFORE THE INDUSTRIAL REVOLUTION

The stress which has been placed over the last thirty years on the importance of road transport in the early modern period can therefore be seen to be an accurate and laudable revision of older negative interpretations. We can agree with the view that the inland trade mattered. Nevertheless, we must not exaggerate the extent to which traffic grew during the two centuries after 1540. Whatever improvements in vehicles and carrying services were made in this period, they were using an extensive and highly developed pre-existing network of bridges and roads. Road improvements of the first half of the eighteenth century were not dramatic improvements, beginning from a low base; rather, they should be seen as changes to an already substantial and sophisticated system, the result of medieval and later investment in the infrastructure.

It is clear that the stock of bridges extant in 1540 appears to have remained adequate for the volume of traffic in the succeeding centuries, and only from the late eighteenth century did it become worthwhile to build new bridges and improve existing ones. The volume of traffic in 1740 was larger than it had been in 1540 and probably larger than in 1340, but was probably not in an altogether different league. By 1840 matters were very different. This statement is inevitably vague and uncertain, but it is worth making as an antidote to the prevailing vocabulary of growth and improvement which has characterized much writing about the early modern period.

It is not altogether surprising that the medieval network of bridges was adequate for traffic levels well into the seventeenth century and later. The road system of 1300 was serving the needs of a population of *c.*5 to 6 million.[31] The population in 1600 of *c.*4 million, in 1650 of *c.*5 million, and in 1750 of *c.*5.75 million lay near to or below the medieval peak.[32]

---

[30] D. Gerhold, 'Productivity Change in Road Transport Before and After Turnpiking, 1690–1840', *EcHR*, 2nd ser. 49 (1996), 496–8, 508.

[31] J. Hatcher, *Plague, Population and the English Economy, 1348–1530* (London, 1977), 68; R. Smith, 'Human Resources', in G. Astill and A. Grant (eds.), *The Countryside of Medieval England* (Oxford, 1988), 191.

[32] E. A. Wrigley and R. Schofield, *The Population History of England, 1541–1871* (Cambridge, 1981), 208–9.

It is, moreover, probable that the output of the economy was of a not dissimilar size. Some comparisons have been made of national income in 1300 and 1688, when Gregory King made his assessment. It is likely that estimated increases have been exaggerated: a case can be made that there was little or no increase in national income over this period. The figures are as follows. G. D. Snooks has argued for an increase in national income from £19 million in 1300 (at 1688 prices) to £50 million in 1688. However, as he notes: 'No direct estimate is possible of GDP in 1300 because there are insufficient data on expenditure, production or incomes received. The best that can be achieved is an approximate figure derived from an empirically-based computer model which simulates trends in real GDP and real GDP per capita between 1086 and 1688.'[33] Given that the figure for 1086 is much disputed, the exercise is rather dubious. Professor Dyer's ingenious analysis of English society and income distribution in 1300 has been used by N. J. Mayhew as a basis for comparison of national income in 1300 and 1688. He comes to a similar conclusion to Professor Snoops, estimating that real GDP doubled over this long period.[34] This estimate, even if right, contrasts with the very rapid growth in the late eighteenth century; Crafts estimates that national product grew at a rate of 1.32 per cent in 1780–1801 and 1.97 per cent in 1801–31 (the rate for 1700–80 is *c.*0.7 per cent).[35] D. N. McCloskey observed that: 'between 1780 and 1860 British national income per head doubled—this even though the population more than doubled.'[36] Total national income probably increased more than fivefold.

In fact, Mayhew's estimate of economic growth between 1300 and 1688 probably overestimates the increase in the output of goods and services. First, it may in part measure the increasing extent of monetization, that is, the change in the volume of monetary transactions taking place, which is not the same as the actual output of goods and services. Secondly, the estimate of a doubling of GDP stands oddly with the Phelps Brown–Hopkins figures of the real purchasing power of building craftsman's and labourer's daily wages. These show conclusively that their real purchasing power was greater in the early

---

[33] G. D. Snooks, 'The Dynamic Role of the Market in the Anglo-Norman Economy and Beyond, 1086–1300', in R. H Britnell and B. M. S. Campbell (eds.), *A Commercialising Economy: England 1086 to c.1300* (Manchester, 1995), 51.

[34] C. Dyer, *Standards of Living in the Later Middle Ages: Social Change in England, c.1200–1520* (Cambridge, 1989); N. Mayhew, 'Modelling Medieval Monetisation', in Britnell and Campbell, *A Commercialising Economy*, 58–9, 72–3; GDP per capita increased by a larger amount since it is assumed that the population was higher in 1300 than in 1688.

[35] N. F. R. Crafts, *British Economic Growth During the Industrial Revolution* (Oxford, 1985), 45.

[36] D. N. McCloskey, 'The Industrial Revolution, 1780–1860: A Survey', in R. Floud and D. N. McCloskey (eds.), *The Economic History of Britain Since 1700*, 3 vols. (2nd edn., Cambridge, 1994), i. 243; Wrigley and Schofield, *Population*, i. 208–9.

fourteenth century than in the early seventeenth century, despite the higher population at the earlier date.[37]

If national income doubled between the early fourteenth and the late seventeenth centuries, if the populations levels were roughly similar, and if the craftsman's purchasing power was higher in the earlier period, then the whole of the doubling of national income must have gone to provide higher profits and rents for landlords.[38] This is unlikely: a doubling of national income might be expected to be reflected in some greater purchasing power for craftsmen and labourers. That their purchasing power did not increase suggests that national income did not double, and may not have significantly increased.

It is worth quoting the conclusions of Phelps Brown and Hopkins, the implications of which have received insufficient consideration by historians:

The simplest impression of the physical equivalent of the wage-rate . . . is of a level much the same throughout, broken through only by a time of much greater prosperity from 1380 to 1510, and a rise that sets in at the last, from 1820 onwards, and carries us up to a new region altogether . . . A drastic fall set in about 1510: the level enjoyed at the accession of Henry VIII was not to be reached again until 1880; the lowest point we record in seven centuries was in 1597, the year of the *Midsummer Night's Dream*. Do we not see here a Malthusian crisis, the effect of a rapid growth of population impinging on an insufficiently expansive economy; such as perhaps we see also in the fall that set in again around 1750, until this time a commercial and industrial revolution came to save Britain from the fate of Ireland?[39]

The principal findings of this book—that at most locations where there was a bridge in 1750 there had been one in the thirteenth century and at many locations there had been a bridge in 1100—probably mirror the fundamental continuities in the economy over this period. This suggests how much the pre-industrial economy of the seventeenth century had in common with the late medieval or even the eleventh-century economy. The findings also demonstrate the capacity of medieval society to invest very heavily in practical civil engineering projects. The creation of a large network of bridges as part of a new road system was one of the most impressive achievements of medieval England. Its importance should be recognized.

---

[37] H. Phelps Brown and S. V. Hopkins, *A Perspective of Wages and Prices* (London, 1981), 28–30. For all its inadequacies, the Phelps Brown–Hopkins index gives a rough idea of purchasing power. They note that 'it is relevant that the building labourer's rate did change in the same proportion as the craftsman's with great consistency from the Black Death to the First World War' (p. 23).

[38] Since by definition national income is comprised of wages, rent, and profits.

[39] Ibid. 23. National product per head fell slightly 1760–80, because a rising national output was consumed by an increasing population (Crafts, *British Economic Growth*, 45).

SELECT BIBLIOGRAPHY

'Account of Lechlade Bridge, Gloucestershire', *Collectanea Topographica et Genealogica*, 1 (1834), 320–4.

ALBERTI, L. B., *The Ten Books of Architecture: The 1755 Leoni Edition*, facsimile edn. (New York, 1986).

ALLEN, T. and WELSH, K., 'Eton Rowing Lake', *Current Arch.*, 148 (1996), 124–7.

BAGSHAWE, R. W., *Roman Roads* (Princes Risborough, 2000).

BARKER, T. and GERHOLD, D., *The Rise and Rise of Road Transport, 1700–1990* (London, 1993): contains a very useful general bibliography of works relating to road transport.

Reprint of Barnstaple Records, ed. J. R. Chanter and T. Wainwright, 2 vols. (Barnstaple, 1900).

BECKER, M. J., *Rochester Bridge, 1387–1856* (London, 1930).

BLACKWALL, A., *Historic Bridges of Shropshire* (Shrewsbury, 1985).

BLAIR, J. and MILLARD, A., 'An Anglo-Saxon Landmark Rediscovered: The Stan ford/Stan bricge of the Ducklington and Whitney Charters', *Oxoniensia*, 57 (1992), 342–8.

Book of Bridges Belonging to the North Riding of the County of York, 1805 (*North Yorkshire County Record Office*).

Book of Bridges Belonging to the West Riding of the County of York, 1752 (*West Yorkshire County Record Office*).

BOYER, M., *Medieval French Bridges: A History* (Cambridge, Mass., 1976).

BRANGWYN, F. and SPARROW, W. S., *A Book of Bridges* (London, 1915).

BRETT, A., 'The Stone Bridge Over the Wharfe at Wetherby', *Yorks. Arch. Jnl.*, 30 (1931), 274–7.

Bridges in Hampshire of Historic Interest (Hampshire, 2000).

BRIERLEY, J., 'The Medieval Exe Bridge', *Proc. Instn. Civ. Engrs.*, part 1, 66 (1979), 127–39.

BROOKS, N. P., 'The Development of Military Obligations in Eighth- and Ninth-Century England', in P. Clemoes and K. Hughes (eds.), *England Before the Conquest: Studies in Primary Sources Presented to Dorothy Whitelock* (Cambridge, 1971), 69–84.

—— 'Medieval Bridges: A Window onto Changing Concepts of State Power', *Haskins Soc. Jnl.*, 7 (1995), 11–29.

—— *Communities and Warfare 700–1400* (London, 2000).

BROWN, S. W., 'The Medieval Bridge and St Gabriel's Chapel at Bishop's Clyst', *Proc. Devon. Arch. Soc.* 40 (1982), 163–9.

BRUCE, J., 'The Three Bridges over the Tyne at Newcastle', *Arch. Aeliana*, NS 10 (1885), 1–11.

BURGES, A., 'Account of the Old Bridge at Stratford-le-Bow in Essex', *Archaeologia*, 27 (1838), 77–95.

—— 'Bridge at Stratford-le-Bow', *Archaeologia*, 29 (1842), 378–80.

CAMPBELL, J., *The Anglo-Saxon State* (London, 2000).

CASSON, H. (ed.), *Bridges* (London, 1963).

CHALKIN, C., *English Counties and Public Building, 1650–1830* (London, 1998).

CLARK-MAXWELL, Revd Prebendary, 'Bridgnorth: the Bridge and its Chapel', *Trans. Salop. Arch. and Nat. Hist. Soc.*, 4th ser., 9 (1923), 118–24.

CLEPHAN, J., 'Old Tyne Bridge and its Story', *Arch. Aeliana*, NS 12 (1887), 135–49.

COCKE, S. and HALL, L., *Norwich Bridges Past and Present* (Norwich, 1994).

COLES, B. and J., *Sweet Track to Glastonbury: The Somerset Levels in Prehistory* (London, 1986).

COLLINGWOOD, W. G., 'Packhorse Bridges', *Trans. Cumberland and Westmorland Ant. Soc.*, 20 (1928), 120–8.

COLVIN, H. M. (ed.), *The History of the King's Works*, 6 vols. (London, 1963–82).

—— *A Biographical Dictionary of British Architects, 1600–1840*, 3rd edn. (London, 1995).

COOPER, L., RIPPER, S., and CLAY, P., 'The Hemington Bridges', *Current Arch.*, 140 (1994), 316–21.

COSSINS, J. A., 'Ancient Bridges, Fords and Ferries', *Trans. Birmingham Arch. Soc.*, 42 (1916), 1–15.

COX, D. C., 'A Medieval Bridge on the Avon at Twyford, near Evesham', *Vale of Evesham Hist. Soc. Research Papers*, 7 (1979), 57–62.

CROAD, S., *London's Bridges* (London, 1983).

CROOK, M., *Medieval Bridges* (Princes Risborough, 1998).

CROW, A., *Bridges on the River Wye* (Hereford, 1995).

CRUMMY, P., HILLAM, J., and CROSSAN, C., 'Mersea Island: The Anglo-Saxon Causeway', *Essex Arch. and Hist. Soc.*, 14 (1982), 77–86.

DARBY, H. C., *Medieval Fenland*, 2nd edn. (Newton Abbot, 1974), 106–18 on fen causeways.

DAVIS, R. H. C., 'The Ford, the River and the City', *Oxoniensia*, 38 (1973), 258–67.

DAVIS, V. G., 'The Rule of St. Paul, the First Hermit, in Late Medieval England', in W. J. Sheils (ed.), *Monks, Hermits and the Ascetic Tradition*, Studies in Church History, 24 (Oxford, 1985), 203–14.

DEFOE, D., *A Tour through the Whole Island of Great Britain*, 2 vols. (London, 1974).

DE MARE, E., *The Bridges of Britain* (London, 1954).

DENT, J., 'Skerne', *Current Arch.* 91 (1984).

DE SALIS, H. R., *Bradshaw's Canals and Navigable Rivers of England and Wales, a Reprint of A Handbook of Inland Navigation for Manufacturers, Merchants, Traders and Others* (Newton Abbot, 1969).

DRINKWATER, C. H., 'Montford Bridge: Tolls, Customs, etc. A.D. 1285 to A.D. 1412', *Trans. Salop. Arch. and Nat. Hist. Soc.*, 3rd ser., 7 (1907), 65–84.

DURHAM, B., et al., 'The Thames Crossing at Oxford: Archaeological Studies 1979–82', *Oxoniensia*, 49 (1984), 57–100.

DYER, C., *Making a Living in the Middle Ages: The People of Britain 850–1520* (London, 2002): contains a brief but useful bibliography of works (including recent studies) relating to medieval transport.

DYMOND, D. P., 'Roman Bridges on Dere Street, County Durham, with a General Appendix on the Evidence for Bridges in Roman Britain', *Arch. Jnl.*, 118 (1963), 136–64.

EMERSON, W. and GROMORT, G., *Old Bridges of France* (London, 1925).

EVELYN-WHITE, C. H., 'The Aldreth Causeway, its Bridge and Surroundings', *Trans. Camb. and Hunts. Arch. Soc.*, 1 (1904).

FIENNES, CELIA, *The Journeys of Celia Fiennes*, ed. C. Morris (London, 1947).

GAUTIER, H., *Traité des Ponts* (Paris, 1714).

—— *Dissertation sur l'epaisseur des culées des ponts . . . sur la largeur des piles, sur la porteé des voussoirs, etc.* (Paris, 1717).

GOODFELLOW, P., 'Medieval Bridges in Northamptonshire', *Northants Past and Present*, 7, (1985–6), 143–58.

GRAY, A., 'The Ford and Bridge at Cambridge', *Camb. Antiq. Soc. Com.*, 14 (1910), 126–39.

GREEN, C., 'Broadland Fords and Causeways', *Norfolk Arch.*, 32, (1961), 316–31.

HAMILL, L., *Bridge Hydraulics* (London, 1999).

HARRISON, D. F., 'Medieval Bridges', *Current Arch.*, 11 (1990), 73–6.

—— 'Bridges and Economic Development, 1300–1800', *Econ. Hist. Rev.*, 2nd ser., 45 (1992), 240–61.

HARVEY, J., *English Medieval Architects: A Biographical Dictionary Down to 1550* (London, 1954).

HASLAM, J., 'The Towns of Devon', in J. Haslam (ed.), *Anglo-Saxon Towns in Southern England* (Chichester, 1984), 249–83.

—— 'Market and Fortress in England in the Reign of Offa', *World Arch.*, 19: 1 (1987), 76–93.

HASSALL, J. and HILL, D., 'Pont de l'Arche: Frankish Influence on the West Saxon Burh?', *Arch. Jnl.*, 127 (1970), 188–95.

HENDERSON, C. and COATES, H., *Old Cornish Bridges and Streams* (Truro, 1928, repr. 1972).

—— and JERVOISE, E., *Old Devon Bridges* (Exeter, 1938).

HEY, D., *Packmen, Carriers and Packhorse Roads* (Leicester, 1980).

HEYMAN, J., *The Stone Skeleton: Structural Engineering of Masonry Architecture* (Cambridge, 1995).

—— and PADFIELD, C. J., 'Two Masonry Bridges: I. Clare College Bridge', *Proc. Inst. Civ. Engrs.*, 52 (1972), 305–18.

—— HOBBS, N. B., and JERMY, B. S., 'The Rehabilitation of Teston Bridge', *Proc. Inst. Civ. Engrs.*, 68 (1980), 489–97.

HILLAM, J., 'An English Tree-ring Chronology, A.D., 404 to 1216', *Med. Arch.*, 25 (1981), 31–44.

HINCHLIFFE, E., *A Guide to the Packhorse Bridges of England* (Milnthorpe, 1994).

HINDLE, B. P., 'The Road Network of Medieval England and Wales', *Jnl. Hist. Geog.*, 2 (1976), 207–21.

—— *Medieval Roads*, 2nd edn. (Aylesbury, 1989).

HOME, G., *Old London Bridge* (London, 1931).

HONEYBOURNE, M. B., 'The Pre-Norman Bridges of London', in A. E. J. Hollaender and W. Kellaway (eds.), *Studies in London History Presented to P. E. Jones* (London, 1969), 17–42.

HOPKINS, H. J., *A Span of Bridges* (Newton Abbot, 1970).

HORSLEY, P. M., *Eighteenth Century Newcastle* (Newcastle, 1991), 1–23 on old Tyne Bridge.

HOSKINS, W. G., 'The Origin and Rise of Market Harborough', in W. G. Hoskins, *Provincial England* (London, 1965).

HUDSON, T. P., 'The Origins of Steyning and Bramber', *Southern History*, 2 (1980), 11–29.

HUDSON, W., 'On an Ancient Timber Roadway Across the River Wensum at Fye Bridge, Norwich', *Norfolk Arch.*, 13 (1898), 217–32.

HUGGINS, P. J., 'Excavation of a Medieval Bridge at Waltham Abbey, Essex, in 1968', *Med. Arch.*, 14 (1970), 126–47.

HUMPHREYS, A. L., *Caversham Bridge, 1231–1926* (Reading, 1926).

HURST, H., 'Excavations at Gloucester 1971–73', *Antiq. Jnl.*, 54 (1974), 46–50, on the bridge.

HUTTON, C., *The Principles of Bridges* (Newcastle-upon-Tyne, 1772).

HYDE, R., *A Prospect of Britain: The Town Panoramas of Samuel and Natheniel Buck* (London, 1993).

LELAND, JOHN, *The Itinerary of John Leland in or about the Years 1535–43*, ed. L. Toulmin Smith, with a foreword by T. D. Kendrick, 5 vols. (London, 1964).

JACK, G. H., 'Ancient Bridges in Herefordshire and their Preservation', *Antiquaries Journal*, 6 (1926), 284–93.

—— 'The Art of the Bridge Builder', *Jnl. of Royal Soc. of Arts* (1931).

JACKSON, D. A. and AMBROSE, T. M., 'A Roman Timber Bridge at Aldwincle, Northants.', *Britannia*, 7 (1936), 39–72.

JERVOISE, E., *The Ancient Bridges of the South of England* (London, 1930).

—— *The Ancient Bridges of Mid and Eastern England* (London, 1932).

—— *The Ancient Bridges of Wales and Western England* (London, 1936).

—— *The Ancient Bridges of the North of England*, new edn. (Wakefield, 1973).

JOHNSON, S. M. and SCOTT-GILES, C. W. (eds.), *British Bridges: An Illustrated Technical and Historical Record* (London, 1933).

JORDAN, W. K., *Philanthropy in England, 1480–1660* (London, 1959).

JUSSERAND, J. J., *English Wayfaring Life in the Middle Ages*, trans. L. Toulmin-Smith, 4th edn. (London, 1950).

KERRY, C., 'Hermits, Fords, and Bridge-Chapels', *Derbyshire Arch. Jnl.*, 14 (1882), 54–71.

Kingston-upon-Thames Bridgewardens' Accounts, 1526–67, ed. N. J. Williams, Surrey Rec. Soc., 22 (1955).

KNIGHT, W., 'Observations on the Construction of Old London Bridge', *Archaeologia*, 23 (1831), 117–19.

LANGDON, J., *Horses, Oxen and Technological Innovation: The Use of Draught Animals from 1066 to 1500* (Cambridge, 1986): contains an extensive bibliography on medieval transport.

LEEMING, J. J. and SALTER, H. E., 'Burford Bridge, Abingdon', *Oxoniensia*, 3 (1937).

London Bridge Accounts, 1381–1538, ed. V. Harding and L. Wright, London Rec. Soc., 31 (1995).

MARGARY, I. D., *Roman Roads in Britain*, 3rd. edn. (London, 1973).

MARTIN, D., 'Bodiam Castle Medieval Bridges', *Hastings Area Arch. Papers*, 1 (1973).

MARTIN, G. H., 'Road Travel in the Middle Ages', *Jnl. Transport Hist.*, NS 3 (1975–6), 159–78.

MASCHKE, E., 'Die Brucke im Mittelalter', *Historische Zeitschrift*, 224 (1977), 265–92.

MASSCHAELE, J., 'Transport Costs in Medieval England', *Econ. Hist. Rev.*, 46 (1993), 266–79.

MAUNSON, D. W. J., 'The Irthling Bridge at Lanercost', *Trans. Cumberland and Westmorland Arch. Soc.*, 79 (1979), 75–84.

Med. Arch., 27 (1983), 195–6 (for Kingston upon Thames Bridge).

MESQUI, J., *Le Pont en France avant le temps des ingénieurs* (Paris, 1986).

MORRISS, R. K., 'Bridges over the Shropshire Severn' in id. (ed.), *The Shropshire Severn* (Shrewsbury, 1994).

MYRES, J. N. L., 'The Campaign of Radcot Bridge in December 1387', *Eng. Hist. Rev.*, 42 (1927), 20–33.

O'CONNOR, C., *Roman Bridges* (Cambridge, 1993).

Ogilby's Road Maps of England and Wales from Ogilby's 'Britannia' 1675 (Reading, 1971).

O'KEEFE, P. and SIMINGTON, T., *Irish Stone Bridges: History and Heritage* (Dublin, 1991).

OLIVER, B. W., 'The Long Bridge of Barnstaple', *Trans. Devon. Assoc.*, 70 (1938), 193–7; 78 (1946), 177–91.

PAGE, J. (ed.), *Masonry Arch Bridges* (London, 1993).

PALLADIO, A., *The Four Books on Architecture*, trans. R. Tavernor and R. Schofield (London, 2002).

PARSONS, E. J. S. and STENTON, F. M., *The Map of Great Britain circa 1360 Known as the Gough Map: An Introduction to the Facsimile* (Oxford, 1970).

PEARS, C. R., 'On the Stone Bridge at Hampton Court', *Archaeologia*, 62 (1910), 309–16.

PHILLIPS, G., *Thames Crossings* (Newton Abbot, 1981).

PIERCE, P., *Old London Bridge: The Story of the Longest Inhabited Bridge in Europe* (London, 2001).

PRADE, M., *Les Ponts monuments historiques* (Poitiers, 1986).

PRESTON, J., 'Rochester Bridge, 1825–1950', in N. Yates and J. Gibson (eds.), *Traffic and Politics: The Construction and Management of Rochester Bridge, AD 43–1993* (Woodbridge, 1994), 221–74.

PRESTON, W. E., 'Notes on the Re-building of some Aire and Calder Bridges', *Bradford Antiquary*, 6 (1913–21), 135–48.

RACKHAM, O., *The History of the Countryside*, paperback edn. (London, 1987).

RENN, D., 'The River Wey Bridges Between Farnham and Guildford', *Research Volume of Surrey Arch. Soc.*, 1 (1974), 75–83.

RICHARDS, J. M., *The National Trust Book of Bridges* (London, 1984).

RIGOLD, S. E., 'Structural Aspects of Medieval Timber Bridges', *Med. Arch.*, 19 (1975), 48–91.

—— 'Structural Aspects of Medieval Timber Bridges: addenda', *Med. Arch.*, 20 (1976), 152–3.

ROWLANDS, M. L. J., *Monmow Bridge and Gate* (Stroud, 1994).

Royal Commission on Historic Monuments:Inventories (1910–).

RUDDOCK, E., *Arch Bridges and their Builders, 1735–1835* (Cambridge, 1979).

RYE, H. A., 'History of Monk's Bridge', *Trans. Burton-on-Trent Arch. Soc.*, 4 (1889–1903).

—— 'The Great Bridge of Burton-on-Trent', *Burton-on-Trent Nat. Hist. and Arch. Soc.*, 5 (1903–6), 4–21.

SALZMAN, L. F., *Building in England Down to 1540*, 2nd edn. (Oxford, 1967).

SILKSTONE, T., *Bridges of the Esk* (North York Moors National Park).

SIMCO, A. and MCKEAGUE, P., 'Bridges of Bedfordshire', *Beds. Arch. Monographs*, no. 2 (1997).

SLACK, M., *The Bridges of Lancashire and Yorkshire* (London, 1986).

STEANE, J., *Medieval Bridges in Oxfordshire* (Oxford, 1981).

—— *The Archaeology of Medieval England and Wales* (1985).

STENTON, D. M., 'Communications', in A. L. Poole (ed.), *Medieval England*, rev. edn. (Oxford, 1958), 196–208.

STENTON, F. M., 'The Road System in Medieval England', in D. M. Stenton (ed.), *Preparatory to Anglo-Saxon England, Being the Collected Papers of F. M. Stenton* (Oxford, 1970), 234–52 (originally published in *Econ. Hist. Rev.*, 7 (1936), 7–21).

STEWART-BROWN, R., 'The Old Dee Bridge at Chester', *Jnl. Chester Arch. Soc.*, NS 30 (1933), 63–78.

—— 'Bridge Work at Chester', *Eng. Hist. Rev.*, 54 (1939), 83–9.

STONE, F., *Picturesque Views of all the Bridges Belonging to the County of Norfolk* (Norwich, 1830–1).

Surrey Bridges in the Time of Elizabeth, Surrey Arch. Collections, 25 (1912), 148–53.

TARBOTTON, M. O., *History and Description of Old and New Trent Bridges* (Nottingham, 1871).

TAYLOR, C., *Roads and Tracks of Britain* (London, 1979).

TAYLOR, P. T., 'An Account of some Discoveries made in Taking Down the Old Bridge over the River Teign', *Archaeologia*, 19 (1821), 308–13.

THOMAS, D. B. L., 'The Chronology of Devon's Bridges', *Reports and Trans. of Devon. Assoc.*, 124 (1992), 175–206.

TOLLIT, H. J., *Report upon all the County Bridges in Oxfordshire* (Oxford, 1878).

TURNER, E. T., 'On the Ancient Bridge Discovered at Bramber in the Year 1839', *Sussex Arch. Collections*, 2 (1849), 63–7.

TURNER, H. L., *Town Defences in England and Wales: An Architectural and Documentary Study A.D. 900–1500* (London, 1971).

WALLIS, A. J., *Dorset Bridges* (Sherborne, 1974).

WALKER, R. J. B., *Old Westminster Bridge* (Newton Abbot, 1979).

WARD, A. W., *The Bridges of Shrewsbury* (Shrewsbury, 1935).

WARD-PERKINS, B., *From Classical Antiquity to the Middle Ages: Urban Public Building in Northern and Central Italy, AD 300–850* (Oxford, 1984).

WATSON, B., BINGHAM, T., and DYSON, T., *London Bridge: 2000 Years of a River Crossing* (London, 2001).

WEATHERILL, J. 'Eighteenth Century Rievaulx Bridge and its Medieval Predecessor', *Yorks. Arch. Jnl.*, 41 (1963–6), 71–80.

WEBB, S. and B., *English Local Government: The Story of the King's Highway* (London, 1920).

WHITING, F. E., *The Long Bridge of Bideford through the Centuries*, 3rd edn. (Bideford, 1997).

William of Worcester Itineraries, ed. and trans. J. H. Harvey (Oxford, 1969).

WILSON, B. and MEE, F., *'The Fairest Arch in England', Old Ouse Bridge, York, and its Buildings: The Pictorial Evidence* (York, 2002), 83–92.

WYNNE, W. A. S., *St. Olave's Priory and Bridge, Hemingfleet, Suffolk* (Norwich, 1914).

YATES, N. and GIBSON, J. (ed.), *Traffic and Politics: The Construction and Management of Rochester Bridge, AD 43–1993* (Woodbridge, 1994).

York Bridgemasters' Accounts, trans. P. M. Stell, Historical Sources for York Archaeology after AD 1100, 2 (2003).

INDEX